HISTORY OF AMERICAN THOUGHT AND CULTURE

Paul S. Boyer, *General Editor*

God's Empire

William Bell Riley
and Midwestern Fundamentalism

WILLIAM VANCE TROLLINGER, JR.

The University of Wisconsin Press

The University of Wisconsin Press
114 North Murray Street
Madison, Wisconsin 53715

3 Henrietta Street
London WC2E 8LU, England

All photos courtesy of Northwestern College, Roseville, Minnesota

Library of Congress Cataloging-in-Publication Data
Trollinger, William Vance.
     God's empire: William Bell Riley and midwestern fundamentalism /
William Vance Trollinger, Jr.
     244 pp.   cm. — (History of American thought and culture)
     Includes bibliographical references and index.
     1. Riley, W. B. (William Bell), 1861–1947.   2. Northwestern Bible
and Missionary Training School (Minneapolis, Minn.)
3. Fundamentalism — History.   4. Middle West — Church history —
20th century.   5. Riley, W. B. (William Bell), 1861–1947.
I. Title.   II. Series.
BX6495.R585T76   1990
286'.1'092 — dc20
[B]
ISBN 0-299-12710-9   90-50099
ISBN 0-299-12714-1 (pbk.)   CIP

Contents

Illustrations

Acknowledgments

CONSIDERING the debts I have incurred in working on this project, I almost feel guilty that my name alone is on the title page. The great virtue of this arrangement is, of course, that I alone receive the blame for the errors within; considering my culpability, that is as it should be.

At the outset I should note that a section of chapter 5 has already been published, in somewhat different form: "Riley's Empire: Northwestern Bible School and Fundamentalism in the Upper Midwest," *Church History* 57 (June 1988): 197–212. This article was chosen for inclusion in the third annual edition of *The Best in Theology* (Carol Stream, Ill.: Christianity Today, Inc., 1989), 115–29.

This book began as a dissertation project at the University of Wisconsin–Madison (although before Wisconsin was Bethel College's Jim Johnson, whose superb teaching was what pushed me to study American history in the first place). At Wisconsin I had the good fortune to have Carl Kaestle as my adviser; Carl not only provided sound suggestions regarding both prose and ideas, but he was and is a good friend who has consistently provided wise counsel. I also benefited from the wisdom and friendship of Paul Conkin, John DeNovo, and Ron Numbers, all of whom have gone far beyond the call of duty as mentors. While at Wisconsin I was also fortunate enough to be surrounded by a host of bright graduate colleagues who provided both friendship and, when needed, criticism; I owe thanks particularly to Ed Agran, Dave Blight, Bob Burk, Tim Dillon, Mary Neth, and Don Rogers.

I am grateful to the following organizations for providing me with financial assistance that enabled me to pursue my research into midwestern fundamentalism: the American Historical Association, which awarded me an Albert J. Beveridge Grant for Research in American History; Messiah College; the School of the Ozarks; the Wisconsin Alumni Research Foundation; and the University of Wisconsin–Madison.

Also of great assistance were scholars, archivists, and librarians who helped me to locate the materials upon which this book is based, including Susan Eltscher at the American Baptist Historical Society, Rochester, New

York; archivists at the Minnesota State Historical Society, St. Paul, Minnesota; and Linda Schmidt of the School of the Ozarks Library, Point Lookout, Missouri. Special thanks go to two scholars who helped me locate research materials: Michael G. Rapp, who pointed me to records documenting Riley's anti-Semitic activities in the 1930s; and Dell G. Johnson, who generously shared with me materials he had gathered in the process of writing his Th.D. dissertation on Minnesota fundamentalism. Also of great assistance was Rev. Thorin Anderson at the First Baptist Church of Granite Falls, Minnesota, who opened up the church archives for my review.

But most important in this regard was Mary Lou Hovda, associate librarian at Northwestern College. Ms. Hovda was wonderfully helpful in guiding me through Northwestern's collection of Riley's publications and in allowing me to rummage through file cabinets for photographs (some of which are reprinted here). In general, the Northwesterners I encountered were immensely generous with their time and assistance. William Berntsen, president of Northwestern when I began my research, ensured that I would have access to the Riley materials. Administrators in the Alumni Office permitted me to go through alumni records for addresses of graduates from the Riley years. Finally, I am especially grateful to the seventy or so Northwestern alumni who completed questionnaires or allowed me to interview them. I hope that this book does their stories justice.

I have been quite fortunate in the number and quality of scholars who have been willing to read and comment on all or part of this work. Special thanks go to Virginia Brereton, Alan Brinkley, Vernon Burton, Nora Faires, Samuel Hays, Dick Pierard, Will Soll, Ronald Stockton, Richard Taylor, and Timothy Weber. In this regard I am particularly indebted to Joel Carpenter and George Marsden, both of whom have provided me with a wealth of good suggestions. I did some of what they and the other commentators suggested. I probably should have done more.

The series editor, Paul Boyer, has been intimately involved with this work for years; he has been not only an astute critic but also a friend who has provided me with an abundance of encouragement. Thanks also to the editors at the University of Wisconsin Press; I am particularly appreciative of Barbara Hanrahan, who provided great assistance while also patiently prodding me through the final stages of this project.

I am most indebted to my family. My mother and father are unwavering supporters. Abigail and Rebekah are a constant joy and a constant reminder of what is truly important in my life. But my greatest obligation is to Gayle, my wife and best friend. While she bolstered my spirits and critiqued my writing, she also advanced her career, furthered her education, and fought (at great cost) for teachers' rights in the hills of southwestern Missouri. She is a remarkable person. This book is for her.

GOD'S EMPIRE

Introduction

SINCLAIR LEWIS began the process of writing his classic satire of popular religion, *Elmer Gantry*, by doing some research into the current state of Christianity in America. As part of his preparation Lewis went to Kansas City in January 1926 and immersed himself in the religious life of the community. While the prominent New York fundamentalist John Roach Straton seems to have been the initial model for Lewis' protagonist, in Kansas City the author fleshed out the character of the infamous Gantry with material from the lives of Methodist minister William "Big Bill" Stidger and Unitarian pastor L. M. Birkhead. In the process Lewis became quite friendly with Birkhead and his wife. After accumulating piles of notes, and armed with a twenty-thousand-word outline, Lewis withdrew with the Birkheads to a summer resort in northern Minnesota, where he began to write the novel.[1]

While in Minnesota Lewis apparently concluded that he needed more data for his portrait of a fundamentalist preacher. He thus made efforts to interview William Bell Riley, strident fundamentalist and pastor of the First Baptist Church of Minneapolis. As Riley recounted later, "when L. M. Birkhead, Universalist Pastor of Kansas City, and Sinclair Lewis brought their half heads together in order to produce the book entitled, *Elmer Gantry*, they . . . invited me to spend a week with them on Long Lake . . . in the hopes of getting something on me that they might work into that rotten volume." Fortunately, Riley observed, "God, who knows all things, knew they were coming" and so filled Riley's week with commitments that the Minneapolis minister was forced to decline the invitation. As a result, Riley chortled, Lewis had "to bring out the book without working me into it as one of the fundamentalists that [he] . . . befoul[ed]."[2]

Considering *Elmer Gantry*'s critical and popular success, it is obvious that Lewis did just fine without interviewing Riley; moreover, Lewis may not have gained that much usable material from Riley, since the austere, upright pastor of Minneapolis' First Baptist Church did not greatly resemble the flamboyant and crassly amoral preacher the author was in the process of creating. But in one regard Lewis' research instincts about Riley were absolutely correct. In seeking to interview William Bell Riley, Lewis was seeking to interview the dominant figure in American fundamentalism in the first half of the twentieth century. More than any other individual, it was Riley who, in the decade after World War I, marshaled the fundamentalist forces into crusades designed to purify both American Protestantism and American culture in general. When defeated at the national level, this organizational dynamo turned his attention to the local level. He and his followers created a powerful fundamentalist network in the upper Midwest, a network which is the prototype for contemporary fundamentalist empires.

This book deals with W. B. Riley, his various national campaigns, and the regional fundamentalist empire he created.[3] Underlying this study is a central assumption that fundamentalism was, is, and will continue to be an important religious and social movement in the United States. This may seem a perfectly commonsensical, even obvious, proposition. But historians (and, for that matter, novelists) have not always viewed fundamentalism in this light. In order to place this work within its interpretive context, it is necessary to make a few comments about the history and historiography of American fundamentalism.

In the late nineteenth and early twentieth centuries evolutionism, comparative religion, and higher biblical criticism challenged orthodox interpretations of Christianity. The latter particularly shook the foundations of orthodoxy, as scholars applying a historical/critical perspective to the Scriptures raised serious doubts about the literal authenticity of much of the biblical record. With Henry Ward Beecher, Shailer Mathews, Walter Rauschenbusch, and Harry Emerson Fosdick in the van, many Protestant theologians and ministers responded by adjusting their beliefs to accommodate these new intellectual currents. The resultant "modernist" theology greatly reduced the contrast between the supernatural and the natural. De-emphasizing God's transcendence, the modernists viewed Christianity as the ever-changing experience of an immanent God. As William R. Hutchison has observed, modernists viewed God as being "immanent in human cultural development and revealed through it"; in keeping with this idea, modernists further believed that "human society is moving toward realization (even though it may never attain the reality) of the Kingdom of God."[4] Enthusiastically accepting the results of higher criticism, modernists questioned the supernaturalness of the Bible and disputed the veracity of biblical accounts of miracles (including the Virgin Birth and bodily Resurrection of Christ). Downgrading the importance of correct belief, modernists proclaimed that the truly Christian life consisted of love and social concern. "Essentially," C. Allyn Russell has nicely summarized, "liberalism was an attitude rather than a credo," with liberals or modernists maintaining "an open mind toward the truth" rather than trusting "in authority and force."[5]

While some Protestants found modernism appealing, a loosely united band of theological conservatives vigorously fought these attempts to adjust Christianity to meet the demands of modern thought. These militant evangelicals, or fundamentalists, staunchly affirmed the supernaturalness and literal accuracy of the Bible, the supernatural character of Christ, including his bodily Resurrection and imminent return to earth, and the necessity of Christians separating themselves from "the world."[6] Most often Baptists or Presbyterians, they struggled to reestablish their denominations as true and pure churches—true to the historic doctrines of the faith as they perceived them and pure from what they saw as the polluting influences of an increasingly corrupt modern culture. But by the late 1920s fundamentalists had lost the fight. Not only were they powerless minorities in the Northern Baptist and the Northern Presbyterian denominations, in which the struggle for control had been the fiercest, but many now perceived them as uneducated, intolerant rustics. The Scopes "monkey trial" cemented this notion in the popular consciousness.

Many historians of fundamentalism perpetuated this perception. In the 1930s observers such as H. Richard Niebuhr, Frederick Lewis Allen, and Stewart Cole concluded that the fundamentalists were but ignorant rural folk desperately clinging to a way of life that was forever passing away. In a similar vein, Richard Hofstadter and others in the years after World War II viewed the fundamentalists as spiritual antecedents of the McCarthyites. According to this interpretation, these religious militants of the 1920s had reacted to natural social change with a paranoid hunt for heretics. Explicitly accepting this premise, Norman Furniss argued in an influential 1954 study that the fundamentalists were intolerant bigots who could not make the transition to modern life. Fortunately for the nation, with the "spread of knowledge" these products of "cultural lag" were destined to be assimilated into the mainstream of American life; in fact, this process was almost complete by the late 1930s. As William Ellis has noted, numerous other historians in the 1950s and 1960s joined Furniss in denigrating the fundamentalists and noting their inevitable disappearance in the face of the American cultural consensus. William McLoughlin capsulized this analysis in a 1967 article in which he argued that the fundamentalists represented not "a significant new religious movement" but instead the usual "effluvia" that accompanied major social change.[7]

By the 1970s, however, it had become apparent that the failure to capture control of the major Protestant denominations and the inability to sustain the antievolutionism crusade did not signal the death of American fundamentalism. The fundamentalist subculture was flourishing, in urban areas as well as in rural regions, in spite of predictions of its inevitable absorption into the mythical consensus. Paul A. Carter thus noted in an prescient article that "the problem for the historian of the twenties is not so much one of accounting for the later decline of Fundamentalism, as Cole [and] Norman Furniss . . . assumed, as it is one of discerning elements in the movement that account for its continuing vitality."[8]

Out of this desire to explain fundamentalism's resilience and vigor has emerged a revisionist historiography. Viewing America as a pluralistic culture, the revisionists dismiss the idea that fundamentalism was and is an aberration. Instead, to quote Ernest Sandeen, they view fundamentalism as "an authentic conservative tradition" within American history. These scholars also reject a monolithic approach and instead emphasize the ideological, temperamental, and regional diversity within the movement. Finally, while the revisionists disagree on the degree of social and cultural causation, they accept with George Marsden that "from its origins fundamentalism was primarily a religious movement" and that "unless we appreciate the immense implications of a deep religious commitment . . . we cannot appreciate the dynamics of fundamentalist thought and action."[9]

This work is part of the revisionist historiography of fundamentalism. As noted above, the assumption here is that fundamentalism is an important religious and social movement in the United States. One important goal of this study is to provide some insights into the continuing vitality of the fundamentalist movement. More specifically, this work is a start toward filling some lacunae in our understanding of fundamentalism. First, this is the first full-length study of W. B. Riley. Riley's importance led Donald Tinder to assert in 1969 that "a good biography of William Bell Riley would reflect more of twentieth century American Fundamentalism than would that of any other man." Two decades after Tinder's observation, that biography still has not appeared.[10] While this work is not a biography per se, much time will be spent on the evolution and nature of Riley's religious and political ideas (including the anti-Semitic conspiratorialism of his later years), his organizational efforts at the national and regional levels, and his impact on religion in America. Because of Riley's prominence in the fundamentalist movement, this examination will shed light upon (among other things) how and why certain conservatives became militant fundamentalists; the nature, success, and failure of the fundamentalist crusades against modernism and evolutionism; and the connections between one branch of the fundamentalist movement and Far Right politics in America.

Another way in which this work differs from most previous works on American fundamentalism is that it concentrates much of its attention on the two decades after the Scopes trial. Despite the recent recognition that fundamentalism did not die or melt into the dominant culture in the late 1920s, there have been few studies of fundamentalism between the denominational defeats and the appearance of national fundamentalist organizations in the 1940s.[11] Perhaps this is because of the decentralized nature of fundamentalism during these years. Thus the topic is not readily amenable to the "history of elites" that characterizes not only traditional religious history but also much of the new historiography of fundamentalism. William Ellis' observation, made in 1981, still rings true: while the revisionists "have provided a valuable service to historiography by describing the intellectual base of fundamentalism," they have failed to give "the grass roots of fundamentalism . . . the full attention it deserves."[12]

In contrast with most of the analyses that have gone before, a good part of this study deals with local and regional fundamentalism. The reason for this is simple: we can not truly understand how the defeated fundamentalists of the 1920s became the successful fundamentalists of the 1930s and 1940s (and beyond) without taking a grass-roots approach to the topic. This is because fundamentalists, in response to their well-publicized defeats at the national level, successfully transferred their efforts to the local level. Some fundamentalists, convinced that it was impossible to preserve doctrinal purity in a large organization, formed independent Bible churches. Others maintained fundamentalist churches that were, at least in name, still affiliated with a mainstream denomination. Some fundamentalist churches eventually joined to form denominations such as the General Association of Regular Baptists. In all three forms grass-roots fundamentalism prospered in the 1930s and 1940s. Such prosperity came at a time when the major denominations were losing members and monies. In fact it appears that, as Joel Carpenter has observed, the growth of fundamentalism in the 1930s marked "the beginning of a shift of the Protestant mainstream from the older denominations toward the evangelicals."[13]

Of course, these fundamentalist churches lacked the resources afforded them by a close relationship with an established denomination. Hence they depended upon a rapidly expanding network of fundamentalist organizations which included publishing houses, mission boards, and radio stations. At the center of this support structure were the approximately seventy Bible schools that dotted the country in the 1930s and 1940s. The Bible school movement began in the 1880s with the founding of New York

Missionary Training Institute (now Nyack College) in New York City and
Moody Bible Institute in Chicago. In the early years these schools sought
to train laypersons for work as missionaries, evangelists, and religious
teachers. But as increasing numbers of fundamentalists became alienated
from the major denominations, they pressed the Bible schools to expand
their services to fill the denominational void. These schools served as
denominational surrogates, providing nearby fundamentalist churches with
ministers, teaching materials, Bible conferences, church secretaries, and a
host of other services. Quite often this fundamentalist network was directed by the local pastor who presided over the Bible school. In effect,
these pastors controlled regional fundamentalist empires.

While there is some evidence of regional empires centered around Moody
Bible Institute of Chicago, Gordon Bible Institute of Boston, and the Bible
Institute of Los Angeles, this thesis has not been fully tested or developed.
While a few historians have asserted the central role of Bible institutes in
the survival of fundamentalism, there have been no case studies dealing
with the work of Bible institutes at the grass-roots level.[14] This work provides just such an analysis, with the focus on William Bell Riley's Northwestern Bible and Missionary Training School of Minneapolis. The meth-
odology will be in keeping with suggestions made by Samuel P. Hays
regarding political history. In a pair of influential articles Hays argued that
historians must take into account in their conceptualization the "different
levels of social organization: the grass roots, the region, and the nation."
These levels "comprise a hierarchy of human involvement, each of which
is a distinctive source of perception and experience, institutional organization and action." Thus, it is at their peril that historians fail to consider
each of these levels, for "an historical perspective limited to any one of
them would be far too narrow." Moreover, study at the regional level holds
the most promise for effective social analysis. It is often here that the local
and the national worlds come into conflict.[15]

Hays's suggestions are particularly applicable here, because central to
much of this story is a conflict between cosmopolitans (denominational
leaders) and locals (fundamentalists). Having examined the failure of Riley
and the fundamentalists to unseat the liberals from control of the major
denominations, the focus turns to Northwestern Bible School, the development and nature of the fundamentalist empire centered around Northwestern and dominated by Riley, and the manner in which this empire promoted and controlled the fundamentalist movement in the upper Midwest.
The climax of this story comes in the 1940s, when the Northern Baptist
Convention attempted to rein in the sizable Baptist wing of this grass-
roots fundamentalist movement. In keeping with Samuel Hays's observa-

tions regarding centralization/decentralization conflicts, the battle between the cosmopolitan and the local forces took place at the state level, at the Minnesota Baptist Convention. After examining this battle, this work concludes with a discussion of the legacy of W. B. Riley and his fundamentalist empire.

I should note that I am not a fundamentalist. I grew up in a conservative evangelical — but not fundamentalist — family; while I remain strongly committed to the Christian faith, over the years my religious (and political) allegiances have shifted even further away from fundamentalism. But while I am not attempting to write an apologetic for fundamentalism, neither do I seek to savage the fundamentalists. Instead, my goal is to understand W. B. Riley and the movement he led.

Toward understanding these midwestern fundamentalists it behooves us to remember that in the early twentieth century many conservative Christians felt alienated from their own culture. The Protestant hegemony of the nineteenth century had crumbled; in its place was emerging a secularized, pluralistic America. Liberal or modernist theologians dominated major denominations. Science and philosophy no longer rested on even a superficially Christian foundation. Social mores now seemed explicitly anti-biblical. With a feeling of being immigrants in their own land, with an overwhelming sense of powerlessness in the face of burgeoning denominational and secular bureaucracies, "fundamentalists" (those conservative Christians who militantly resisted modernist theology and modern culture) sought to hold onto their truth. Whatever one might think of certain aspects of the fundamentalist ideology — for example, the virulent nationalism and (in Riley's case) vicious anti-Semitism — it must be realized that, as Jackson Lears has said of the Right in general, fundamentalism "embodies a wholly understandable yearning for an authentic, unchanging bedrock of moral values and beliefs that can withstand the disintegrative effects of modernization."[16]

William Bell Riley's fundamentalist empire provided its inhabitants with certain and unchanging truth. More than this, Riley's empire offered midwestern fundamentalists a community of the like-minded in the midst of a hostile world. Hence Riley's empire was remarkably vital. And as this monograph will show, the vitality of this empire explains much about the survival of fundamentalism in America.

1

The Leader

In 1911, when W. B. Riley turned fifty, he was the pastor of a large Baptist church in Minneapolis and the president of a tiny Bible school connected with the church. He was also a popular evangelist in the upper Midwest, as well as a dabbler in denominational and urban politics. In short, he was a local figure of some renown but certainly not a national religious leader. If W. B. Riley had died at age fifty he would merit, at best, a footnote in the history of religion in America.

But the past is indeed prologue, and there is much in these five decades of relative obscurity that illuminates W. B. Riley's final four decades as fundamentalist crusader, political controversialist, and builder of a religious empire. Most important, there are ample clues in these years to explain why W. B. Riley reacted to modernism with militant opposition and to indicate that he would not be content to serve as a foot soldier in the post–World War I fundamentalist movement.

William Bell Riley was born March 22, 1861, in Green County, Indiana. His mother was of Pennsylvania Dutch stock. His father was a native Kentuckian and, like many in lower Indiana, a Southern sympathizer. In keeping with such sympathies Branson Radish Riley moved his family, "depleted alike in purse and prospects," back to Kentucky shortly after the Civil War broke out. There they rented a farm and raised tobacco for cash, along with livestock and foodstuffs. Survival was a family concern. Riley recounted years later: "In my ninth year father told me that I could 'make a hand.' This meant that I could follow the plow from morning until night, and I did it. . . . [For the next eight years] I hoed beans, hoed cabbage, hoed corn, and hoed tobacco in summer, together with every green thing that a garden grew or a farm could produce, and with the same hoe cut stalks on frosty winter mornings."[1]

Riley had no intention of wielding a hoe for the rest of his life. From

a very young age he had been enchanted with the idea of becoming a law-
yer, and he slipped into the county courthouse to observe trials whenever
possible. These trials so stimulated the youngster that, according to Marie
Riley, Riley's biographer and second wife, "when he returned to the corn-
field he took it out on the stalks of corn by delivering many a 'court address' either for or against an imaginary plaintiff or defendant!" Because
the country school Riley attended had a debate program, he had the opportunity to develop his oratorical skills. In an interesting foreshadowing
of his battles fifty years hence against evolutionists, by the age of sixteen
he was participating in public debates in schoolhouses throughout the
county, arguing such topics as "RESOLVED; That the Democratic Form
of Government is Preferable to the Monarchical" and "RESOLVED; That
Liquor is an Unmitigated Evil." This experience and the acclaim that came
with it further fired his ambition to become an attorney.[2]

To achieve his dream Riley needed a college education. In the spring
of 1879 he devised an ingenious plan whereby he could attain the funds
necessary for one year of precollege preparation. He rented the farm from
his father, promising to pay all expenses, plus a thousand dollars to his
father after the crop was sold. While the farm had never produced such
a profitable yield, Riley, as he put it later, was "desperate in my desire for
an education, and decided upon that method of testing myself and the
promises of God." The scheme was successful. With a "considerable balance" in his pocket, Riley set out for Valparaiso Normal School in Indiana.
Enduring a diet of crackers and corn syrup and equipped with but one
suit of clothes, Riley succeeded in securing a teacher's certificate by the
spring of 1880. With this certificate Riley planned, as he noted later, "to
teach my way through College" and then "adopt Law as my permanent
profession."[3]

Riley wanted to begin college in the autumn of 1880, but a lack of funds
and his brother's attack of typhoid forced him to return to the farm. As
he worked the fields, awaiting the chance to begin legal training, he felt
the tug of "the divine will" pulling him toward the ministry. Certainly Riley
was a prime candidate for a call to the pastorate. Marie Riley observed
that in his boyhood years he had been "bathed . . . in the waves of the
warm evangelical revival" that washed over Kentucky throughout the nineteenth century. His parents were deeply religious, and he had professed
faith in Christ at the age of seventeen. Finally, and perhaps crucially in
Riley's sense of providential calling, his father deeply regretted that family
responsibilities had kept him from becoming a preacher.[4]

The young Riley nevertheless resisted the change in career plans, un-
enthused as he was about the poverty and strict moral demands of the

William Bell Riley with his father and brothers, 1882. Standing (left to right): Orlando, William, Theophilus, and Fletcher. Seated: Branson (father) and Walter.

ministerial life. Decades later he recalled his struggle against God's call: "Days of ill-content about my choice followed each other in what seemed interminable succession; and in spite of the physical weariness with which I fell into my bed night after night, sleep refused to come. The fight was on! After some months of turmoil . . . my roughly-clothed knees were driven into the black loam of the Kentucky hillside, [and] as I knelt between two rows of tobacco . . . I reluctantly said, 'I will! I will preach!'"[5] The career of fundamentalism's most important minister had begun.

Through the benefactions of a prosperous neighbor Riley began attending Hanover College in southern Indiana in the autumn of 1881. He chose this Presbyterian school because, Marie Riley explained, it was "an Institution of student sobriety and also a College that was fundamental in the Christian faith." He lacked the four years of high-school training most of his classmates had enjoyed. Nevertheless, by dint of hard work Riley graduated fourth in his class, and first in debate, which further testified to his oratorical skills.[6]

Leaving Hanover in 1885, he proceeded immediately to the Southern Baptist Theological Seminary in Louisville. There he imbibed the teachings of Bible teachers whose message, much to Riley's delight, "confirmed and established" the faith of his upbringing. According to Riley's recollections near the end of his life, the seminary at Louisville in the 1880s was a solid wall of orthodoxy: "There was not a heterodox note in the tongue of any one of [the professors], as the two hundred men who studied with me would every one bear witness."[7] Riley's reminiscences about his Louisville days might have been somewhat idealized; they came in the context of his anguish in the 1940s over the fact that, in his eyes, his alma mater had become "a fount of modernism." Nevertheless it is undoubtedly true that Riley's seminary training solidified his strong loyalty to a conservative interpretation of the Christian faith.[8]

Riley's commitment to orthodoxy was further reinforced by his frequent contact with Dwight L. Moody. Riley first encountered Moody at a revival led by the famous evangelist in 1887 on the grounds of the Southern Baptist Theological Seminary. Riley was one of the many seminary students who helped Moody in this five-week campaign. Riley's biographer observed in 1935 that "here young Riley had an experience which he has prized all through his subsequent ministerial life — learning how to deal with men individually — and became an ardent admirer of Mr. Moody, both from the standpoint of his messages and his methods." The Louisville revival was just the beginning of Riley's exposure to Moody. While Riley was pastoring in Lafayette, Indiana, Moody held revival meetings in the young minister's church. More important, during Riley's years in Chicago he frequently had the opportunity to work with and learn from the famous evangelist. From these encounters Riley became a great admirer of Moody, gaining a deep respect for Moody's staunch faith and forceful personality.[9]

Riley graduated from Southern Baptist Theological Seminary in 1888.[10] But his ministerial career had begun years before. While at Hanover he earned extra money preaching at country churches in the region. In 1883 he accepted the pastorate of a Baptist church in Carrollton, Kentucky, agreeing to preach every other Sunday. Soon thereafter he began to serve the other two Sundays each month in a church in Warsaw, Kentucky, and he maintained both posts until 1886. He soon progressed to full-time posts, accepting calls to the Indiana cities of New Albany (1887–1888) and Lafayette (1888–1891), and then to Bloomington, Illinois (1891–1893). While in Lafayette Riley married Lillian Howard, to whom he was wedded until her death in 1931.[11]

According to Marie Riley, Riley's years at Bloomington were so successful that the church was almost always packed to the limit for his services, and he gained a statewide reputation. In early 1893 the newly formed Calvary Baptist Church of Chicago offered the up-and-coming Riley the post of minister. Riley jumped at the chance to minister to a large city. He succeeded in increasing the church's membership from sixty in 1893 to five hundred in 1897. Nevertheless, it was a time of disillusionment for Riley. One reason was the devastating economic depression of those years. Not only did the hard times tax the resources of the church, but the depression also forced members to cut their contributions to the extent that the young pastor was not paid the salary for which he had contracted. A more important factor in his disillusionment was Riley's sense that the very size of Chicago dwarfed the importance of his work.[12] As he commented in a revealing admission, he had taken the Calvary post because he had "the false impression that the bigger the city, the greater the opportunity for service." But during his first year in Chicago he came to the conclusion that "a big city is the poorest place in the world for any preacher except its most notable one. Its very extent suffices to reduce opportunity, to circumscribe influence, and even to destroy the reach of personality. It is like standing up before the General Grant, the giant of the Sequoias; it dwarfs a man."[13]

Increasingly Riley yearned to pastor a downtown church in a medium-sized city. The First Baptist Church of Minneapolis proved to be the fulfillment of his dreams, and a detailed examination of his early years there reveals much about both Riley and his followers.[14]

The First Baptist Church of Minneapolis was established in 1854. The church soon acquired an elite membership that included business leaders George A. Pillsbury, C. E. Reynolds, and A. L. Bausman, among others. Originally in the heart of the city, the upwardly mobile laity voted in 1886 to move the church to a site near the edge of a new, affluent suburb. A beautiful stone edifice was constructed, and there Minneapolis bluebloods gathered to hear the cultured sermons of Dr. D. Wayland Hoyt.[15]

Hoyt resigned in 1896. Late that year the church pulpit committee invited young W. B. Riley of Chicago's Calvary Church up to Minneapolis

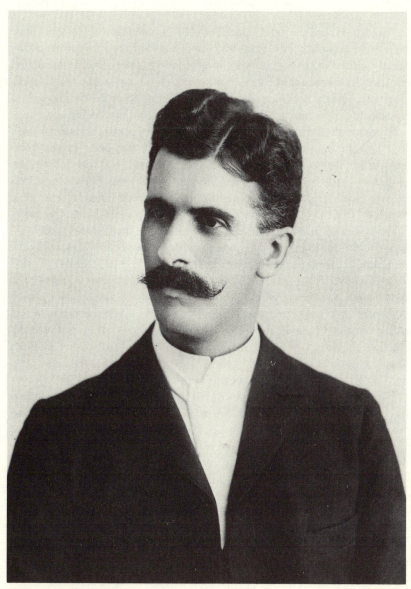

William Bell Riley, 1895

to "candidate" for the post. Even before Riley arrived, some committee members had misgivings about this son of a poor Kentucky farmer. Riley greatly added to their doubts by inadvertently leaving his dress suit on the train, a mistake that forced him to preach his trial sermon in a sackcloth suit. "The aristocracy of the church," Marie Riley gently noted, "did not take kindly to his garb, and thus the [pulpit] committee were not agreed that he was their man."[16] Despite his unstylish apparel, however, the tall (6' 1") young man with the prominent nose and deep-set eyes had managed to impress many in the First Baptist congregation with his powers of oratory. After considering an additional twenty-five to thirty candidates, the committee finally bowed to popular sentiment and asked Riley to serve as pastor. In a move which must have shocked many committee members, Riley replied by insisting that certain conditions be met before he accepted their invitation. Rural upbringing notwithstanding, Riley was no country bumpkin. He recognized that those individuals who had initially opposed him were church officers with a great deal of vested power. Fearing the day when these officers would limit his prerogatives, the ambitious Riley demanded that the church's government be taken "from the hands of five ruling trustees, the majority of the trustee board, . . . putting it into the hands of the Advisory Board, made up of all officers — twenty-five to thirty people." In a decision some members would come to rue, the committee agreed to this demand. Riley began his pastorate March 1, 1897.[17]

Riley saw his work at First Baptist as crucial to the health of Minneapolis; as he said about urban churches in general, "evangelical ministers and evangelistic churches will either shine [in the city] or darkness will reign; we will either be the salt to the city, or corruption and decay are its destiny."[18] While he believed that the church had a political role to play in fighting urban immorality (see chapter 3), the most certain way to create a moral metropolis was to evangelize the citizenry. The forceful and aggressive young minister was thus determined to remake First Baptist into a metropolitan center of soul-winning. His model was Boston's Tremont Temple, which, despite a number of disastrous fires, had more members than virtually any other church in Boston in the late nineteenth century. The size of this large congregation was due in great part to the popular preaching of Baptist minister George Lorimer. In 1889 Riley was in the Massachusetts capital for denominational meetings. He visited Tremont. A church officer gave him a tour of the building, in the process explaining fully "Lorimer's ideal institution for the heart of a city." Riley was "enamored and enthralled" and decided then that "some day I should attempt for some other city what George Lorimer had accomplished for Boston."[19]

In keeping with efforts by a number of other urban evangelical pastors

First Baptist Church, Minneapolis

of the time, including A. J. Gordon and A. B. Simpson,[20] Riley's first step in creating his "City Temple" was to open his wealthy Minneapolis church to all people, regardless of class. This campaign for a classless church was not the product of radical leanings. While in these years Riley was moderately reformist, he was certainly no left-wing critic of capitalism.[21] For example, in one of his earliest First Baptist sermons entitled "Ananias — or the Dangers in Handling Wealth," Riley attacked those individuals who engaged in dishonest business practices; however, he then went on to indict those with "anarchistic feeling[s]" who indiscriminately criticized the rich: "I believe a man may be wealthy and yet most honorable, most righteous, most religious." Riley called for an open church not because of a social radicalism but because of his desire to evangelize the entire citizenry and because of his ecclesiology. He strongly believed that the true church was a democracy. As he reminded prospective ministers in an article many years later: "The democratizing of a church is essential not alone to its spiritual life, but to its normal and healthy growth. God Himself is no respecter of persons, and the house in which the rich and the poor, the ignorant and the learned, the high and low *cannot* meet together to recognize God as the maker of them all, may be called the church house but it can never become the place of His holy presence."[22]

Riley was so determined to open First Baptist to all persons that, according to a story which may or may not be fictitious, he even went to the extent of lecturing "one lady of stature [that] she should be ashamed to allow her footman to stand outside tending horses while she warmed herself at the fires of the gospel of grace."[23] Riley also pushed for the abolition of pew rentals in First Baptist. The wealthiest trustee led the opposition to Riley's proposal. Nevertheless, the congregation followed their new pastor and overwhelmingly adopted this change.[24]

But Riley had just begun his reform of First Baptist. Next he requested that the Ladies' Aid Society end their practice of raising money for the church by holding suppers, bazaars, and the like. His reasoning was that tithing was the biblically sanctioned method of financially supporting the church. Using arguments he had used against pew rentals, he noted in a talk to the Ladies' Aid Society that these "money-making schemes" allowed prosperous members "the impression that they have contributed something to the Church." They were thus less willing to give the large sums "the Church needs and [they are] able to give."[25] The Society responded favorably to Riley's plea and eliminated their money-raising activities, although, according to Marie Riley, most of the women who opposed the free pew also voted against this proposal.[26]

Riley was not finished. He also launched attacks on dancing, card-playing, and theater attendance, distributing to the congregation booklets damning these practices. Moreover, he participated in a move by the advisory board to shorten the liturgical part of the church service. Not only did this eliminate complaints about the length of Sunday morning worship services, but it also gave greater prominence to his sermons.

All of these changes are directly related to what Riley saw as his primary goal — to make First Baptist a center of evangelism. Every one of Riley's

Sunday morning sermons concluded with an invitation for individuals to come forward and accept Christ. On Sunday nights Riley established what he termed permanent revivals, with "attractive" sermon topics, musical specials, and youth participation in the services. Throughout the year there were weeks of revival meetings and Bible conferences, conducted by visiting evangelical leaders. In the Sunday morning, Sunday evening, and special services there was one primary goal — soul-winning.[27] At times this even meant that, as one church member recalled, the "converted members of the church [would] walk among those who had not yet made the decision and personally urge them to come forward."[28]

Riley's campaign to remake First Baptist had immediate results. Membership rolls expanded from 585 in 1897 to 855 in 1898 and continued to expand rapidly over the next decade. Reflecting on his early years at First Baptist, Riley commented that by "the abolition of the pew-rental system, attendance was popularized and outsiders began to frequent the services."[29] While more was involved than simply the elimination of rented pews, Riley was indeed correct in claiming that he had, indeed, succeeded in attracting "outsiders" to the church. In his excellent dissertation chapter on First Baptist Walter Ellis has established that when Riley began his pastorate, 50 percent of the First Baptist families were professionals, merchants, or entrepreneurs, and only 10 percent were tradesmen, industrial workers, or laborers. But of the families that joined in the first year of Riley's efforts only 26 percent were professionals, merchants, and managers, while 36 percent were blue-collar workers and laborers, and 38 percent were in white-collar or service occupations. Granting that many of these new members were young and thus not yet at the height of their careers, it is nevertheless striking that First Baptist Church of Minneapolis, once the church of the city's elite, now had a large constituency of members from the lower middle class. This expansion of First Baptist membership rolls through the addition of lower-middle-class communicants continued for years to come.[30]

The First Baptist experience foreshadowed the broader fundamentalist movement. The limited evidence on the social roots of fundamentalism points to a lower-class and lower-middle-class constituency.[31] But the question here remains: Why did lower-middle-class individuals flock to W. B. Riley's First Baptist Church of Minneapolis? As noted above, it was not because Riley preached an antiestablishment social radicalism. Nor was it because Riley engaged in flashy showmanship. Riley's style was much more in keeping with Dwight Moody than Billy Sunday. But while he eschewed emotional outbursts in the pulpit, Riley's oratorical skills were certainly a major reason for his success at First Baptist. The tall, handsome Riley had a resonant voice and a forceful, even impassioned, delivery. His messages were down-to-earth, loaded with vivid imagery, and simple to understand. His sermons were thus appealing to individuals equipped with a nonelite education, much more so than the scholarly discourses of First Baptist's previous ministers.

But style is not the only reason "outsiders" flocked to hear Riley at First Baptist. There was also the content of these messages, which will be discussed at length later in this chapter. For now, suffice it to say that Riley's pessimistic view of the future and rejection of human progress was in keeping with the personal experiences of those in the bottom reaches of the middle class. Moreover, his concomitant emphasis on the premillennial return of Christ provided those not enjoying worldly success an otherworldly hope. Finally, Riley's emphasis on correct belief and total spiritual commitment encouraged a group cohesion that was quite attractive to anxious people at the lower end of the socioeconomic scale.

As might be expected, Riley's remaking of First Baptist antagonized many of the old guard. Marie Riley described their discontent: Riley's "very success was disturbing to certain elements in the Church. The ruts in which it had so long run were being left; the methods it had employed were being changed; a revolution was being wrought—and the masters of the Church realized this."[32] The "officially ambitious" old guard not only opposed the abolition of pew rentals and church bazaars but also disliked being lectured on their amusements and their insufficient financial support of the church. They also chafed under the changes that rendered their church less ritualistic and more evangelistic. Most of all, they resented the invasion of a lower-middle-class constituency into their church. Issues of class underlay many of their complaints about the new First Baptist. At one point some of the old guard, many of whom lived in the suburbs, condescendingly suggested that because the new majority might not feel comfortable attending a church at the edge of an affluent suburb, they should consider starting their own church closer to downtown.[33]

But suggestions of schism came late in the conflict. The old guard's original goal was to rid themselves of Riley. They eagerly awaited the opportunity to generate congregational opposition to the young minister. Their best chance came with Riley's response to the Filipino-American War. The southern-bred Riley was a staunch Democrat, and he lined up with anti-imperialist Democrats in opposing the American war against Filipino insurgents. When the Republican administration in Minneapolis denied Filipino veterans who had served with the United States forces the right to march in an 1899 veterans parade, Riley joined with other local Democrats in an anti-imperialism rally. In the invocation the First Baptist minister intoned: "We cannot ask Thee that our soldiers in the Philippines may be victorious, for we do not believe that this is Thy will; but we do ask that their lives may be preserved and that they may return to their homes and friends."[34]

The Republican newspapers in the Twin Cities had a field day blasting the young minister for these words. The *Minneapolis Tribune* even managed to "wave the bloody shirt": "It remains to be seen whether or not Mr. Riley's Church will remain silent when its official head and spokesman uses the position given him by its members to invoke a curse upon the President and his administration, to express his sympathy with conspirators and murderers in the Philippines, and to strengthen the hands of the pitiful band of Copperheads who would, if they could, paralyze by disloyal action the efforts of the American nation to maintain the honor of the flag and to extend the area of American freedom."[35]

Perhaps Marie Riley exaggerated when she reported that the *Tribune* (and other Twin Cities newspapers) had been "egged on by the minority group" at First Baptist. But it is certainly true that these newspaper attacks on Riley played right into the hands of the pastor's opponents at First Baptist. Most of them were indeed Republican, and they sought to use the negative publicity to force out the obstreperous pastor. But their blatant attacks on Riley's patriotism failed. He refused his opponents' demand that he leave by his own volition; the deacons refused the demand that they ask for his resignation. Instead the congregation rallied to their pastor's defense by passing a motion in December 1899 criticizing the local press's vituperative attacks on Riley and reaffirming that their pastor had, "as [did] every other member of [the] church, the right of free speech."[36]

Foiled, the leaders of the old guard changed tactics. In May of the next year they circulated among the members a list of grievances. The complaints charged that certain organizational methods within the church bred distrust and dissension; true and tried church leaders were removed from power by "purely political and discreditable means" of choosing officers; "some of the church's old and most loyal members" had left the church or ceased to give money; many acceptable teachers and workers had resigned instead of serving under Riley; and the minister persisted in teaching disputed doctrines (the imminent return of Christ). Citing these grievances, the dissidents called for the formation of a council made up of leaders of other Baptist churches in the area which would mediate between the feuding First Baptist factions. Their hope was, of course, that this council would remove Riley from the pastorate.[37]

The new members, however, were solidly behind Riley, and so the church voted against the establishment of an investigative council. As a last resort, in 1901 the frustrated minority called an ex parte council to hear their complaints. The council consisted of seven representatives from the University of Chicago and two from Rochester Theological Seminary. Considering that Riley had frequently engaged in theological battles with representatives of the former institution when he was a pastor in Chicago, it was not terribly surprising that the council, in Riley's words, "condemned me . . . and called upon the church to end my pastorate." Because of the Baptist emphasis on the independence of the local congregation, First Baptist was under no compunction to respond to the council's investigation. The council's recommendation was ignored. The dissidents called a second ex parte council in 1902. Its similar recommendation was similarly ignored.[38]

Soon after this last victory Riley learned that his opponents had withdrawn their financial contributions to the church. According to his sympathetic biographer, Riley sensed here an opportunity "to end an opposition with which he had long been patient." Riley began actions to exclude the dissidents from the church on grounds of "refusing to contribute, . . . refusing to walk in fellowship, . . . [and] refusing to be reconciled." Beating Riley to the punch, 146 members withdrew from First Baptist. As further evidence that issues of class were central to this dispute, Walter Ellis has documented that it was the "establishment members who seceded": 64 percent of the separating families were professionals or merchants, and no laborers or manufacturing workers joined the exodus. On April 2, 1903, the separating families formed Trinity Baptist Church. Ex parte council member and University of Chicago board member Lathan Crandall was their first minister.[39]

According to Marie Riley, young ministers could learn invaluable spiritual lessons from this tale of conflict: "From it they will see that the man who is faithful to God is never forsaken by Him, but, on the contrary, is certain of His blessing. They will also learn what the subject of his biography discovered, namely, that the days which seem darkest are frequently the ones in which God is doing the most for His own. Situations, therefore, of apparent hopelessness may, by faith, be converted into opportunities for the achievement of victory."[40] Riley certainly had achieved victory in his five-year battle to consolidate his control of First Baptist, in the process displaying a relish for conflict he would never lose. Much to his delight, Trinity Baptist Church had a lackluster growth record over the years. On the other hand, the forced withdrawal of the dissidents gave the ambitious minister the freedom to lead First Baptist into an era of remarkable success. By the time of Riley's retirement in 1942 the Minneapolis church had 3,550 members, one-tenth of Minnesota's Baptist popula-

William Bell Riley preaching at First Baptist Church, Minneapolis

tion. His dream had come true. He had indeed created an evangelistic "City Temple."[41]

Church growth was not the only benefit of purging his opponents from the congregation. Having solidified his church base Riley in the fall of 1902 founded Northwestern Bible and Missionary Training School. As we shall see in chapters 4 and 5, this school allowed Riley to build a fundamentalist empire in the upper Midwest.

The school remained tiny in the early years of the twentieth century. But in these years Riley was, in essence, laying the foundation for his regional empire, since his evangelism was not limited to the pulpit of the First Baptist Church of Minneapolis. He also spent a good deal of time in the pulpits of other churches. First Baptist officials made this possible, by writing into Riley's ministerial contract a provision which permitted him to spend four months a year as a traveling evangelist. While later in life Riley concentrated on other concerns, from 1897 to the early 1910s Riley held revival meetings throughout the Midwest and Northwest, and he conducted one evangelistic tour of England.[42]

Generally, Riley would hold two to four weeks of services in a city. The content of Riley's messages was standard revival fare. Typical messages dealt with the folly of vice and arrogance, the destruction awaiting those who defy God, the glory awaiting those who accept Christ, fearful and backsliding Christians, and the value of church membership.[43]

As noted earlier, Riley's evangelistic success certainly was not due to Billy Sunday–like showmanship. A Seattle reporter observed in 1913: Riley "upsets all the usual notions of an evangelist. He doesn't look the part and he doesn't act the part. He dresses like a prosperous banker. . . . And, save for the unusual earnestness of his speech, his tone of voice is that of the same banker. He doesn't rave and he doesn't rant. He doesn't wail and he doesn't weep. He has never wilted a collar in all his years of preaching. He has never torn an ounce of hair from his iron gray pompadour."[44]

Riley's restraint and dignity, combined with the clarity of his message and the power of his voice, actually seemed to enhance his appeal. The *Waterloo Daily Courier* extravagantly lauded Riley for all of these qualities:

Frank and sincere in his desire to help everybody . . . ; with a voice that is neither loud nor harsh and yet one that reaches every part of the large new Walnut Street Church; *a master in swaying the emotions of his listeners and yet not an "emotional" evangelist;* with the healthy optimism of a June day, and yet warning against sin and pointing out the pitfalls which are apt to trap the unwary — Dr. Riley is a wonderful man and has performed a wonderful work. Some have gone so far in the estimation of his character and in the measure of his good work as to call him a second Dwight L. Moody [emphasis mine].[45]

The Waterloo paper exaggerated. The reality was that as a revivalist Riley was but a lesser light among the large company of would-be successors to Dwight L. Moody in the early years of the twentieth century.[46] Still, the comparison to Moody had some merit, and not only because Riley emulated Moody's style. Riley's "protracted meetings" did get results. In Dayton, Duluth, Peoria, Sioux Falls, and numerous other midwestern cities and towns, hundreds, sometimes thousands, of individuals responded to Riley's call for them to confess Christ as their Savior.[47] If W. B. Riley had concentrated his efforts on professional revivalism, perhaps he would indeed have earned the label "the second Dwight L. Moody."

As we have seen, the young W. B. Riley possessed administrative talent, oratorical skills, driving ambition, enormous energy, and a love of controversy. All of these qualities would contribute to his decision to organize a fundamentalist crusade after World War I. More important than these personal traits was Riley's participation in the revivalist tradition, with its emphasis on biblicism and the distinction between the supernatural and the natural. In the same vein, and because fundamentalism was first and foremost a religious movement, understanding the details of young Riley's theology is crucial to understanding why he ended up in the fundamentalist camp. Preeminent here are two doctrines that would prove to be the chief pillars of the fundamentalist movement — the infallibility or inerrancy of the Bible and the personal and premillennial return of Christ.

In 1891 Riley delivered a series of ten sermons at the First Baptist Church of Bloomington, Illinois, on the "Greater Doctrines of Scripture." These sermons expanded upon various tenets contained in the New Hampshire Confession of Faith, which Riley accepted, and they serve as a summary of much of Riley's theology. The Bloomington minister began with a sermon on "The Inspired Word," a natural choice not only because this is the point at which the New Hampshire Confession started but also because Riley's view of the Bible was central to his belief system. Riley quoted the confession in asserting that *"God is the one and only author!"* Riley then went beyond the explicit claims of the confession to inform his congregation that God had written "every book, chapter, verse, sentence, and even word." According to Riley, the Bible itself stated over and over again that God had authored every word. But as any intelligent observer knew, much more than the Bible's own claims gave evidence of God's authorship. To those skeptics who cried out for a more detailed defense of the doctrine of verbal inspiration, Riley proclaimed that "the external evidences in *Prophecy, Miracles, Gospel success,* etc., are always ready to speak again of the Word, saying, 'It came from God'; while the testimony from within invites every doubting soul to consider the *wisdom* in this word, its *matchless code of morals, its superhuman revelations,* and the *depths of its mystery,* and know that it is divine!"[48]

In proclaiming God's authorship, Riley was not concerned by the fact that human hands actually wrote the biblical record. Human beings only "played the part of becoming the mediums of divine communication, and at times, like reporters of less important thought, wrote better than they themselves knew." Riley granted that the different "mediums" had different writing styles, but he felt that there was no contradiction between this multiplicity of styles and the fact that God was the Bible's sole author. He used as his example a businessman who dictates letters to his secretaries: "Grant that the very words employed by the manager are put into the letters, will not each of them bear the marks of the writer's mind and style? They are essentially the letters of one man. He stands responsible for every word they contain, and yet each scribe has shaded into his batch something of his own personality."[49]

Riley did not explain to his audience how individuals taking dictation could "shade in" their own personalities. But while Riley might have strained the bounds of logic in his attempt to reconcile verbal inspiration with the presence of stylistic variations, the central premise of his sermon was clear: God was the author of every word in the Bible. This tenet led quite naturally to another proposition contained in the New Hampshire Confession and quoted by Riley: "The Holy Bible has . . . truth without any mixture of error for its matter." According to Riley, the Scriptures were the infallible product of the Holy Spirit's guidance. This infallibility, or inerrancy, applied to the entire biblical record, and not simply to certain "religious" sections. In a sermon published in 1909 Riley neatly capsulized his views on this subject: The Bible is "infallible, inerrant; . . . its integrity extends to history as well as to morals and religion, and involves expression as well as thought."[50]

In arguing the Bible's infallibility or inerrancy, however, Riley was only referring to the original manuscripts. Riley refused to claim that the translators of the original manuscripts were also God's infallible "mediums." As he granted in his sermon "The Inspired Word" there was occasionally "some interpolation or mistake in translation." But he went on to say that this "ought not to cast any discredit upon the genuineness of the Word, nor indeed create a dread in the devout mind." Instead Riley emphatically reassured his listeners that "the jealous care with which the scriptures are guarded, and the original autographs which remain to measure every translation and show its fault and faultlessness, will forever secure the Bible against other authorship than that of God."[51]

Riley's view of the Bible, as delineated in this 1891 sermon, was certainly not original or even unusual. In response to higher criticism and its perceived threat to the authority of Holy Scripture, numerous conservatives in the late nineteenth century were advancing similar, albeit sometimes more sophisticated, defenses of a verbally inspired and errorless Bible. While inerrantists were found in all denominations, the most articulate exponents were Presbyterian, most notably Princeton professors Charles Hodge, A. A. Hodge, and Benjamin B. Warfield. By the early twentieth century the doctrine of a verbally inspired and errorless Bible had become for many conservatives a test of Christian orthodoxy. Riley passed.[52]

From "his start with an infallible book as his standard of religious authority," C. Allyn Russell observed, "Riley's other convictions followed quite naturally." As summarized in *Ten Sermons on the Greater Doctrines of Scripture*, these beliefs included the unity of the Godhead in three persons, the deity of Jesus, the sinfulness of human beings, Christ's vicarious Atonement and bodily Resurrection, justification by faith, the "gospel church" defined as a congregation of baptized (by immersion) believers, the perseverance of the saints, and God's final Judgment that would result in eternal life for the saved and eternal punishment for the unsaved.[53]

Interestingly enough, in these 1891 sermons Riley made no reference to a doctrine dear to his heart—the personal, premillennial, and imminent return of Jesus Christ. This could be because there is no statement of premillennialism in the New Hampshire Confession, upon which Riley based his doctrinal expositions. But perhaps it was because in 1891 he had just adopted or was in the process of adopting premillennialist views. Riley had not been taught a premillennial eschatology at Southern Baptist Seminary, whence he graduated in 1888. But as he observed in a 1940 article, "two years after graduation . . . my Pre-millennarianism [was] adopted as a result of deep and careful Bible study."[54] Perhaps the fact that his hero, Dwight L. Moody, was an ardent premillennialist also had something to do with his conversion to this doctrine. Whatever the reason, by the mid-1890s Riley was delivering sermons on the personal, premillennial, and imminent Second Coming of Christ.[55]

In his premillennialism, as in his inerrantism, Riley certainly had much company in the late nineteenth century. In the years prior to the Civil War a solid majority of American evangelicals were postmillennialists. They believed that Christ would return after the Spirit-empowered church had established the millennium, a prospect that seemed bright indeed in antebellum America. But in the less sanguine atmosphere of the post–Civil War years, increasing numbers of evangelicals in the United States became premillennialists, who believed that the millennium would not occur until Christ returned to establish it. More specifically, what most of these evangelicals adopted was a version of premillennialism known as dispensationalism. This eschatological system was brought to America in the 1860s and 1870s by a founder of the Plymouth Brethren movement, John Nelson Darby. His ideas, or variations on his ideas, were spread throughout American evangelicalism primarily through a series of major prophecy and Bible conferences in the United States that began with the founding of the annual Niagara conference in the 1870s.

At the heart of dispensationalism is the notion that the Bible must be read literally. If this is done, biblical prophecies will prove to be a sure guide to human history—past, present, and future. Read properly, the Bible reveals that history is segmented into sharply separated eras, or "dispensations." (Most dispensationalists saw seven such eras in the biblical account.) Christ's kingdom belongs wholly to a future era. The present dispensation is the "church age," which is characterized by large-scale and ever-growing apostasy in the institutional churches and the gradual moral decay of what had been "Christian civilization."[56]

Riley was a dispensational premillennialist. For him, as for his eschatological allies, premillennialism was the natural outgrowth of viewing the
Scriptures as being without error and literally accurate. In a 1897 sermon
entitled "The Promised Return" Riley proclaimed: "The plain language of
Holy Writ ought to be the end of controversy for a Christian, and I declare it is my profoundest conviction, in the face of a theological training
to the contrary, that if that rule was adopted by scripture students today,
post-millennialism would have its grave dug today, and the promise of
[Christ's premillennial return] would become immediately a permanent factor in our faith."[57]

In keeping with his fellow dispensationalists, Riley argued that in the
current age the Church was but "a small fraction of the race, much of it
[the Church] apostate, and according to prophecy, more of it to become
so."[58] But while these were bad times for the tiny minority of true believers, they would miss the worst of times. Like most of his fellow dispensationalists, Riley was also a pretribulationist: he believed that true believers will be spirited out of the world (in an event known as the Rapture)
prior to the Tribulation, a seven-year span which will see the emergence
of a world dictator, the Antichrist, and the intense persecution of the Jews.
At the end of the seven years Christ will return to earth.[59] Christ's return
will not simply be a spiritual return; as Riley told his First Baptist congregation, to say that biblical statements about Christ's Second Coming
referred to his "spiritual supremacy" was simply a "distortion of the plain-
est speech."[60] Instead Christ's return will be personal. He will bring the
saints with him, and together they will end the Tribulation by defeating
the forces of Satan and the Antichrist in battle. With this victory the millennium will commence, a literal one-thousand-year span in which Christ
rules in peace and love from his throne in Jerusalem. In the fourth sermon
of his 1897 series on the Second Coming, Riley effused about the prospect
of Christ's millennial rule: "To see Satan put down; to see sin brought to
an end; to see suffering and sorrow banished; to see the whole earth clothed
in natural and spiritual beauty, and God dwelling in visible presence among
His people. What want we more?"[61] But there will be more. At the end
of the millennium all non-Christians will be banished to hell, a place of
eternal and horrible suffering. The saints will thereafter and forever in-
habit heaven, "The place of perfect happiness" where not "one bright eye
shall ever be dimmed by tears" and where "not one sob of sorrow shall
ever be heard."[62]

Riley frequently proclaimed that Christ's return was imminent, meaning "the possibility of Christ's coming at any moment." While he strenu-
ously denied that "imminent" necessarily meant "immediate," he often ob-

served that biblical prophecies regarding the last days were being fulfilled, thus indicating that the Rapture of the Church was near. For example, in his 1897 sermon "Present Signs of His Speedy Appearance," Riley joyfully enumerated these contradictory indicators of Christ's return: the massive conversion of Jews to Christianity and their return in great numbers to Palestine; the massive evangelization of Japan, China, Africa, and the South Sea islands; the awful wickedness of modern cities; and the Church's massive compromise with the world.[63]

Riley also spoke on "The Significant Signs of the Times" at the 1914 prophecy and Bible conference at Moody Bible Institute, a meeting which Riley also helped organize. This conference at Moody was but another in the long line of major prophecy and Bible conferences in the United States that had proven to be quite important in the spread of dispensational ideas among American evangelicals. Prior to the 1914 meeting Riley had made a name for himself as an articulate and persuasive teacher of dispensational dogma, but this conference at Moody marked Riley's move to a position of leadership among American premillennialists. This was underscored by the prominent role he played at the next major prophecy conferences, which were held in 1918 in New York and Philadelphia. The alliances Riley made at these conferences were to be crucial in his establishment of a fundamentalist crusade.[64]

At the core of the post–World War I fundamentalist movement was the opposition to modernism, an opposition that at first focused on modernist or liberal theology and then broadened to include a variety of other trends in modern culture.[65] In this regard, the above portrait of the pre–World War I W. B. Riley reveals a man who was intellectually predisposed to becoming a fundamentalist. This is certainly true in his emphasis on a supernatural and inerrant Bible, which was at great odds with the sociohistorical approach to the Bible advocated by theological liberals. It is also evident in Riley's dispensational premillennialism, not only in its hyperliteral approach to the Bible but also in its view of history as shaped by supernatural forces, a view at odds with the tendency in modernist theology to minimize the difference between the natural and the supernatural. Riley's premillennialism also informed him that the modern institutional church was essentially apostate, and that modern civilization was corrupt and growing more corrupt. Finally, and perhaps most important, there was W. B. Riley's participation in the revivalist tradition. George Marsden has asserted that revivalism was the primary seedbed of American fundamentalism.[66] American revivalists had always emphasized biblical primitivism as well as strict distinctions between the supernatural and the natu-

ral, the saved and the unsaved; these notions would be central to fundamentalism. On the road or at home at First Baptist, W. B. Riley was just
such a revivalist.

Revivalist, inerrantist, dispensationalist — the pre–World War I Riley had
all the makings of a post–World War I fundamentalist. What also needs
to be added into this mix is his distinct love of conflict. Riley the controversialist was more than willing to take militant action in defense of the
faith. His first opportunity to put this conviction into practice came in the
1890s, when he was still in Chicago. While pastoring at Calvary Baptist
he encountered the enemy in the form of ministers and professors from
the University of Chicago. This Baptist super-university was founded in
1892 by John D. Rockefeller and William Rainey Harper. Besides Harper,
the key figures included Shailer Mathews and George Burman Foster. Their
dominant emphasis was a scientific, empirical approach which, as Sydney
Ahlstrom has observed, eventually led them to view "religion as a human
phenomenon, the Bible as one great human document among others, and
the Christian faith as one major religio-ethical tradition among others."[67]
While the modernism of these men from the University of Chicago probably had not developed to this extent in the years Riley pastored in Chicago, the Calvary Baptist minister was nonetheless horrified at their approach to the Bible and Christianity. With other orthodox ministers he
spent the weekly meetings of the city's Baptist Association debating the
University of Chicago representatives. The liberals wearied of arguing with
the forceful young conservative. According to Marie Riley, William Rainey
Harper told the pulpit committee from First Baptist Church, "If you want
Riley, we can well afford to spare him from Chicago."[68]

Defense of the faith required more than private debates with the enemy.
Responding to George Burman Foster's *The Finality of the Christian Religion,* in 1909 Riley leveled a book-length attack on the theology promul-
gated by Chicago and schools of its ilk. *The Finality of the Higher Criticism* was Riley's opening salvo in his lifelong war on modernism. Riley
attacked Foster and his fellow modernists for denying the divine inspiration, the infallibility, and the sacredness of the Scriptures. He argued that
their naturalistic, sociohistorical view of the Bible naturally led to apostasy, as witnessed by their rejection of the Virgin Birth, miracles, bodily
Resurrection, and Second Coming of Christ. He bemoaned the fact that
Chicago and seminaries like it permitted individuals "to stand in its walls,
and deny, in the presence of its theological students, every fundamental
of our holy faith." Much more distressing, the "infected graduates" of these
schools graduated to church pulpits, seminary professorships, and places
of importance in the denomination. In a characteristic swipe at "middle-

of-the-roaders," Riley asserted that the rejection of such doctrines as inerrancy and the literal Second Coming of Christ by supposedly orthodox believers opened the door for radical critics: these well-meaning conservatives have "provided some of the seeds which [the modernists] have sown in the great world-field," and the result is an "awful harvest of skepticism." The day for tolerating or inadvertently encouraging the "doubting spirit" was past. Instead Riley queried in the foreword to *Higher Criticism:* "We confess to a conscious call in this publication, being fully persuaded that the honor of Christ and the very life of His church are alike endangered by the doubting spirit now brooding over the educational institutions of America. Is it not high time the conservative and constructive ministers of our country united forces for the successful defense of 'the faith once delivered?'"[69]

This is a telling passage, since it reveals that by 1909 W. B. Riley was ready to organize a crusade against the growing influence of modernism in Protestantism. The choice of the University of Chicago as the site of the 1910 Northern Baptist Convention spurred him, as Ferenc Szasz has documented, to formalize plans for a gathering of militant conservatives. The Minneapolis minister "carefully compiled lists of men of whom he was suspicious and those he felt to be solid in the faith." He suggested that the latter sign a joint statement blasting modernism and complaining about holding the convention at the liberal Chicago school. He also prepared a call for a preconvention conference in order for conservatives to make further plans against the "creeping modernism" in the Baptist denomination. Riley did not make the public call himself, arguing instead that it should come from someone in the city in which the convention was to be held. Riley's hesitation may have stemmed in part from his awareness that he lacked national leadership experience. Whatever the reason, Riley designated Johnston Meyers of Chicago to be the official spokesperson. Meyers supported the conference but, unfortunately for Riley would not accept the responsibility of issuing the call. The proposed conference of antimodernists died aborning.[70]

Riley's energies were subsequently diverted into extensive revival campaigns as well as a speaking tour in England. As of the early 1910s, then, his proposed revolt against modernism seemed remote indeed. But W. B. Riley had not permanently abandoned his plan. As a revivalist who stoutly held to the inerrancy of the Bible and the imminent and premillennial Second Coming of Christ, he simply could not abide modernism. Moreover, and as we have seen, Riley possessed relentless "up-from-the-bootstraps" determination, enormous ambition, and a hearty love of conflict and debate. These personal traits, combined with his theological beliefs and the further spread of modernist ideas in the major denominations, continued to drive W. B. Riley toward creating a confederacy of conservatives.

Then came World War I. The cultural crisis engendered by the Great War sharpened and intensified the tension between Protestant liberals and conservatives. This tension provided W. B. Riley with a wonderful opportunity to organize a national antimodernist crusade. He would not squander the chance.

2

The Crusade

With the possible exception of William Jennings Bryan, W. B. Riley was the dominant figure in American fundamentalism in the 1920s. Stewart Cole pointed out in 1931 that Riley was "the ablest executive" the fundamentalist movement produced.[1] Moving out of relative obscurity into the national spotlight, Riley marshaled the fundamentalist forces into an antimodernist crusade in the decade after World War I. The industrious Riley was the founder and leading spokesperson of the World's Christian Fundamentals Association (WCFA), the first organization that attempted to unite conservative Christians of all denominations in an international association. An indefatigable polemicist, he was one of the most active and effective debaters among American antievolutionists. At the denominational level, he was a recognized leader of the fundamentalist faction within the Northern Baptist Convention (NBC). Throughout the 1920s he wrote innumerable articles, pamphlets, and books for the fundamentalist cause, and he also edited magazines such as the *Baptist Beacon* and *Christian Fundamentals in School and Church.*

For all of Riley's efforts, however, the national crusade was dead by 1930 at the latest. The WCFA was moribund. The momentum for antievolutionist legislation had been reversed. At the denominational level, the modernists were in firm control of the Northern Baptist Convention, and Baptist fundamentalists were badly divided. What had happened to this once-promising national movement?

Because W. B. Riley was the chief executive of the fundamentalist movement, an examination of his interdenominational and then his denominational labors will help explain both the early victories and the eventual failure of the national fundamentalist crusade. As we will see, a combination of Riley's remarkable abilities and external social forces contributed to the crusade's early success, and a combination of internal problems and external social forces led to the crusade's swift collapse.

Riley's rise to prominence on a national level coincided with American entry into World War I. This was probably due in great part to the fact that the war created a more receptive audience for his message. As George Marsden argued in *Fundamentalism and American Culture*, the Great War had an enormous impact upon conservative evangelicals in the United States. Prior to America's entry into the war in 1917 most conservatives were rather moderate in their criticisms of theological liberals; at times conservatives even cooperated with liberals in denominational and inter-denominational ventures. But Wilson's holy war against German barbarism engendered a crisis of culture in the United States, as Americans feared, in Marsden's words, for "the survival of civilization and morality." Like many other Americans, conservative evangelicals were swept up in this spirit of cultural alarm. Moreover, they had at hand a ready explanation for "the astounding moral collapse of German civilization" — its acceptance of modernist theology and its natural partner, Darwinian evolutionism. Alarmed that America might follow the same moral course as had Germany, during the last two years of World War I evangelical conservatives in the United States began to move, Marsden observed, "from moderation to militancy" in their opposition to modernism in America.[2]

As conservative evangelicals became more militant it was only natural that they would find Riley's message more congenial. By 1909 Riley was already a strident antimodernist, even to the point of calling for the formation of a conservative organization to ward off modernism. In this regard Riley stands outside Marsden's analysis, since he did not need World War I to move him toward militancy. This said, it is certainly true that, although it is not at all clear what role the war played, Riley's antimodernism both intensified and broadened during the war years. This is best reflected in his 1917 publication, *The Menace of Modernism*.

At the heart of *Menace* is Riley's horror at the rapid spread of modernism in American culture, particularly within higher education. Riley proclaimed that in the past few years colleges, seminaries, and universities across the United States had been infiltrated by numerous Antichrists who taught that the Bible was of human origin and filled with errors, that Jesus was not God in the flesh, and that social reform (man's work) was more important than salvation (God's work). Modernism had even triumphed in a host of once-Christian colleges, where students were now taught Darwinism and the concomitant "sneer at Scripture." As a result of the modernist invasion of higher education, many American youth received a viciously anti-Christian indoctrination that could blight them for life. Such education not only destroyed individuals but, even more important, also threatened the moral underpinnings of American society. In his chapter

"Has the State University Become a Hot-Bed of Heterodoxy?" Riley explained that "faith in God and His Word have produced the flowers of civilization," including America, which is "what she is . . . solely because the foundations of the State were laid in biblical teaching." On the other hand, "history attests that unbelief has never helped anything, and that skepticism has never resulted in righteousness or fruited in strength." Given the nation's Christian heritage and the cultural ill effects of religious unbelief, the modernist infiltration of higher education constituted an "outrage," an "attack" upon the moral underpinnings of America.[3]

The Menace of Modernism is saturated with Riley's sense of alarm about an American culture in grave danger. But even more striking about this 1917 volume is its personal tone. W. B. Riley deeply resented the modernists, not simply because they held heretical ideas or even because they threatened America. According to the Minneapolis minister, the modernists had arrogantly designated themselves the "solitary progressives of the hour," the "men who really think." Only uneducated folks disagreed with them. This assertion obviously hit very close to home, and Riley complained that the modernists ignored or scorned the educational qualifications of the innumerable well-educated laypersons, ministers, and Bible school teachers who believed that the Bible is inerrant and that "Darwinism is without verification."[4]

Much more than the modernists' arrogant dismissal of conservatives bothered Riley. Unlike *The Finality of the Higher Criticism* (1909), in which he focused almost solely on the modernists themselves, in *The Menace of Modernism* what really distressed Riley was the fact that the modernists had secured America's educational elite as allies. Not only did university professors sarcastically and "scientifically" attack the veracity of the Bible and hold Christianity up to ridicule, but they also enthusiastically welcomed modernist ministers into the university as speakers and, on occasion, as fellow professors. On the other hand, as Riley observed about a colleague, conservative ministers had "about as good a chance to be heard in a Turkish harem as to be invited to speak within the precincts of a modern State University." Riley attempted to soften this blow by repeatedly noting that conservative ministers had much larger congregations than did their modernist counterparts. Nevertheless, Riley was extremely bitter about the alliance of modernist ministers and skeptical professors, an alliance that, in Riley's view, permitted mediocre but liberal ministers to attain the status of scholars:

I have seen a little two by four preacher, who could not get four hundred people to hear him on any occasion, and who could not find a publisher in all the land

that would take a manuscript from him and risk the expense of printing it, called
to a professorship in a great University; and instantly he blossomed into authority
on all scientific subjects; and I have seen that occur so often that I know what
takes place behind the curtains, and am not deceived when the play is staged, and
a fine scholar (?) faces the crowd and calls himself Prof. Edwin Booth, or Prof.
Henry Irving, or even Prof. Wm. Shakespeare.[5]

The unsaid message here is most telling: while the university conferred
intellectual legitimacy upon modernists, it did not confer intellectual legitimacy upon W. B. Riley and his conservative compatriots. Riley's painful awareness of this fact, well reflected in the above passage, is central
to his bitterness in *The Menace of Modernism* and sets this volume in
marked contrast with his 1909 diatribe against modernism.[6] If *Menace* is
any indication, by 1917 Riley suffered from a severe case of status anxiety.
He had reason to be anxious. The cultural authority of Riley and other
ministers rested both on traditional professional status and popular appeal; it is noteworthy that Riley, who in *Menace* repeatedly boasted that
pastors of his ilk had the largest congregations, indeed presided over a
church of more than three thousand members. But an academic revolution in the years at the end of the century severely challenged the authority of ministers such as Riley. Chronicled by Burton Bledstein and others,
this revolution involved the professionalization of learning and the rise
to academic preeminence of the secular universities. The professors at these
universities prided themselves on being "scientific," which meant, among
other things, specializing, being "objective," and removing religious beliefs and principles from their field of study. For many in the cultural elite,
the authority of ministers was now supplanted by these academic experts,
many of whom had an antagonistic view of orthodox Christianity.[7]

W. B. Riley claimed not to be threatened by the experts' challenge to
his religious beliefs: "Pardon me if I am not scared when the Herr Professor shoots his little paper wad of science at my theological form."[8] Nevertheless, *The Menace of Modernism* clearly reveals that Riley was indeed
anxious about the experts' challenge to his status, and his anxiety was greatly
exacerbated by the fact that his theological enemies had allied themselves
with the new arbiters of knowledge. While Riley had been a militant antimodernist since at least 1909, these concerns about status certainly heightened and sharpened his antimodernism. In this regard, Riley's crusade
against evolutionist teachings in the schools, which will be discussed below, probably owed some of its extreme fervor to Riley's general animos-
ity toward the university professors who propagated such views. All of
this lends some credence to R. Laurence Moore's contention that the fun-

damentalist movement was, at heart, a response to declining intellectual prestige.[9]

World War I not only moved many conservative evangelicals toward militant opposition to modernism, but it also heightened their interest in interpreting biblical prophecy. Premillennialist and prophecy conferences had been a mainstay of conservative Protestantism for four decades, but the magnitude of the war's horror seemed to vindicate the premillennialists' cultural pessimism and give rise to the idea that the last days were indeed occurring. This feeling was heightened by reports that British forces led by General Allenby had captured Jerusalem from the Turks. Premillennialists had long argued that one of the signs of the last days was the return of the Jews to Palestine, and the removal of the Turks cleared the way for fulfillment of biblical prophecy. In 1918 huge crowds attended prophecy conferences in Philadelphia and New York City. As proclaimed in the statement announcing the Philadelphia conference, the conferees heard addresses confirming that the "Lord's prophetic Word is at this moment finding remarkable fulfillment," which indicated "the nearness of the close of this age, and of the coming of our Lord Jesus Christ."[10]

Already a regular on the premillennial conference circuit, Riley was active in these conferences. But having concluded *The Menace of Modernism* with another call for a "Christian confederacy" of "true and evangelical conservatives," he yearned for the chance to move these premillennialists beyond, as George Marsden had described it, "just evangelizing, praying, and waiting for the end time."[11] In the summer of 1918 Riley and other leaders in the prophetic conference movement met at the summer home of Reuben A. Torrey, the dean of the Bible Institute of Los Angeles, in Montrose, Pennsylvania. There they sought to lay plans for a second prophecy meeting to be held in Philadelphia the next year.[12] Riley skillfully worked to broaden the emphasis of the upcoming meeting from prophecy to the preservation of the fundamentals of the faith. He also gained the group's commitment to the formation of an interdenominational association of conservatives. When the matter drifted in the months after the Montrose meeting, Riley took control. He used the New York meeting in December to make preparations for a "world conference on fundamentals." Riley made absolutely clear in a promotional article that the conference on fundamentals was not to be just another discussion of prophetic fulfillments.[13] It would be, instead, the first meeting of a new organization dedicated to "the persistent propagation of 'the faith once for all delivered' as the only antidote to that infidelity which is forcing its way beyond the very altars of our churches, and which has already slimed our schools with its deadly saliva."[14] In typically vivid and forceful language W. B. Riley had launched his fundamentalist crusade.

More than six thousand people attended the first World Conference on the Fundamentals of the Faith in Philadelphia May 25 to June 1, 1919. The importance of the Bible schools in the nascent fundamentalist movement was graphically illustrated by the roster of speakers, which included the aforementioned Reuben A. Torrey, dean of the Bible Institute of Los Angeles; James M. Gray, dean of Moody Bible Institute; William M. Pettingill, dean of the Philadelphia School of the Bible; and of course, W. B. Riley, president of Northwestern Bible and Missionary Training School. Riley gave the opening address, and he set the tone for the conference by pronouncing that this was "an event of more historic moment than the nailing up, at Wittenberg, of Martin Luther's ninety-five Theses."[15] In Riley's eyes, what made this event so momentous was that it marked the establishment of the World's Christian Fundamentals Association. He proclaimed in a 1922 retrospective that the creation of the WCFA gave the beleaguered faithful in America a means to combat the advances of menacing modernism:

Orthodox believers by the millions, members of the greater evangelical bodies, had long waited; multitudes of them had ardently prayed for the . . . realization of just such a fellowship. Sick at the sight of menacing skepticism, convinced that our colleges and theological seminaries were being debauched by the introduction of a science, falsely so-called; realizing that their sons and daughters were being, in four short years away from home, changed over from devout believers to scoffing skeptics, many fathers and mothers hailed this association as the sure sign of a new day for both faith and fellowship. They saw in it not a blind devotion to dogmatism, nor yet a thoughtless return to worn-out creeds, uninspired ceremonies and meaningless formulas; but, rather, the return to God's 'tidings for the meek,' healing balm 'for the broken-hearted,' the announcement of 'liberty to the captives' of college infidelity, and 'the opening of the prison' to them that had been bound and shackled with skepticism, the proclamation of the acceptable year of our Lord, and the day of vengeance of our God against Modernism, a comfort to both mourning parents and believing friends.[16]

As might be expected, much time at Philadelphia was spent attempting to convince these "mourning parents and believing friends" to join this new organization. They could become members by affirming the nine-point World's Christian Fundamentals Association creed, which Riley helped write and which proclaimed, not surprisingly, the inerrancy of the Bible and "the personal, premillennial and imminent return of our Lord Jesus Christ," among other doctrines.[17] They could join at either the associate or active level: associate members paid a one-dollar annual fee and received "as much free literature as the Association happens to produce during the year," while active members paid five dollars for voting and officeholding privileges. Institutional memberships were also available. Churches, Bible conferences, and other fundamentalist organizations could join at the ten-dollar level, with one vote for every hundred members. Inducing organizations to join was crucial to Riley's strategy; as he noted in 1922, one of his chief goals at Philadelphia was to bring under the WCFA umbrella the just-emerging interdenominational network of fundamentalist Bible schools and publications.[18]

Not surprisingly, Riley was chosen to preside over the organization he founded. Under his leadership five standing committees were created to correlate the efforts of the various fundamentalist organizations. The Committee on Bible Schools, chaired by Moody's James M. Gray, set itself the task of standardizing the curricula and creeds of the various Bible schools. Charles A. Blanchard, president of Wheaton College, and his Committee on Colleges and Seminaries called on "Christian people not only to have no fellowship with . . . infidel, atheistic education" but also "to seek out institutions which endeavor to be faithful to the Word of God." Toward this end the executive committee proposed the creation of a list "of such colleges, seminaries, and academies as refuse to employ text books and teachers that undermine the faith in the Bible." The Committee on Religious Magazines and Periodicals, presided over by *Sunday School Times* editor Charles G. Trumbull, promised that member magazines would actively promote the WCFA. This committee also recommended that WCFA headquarters "supply the religious press of North America with official information on the Fundamental Conference Movement, with syndicate articles for publication, and with lists of sound books worthy of recommendation." The Missions Committee suggested that members of the association withdraw their support from foreign mission boards that "are knowingly sending forth unregenerate men or those unsound in the faith" and instead send their money to seven interdenominational mission boards that were safe from the ravages of modernism — Africa Inland Mission, Central American Mission, China Inland Mission, Inland South America Missionary Union, South Africa General Mission, Sudan Interior Mission, and Woman's Missionary Union. Finally, the Committee on Conferences proposed a plan whereby the WCFA would organize and conduct a series of smaller conferences on the fundamentals of the faith throughout the United States and Canada.[19]

The Committee on Conferences was easily the most successful committee. Not coincidentally, its chair was the WCFA head, W. B. Riley. Immediately at the conclusion of the Philadelphia conference Riley launched an extraordinarily ambitious cross-continent tour. The religious troupe included an array of pianists and singers as well as fourteen speakers, including fundamentalist leaders Amzi C. Dixon, J. C. Massee, Mark Matthews, Charles A. Blanchard, W. B. Hinson, and Riley himself. Riley arranged the itinerary so that when a speaker finished his part of the program he went on to the next conference, without waiting idly for the rest of the group to finish. By this method the tour could cover many more cities "without the loss of time on the part of any speaker and with the least possible expenditure in travel and entertainment."[20] The logistic problems attendant upon such a scheme were enormous. Moreover, a minimum of three thousand dollars a week was needed to keep the show on the road. But Riley proved equal to the task. The six-week trip reached eighteen cities, including New York, Chicago, Denver, Calgary, Vancouver, Seattle, San Francisco, and Los Angeles, and ended, remarkably, with a small financial surplus.[21]

How did such a costly campaign turn a profit? More generally, how was the World's Christian Fundamentals Association financed? Without the WCFA financial records, this question is impossible to answer with any certainty. Riley repeatedly claimed that the organization was financed at the grass-roots level. He observed in his report on the 1922 WCFA convention that, "aside from one great gift made for the publication of booklets on the fundamentals years before the movement took on either name or organization, it has had no single fostering friend to finance it." But as we will see in chapter 4, Riley's own Bible school depended heavily on the support of wealthy donors. Moreover, Ferenc Szasz has documented in *The Divided Mind of Protestant America* that wealthy men, including J. C. Penney and George F. Washburn, contributed liberally to the fundamentalist crusade. In light of this, it seems likely that, as Szasz concluded, "there was financial support from both above and below and more from above than Riley was willing to admit."[22]

However it was financed, the huge 1919 campaign provided the nascent fundamentalist movement with enormous publicity and spurred the creation of local fundamentalist Bible conferences. Put another way, this tour transformed the concerns of Riley and other conservative Protestant leaders into a national crusade. This is exemplified by one Indiana minister who, in the wake of the conference tour, sent a letter of testimonial to Riley's *Christian Fundamentals in School and Church*: "I regard Dr. W. B. Riley as the Apostle Paul of our American ministry. . . . His Bible Conference work is doing more than any other agency I know of to clear the atmosphere for right thinking about what the Scriptures teach, and to fortify the Lord's people against the menace of modernism. These conferences are also having a wonderful effect in quickening and energizing the churches for aggressive Evangelism and missionary work."[23]

At the conclusion of this strenuous tour Riley trimmed the company to four assistants and returned to the road. By the summer of 1921, he claimed, he and his associates had conducted over two hundred conferences, touching "practically all of the larger cities of America and Canada, scores of cities of the second grade, and in some instances have taken towns and villages." Flushed with evangelistic success, the WCFA head pronounced at the opening of the fourth annual convention that "the very men who took the initial steps in this organization stand amazed at its unprecedented growth, its wide-spread influence, its conceded power, and its unlimited prospects. If the period of three years has sufficed to shake the continent, bring Conservatives to a consciousness of their numbers and strength, and smite the enemies of Truth with overwhelming fear, what may be expected when this Association shall come to the celebration of its Tenth anniversary?"[24]

Riley's exuberance about the future was misplaced. By 1922 the World's Christian Fundamentals Association was already displaying signs of collapse. Although Riley's speaking tours and related activities heightened antimodernist sentiment, they were of minimal value in banding fundamentalists together in a tightly structured organization. While Riley's Committee on Conferences was spectacularly successful, the other four committees achieved little over the years besides publishing lists of recommended Christian books and schools. Within a few years after the formation of the WCFA, the plans for standardization and accreditation of Bible schools, establishment of a Fellowship Foundation to rival the Rockefeller Foundation, and creation of a fundamentalist theological seminary had all been quietly scrapped.[25] By 1925 the program of the annual convention had been trimmed down to cut costs, and in the next few years attendance took a precipitous plunge. A discouraged Riley resigned as president in 1929, although he continued to serve as executive secretary. While the WCFA continued to limp along for the next few decades, the association of fundamentalists that would "roll back the tide of modernism" had failed to materialize.[26]

Three major factors account for the early demise of the World's Christian Fundamentals Association and go far toward explaining the failure of the national fundamentalist crusade. Marie Riley put her finger on the first problem when she observed that "some personal incompatibilities, and a constant tendency towards independent leadership combined to retard the progress of what was intended to be an 'all-inclusive fellowship' in the Association itself."[27] Fundamentalist leaders were proud, stubborn, and independent men who jealously guarded their personal fiefdoms. They were quick to split with those whom they thought were encroaching on their prerogatives or whom they felt had erred in their ways. Cooperation among fundamentalist leaders was extremely rare, and feuds were common. More to the point concerning the WCFA, submission to the leadership of a fellow fundamentalist leader was anathema. While Riley claimed that running the WCFA was a cooperative effort, there was little doubt that he held the reins of power, tightly. From the beginning other fundamentalist leaders resisted putting themselves under Riley's command, much to his chagrin: "Some fundamentalists are laws unto themselves, and even those who have no such disposition are not as yet in the close co-ordinated fellowship that would accomplish the best and most to be desired results."[28]

By the end of 1924 Riley had lost whatever control he did have over his fundamentalist colleagues. On June 7 of that year Riley was involved in a serious auto accident while returning from a fishing trip in northern Minnesota. He suffered a severe concussion that left him with a painful and insistent headache. The following day the WCFA convention opened in Riley's First Baptist Church of Minneapolis. Riley ignored his physician's orders and participated fully in the meetings, although, as he admitted later, he was "living in a daze." After the convention he resumed his normal schedule, which included conducting a Bible conference in Arkansas and a preaching tour through northern Minnesota. But on July 13 he collapsed in his own pulpit, and for a month he wavered between life and death. When he was well enough to travel, he retired to southern California, where it took another six months for the exhausted leader to make a full recovery.[29]

When Riley finally returned to the fray he faced a bewildering array of new fundamentalist organizations: "There is constant complaint coming to our headquarters concerning the multiplication of Fundamentalist organizations. We have the Fundamentalist League of the Pacific Coast, the Anti-evolution League, American Bible League, the Defenders of Science and Sacred Scriptures, and the Bryan Bible League, and many other organizations. It should be remembered that the original movement is the World's Christian Fundamentals Association, and in our judgment, [most] of these movements ought to be simply a state organization of the World's Christian Fundamentals Association."[30]

At the association's 1926 meeting in Toronto Riley made a last-ditch effort to bring together the different fundamentalist groups under the WCFA umbrella. He had little success.[31] Hard on the heels of this failure came his spectacular split with WCFA associate and Southern Baptist firebrand J. Frank Norris. Earlier in the decade, when Norris was embroiled in an ongoing controversy in his home state of Texas, Riley defended his colleague as one who "never lined up on the wrong side of any question," and who was unquestionably "a servant of the Lord."[32] But in 1927 Norris changed the title of his magazine from *The Searchlight* to *The Fundamentalist*, in an apparent effort to fool fundamentalists into thinking that his periodical was the WCFA's official organ, instead of Riley's *Christian Fundamentals in School and Church*. Riley angrily broke with Norris over this injustice. His anger did not wane over the years. In a 1938 article entitled "Fundamentalism and Religious Racketeering," Riley used Norris as an example of religious frauds who trade in on the good name of fundamentalism: "Such men almost uniformly edit magazines. Some of them have dared to do the dastardly thing of stealing the name of the Movement itself and calling their sheets THE FUNDAMENTALIST. The fact that they have been . . . discredited by the officers of [the WCFA] is kept in the background, and, like the public auctioneer on a street corner they halloo so loudly that all other sounds are drowned by the voice that calls attention to SELF."[33]

Hence division among fundamentalist leaders was a key factor in the demise of the World's Christian Fundamentals Association. A second factor was the failure of the WCFA to provide an institutional alternative to the modernist-tainted denominations. In an article celebrating three years of the World's Christian Fundamentals Association Riley observed that the purpose of the association was to expose the agents and methods of modernism in the major denominations. He asserted that these efforts in publicity would bring victory to the fundamentalists. But fundamentalist catcalls did not remove the enemy. In both the Northern Baptist Convention and Northern Presbyterianism in the early 1920s modernists used pleas for denominational unity and sophisticated bureaucratic maneuvers to deflect fundamentalist criticisms and maintain their power. What then would happen to the WCFA? At times in the mid-1920s Riley gave the impression that he and his fundamentalist followers would separate from the besmirched denominations. "Some of us," he commented in 1923, "have reached the point where we are perfectly willing to have . . . cleavage come. We are tired of fellowshipping men who deny the veracity of the Scriptures, dispute the Deity of Christ, and decry the blood atonement!" In that same year Riley even went to the extent of announcing that he stood "ready to throw the working force of the Christian Fundamentals Association" into the founding of hundreds of independent "fundamentalist tabernacles" throughout the nation.[34]

These WCFA churches never materialized. Riley's call for tabernacles seems to have been a desperate tactic designed to shock denominational leaders into line, although it should also be noted that throughout his life Riley genuinely struggled with the question of separatism. Until his final years, however, the fundamentalist chieftain maintained confidence that God would work within the major denominations; certainly God and the fundamentalists would eventually triumph in Riley's beloved Northern Baptist Convention. Riley thus had no intention of having the World's Christian Fundamentals Association serve as a new denomination.[35] But this meant that when the publicity campaign failed to budge liberals from their places of power in institutional Protestantism, the WCFA had little to offer disaffected conservatives. Stewart Cole was thus correct in his 1931 observation that because the WCFA refused to take the "logical step" and "withdraw its members from the denominations and become an independent sect," then "this spectacular and most vigorous and inclusive of all fundamentalist Christian causes seems to have run its full course."[36]

By 1923 at the latest, the World's Christian Fundamentals Association had abandoned its goal of eliminating modernism from the major Protestant denominations. The organization's new goal was to drive evolutionism out of the public schools. But while antievolutionism enjoyed fleeting success, this shift in focus proved to be the third and final nail in the WCFA's coffin. By abandoning its original raison d'être and instead adopting antievolutionism as its cause, the WCFA was left without a unifying purpose when the antievolution crusade stalled in the late 1920s.[37]

W. B. Riley nevertheless found it natural to include antievolutionism as part of the fundamentalist crusade. As early as the first decade of the twentieth century Riley recognized in evolutionism a deadly threat to both church and society.[38] In his sermon "The Theory of Evolution and False Theology," which was published in 1909, Riley summarized much of his argument against evolutionism.[39] Central to his critique was the belief that the theory of evolution was un-Christian. According to Riley, the evolutionists had replaced the scriptural account of Genesis with a theory that not only rejected the notion that God created each species separately but in fact left out the role of God in creation. While there were "brethren in the pulpit" who attempted to claim that "evolution is true, and so is the Bible," the reality was that to accept evolutionism was also to accept that God was not a "personal heavenly Father" but an impersonal force; Jesus was not divine but "only a remarkable man"; and the Bible was not infallible but filled with errors. That evolutionism was un-Christian was obvious when one looked at those in the church who accepted it as true: "It is doubtful if there is a single skeptical professor in the Old World or the New, who is not also a fairly-fledged evolutionist."[40]

That evolutionism was at odds with Scripture did not mean for Riley a choice between religion and science. He saw continual demonstrations throughout history of the perfect agreement of science and Scripture. The problem was that evolutionism was not a science. According to Riley, science was "knowledge gained and verified by exact observation and correct thinking." Evolutionism, on the other hand, was simply a theory, defined by Riley as "mere hypothesis or speculation."[41] To call evolutionism a science was to misuse the word and to ignore that this theory lacked even the fragments of substantiating evidence:

What evidence is there that the universe began in fire mist? What evidence is there that life originated out of death? What evidence is there that mineral became the vegetable, and vegetable became the animal, and the animal became the man? What proof have we of the eternity of matter beyond the atheistic desire to have it so? And if these premises are false how can conclusions resting upon them be true? If within the knowledge of man the reptile has never become a bird, a fish has never become a mammal, a monkey has never become a man; if the depths of the earth and the sounding of the seas refuse to deliver up a single instance of such a metamorphosis, what are the premises of this argument? It may be very convenient to push your claims back to the time where the knowledge of man utterly fails, but do not do violence to the splendid attainments of human speech by calling such conduct 'scientific.'"[42]

Riley's distinction between science and theory was at the heart of the fundamentalist critique of evolutionism, and in this distinction we see a conflict of scientific paradigms. George Marsden has noted that the fundamentalist view of science, so neatly represented by Riley, was an older, commonsensical view, with its demand that science be limited to observable facts and demonstrable laws. Speculations were not scientific conclusions. But the opponents of the fundamentalists, on the other hand, saw "perception as an interpretive process." They were "open to speculative theories," although they "considered these theories to be reliable inferences from the facts, and felt that no modern scientific person could seriously doubt them." Such notions were anathema to Riley and his fellow fundamentalists.[43]

World War I and its attendant crisis of culture intensified and, more important, expanded Riley's attacks on evolution. Now Darwin's theory was not only wrong, it was also socially destructive. Riley claimed that the doctrine of "the survival of the fittest," which he saw as an integral part of evolutionism, encouraged in people a self-centered aggressiveness that inevitably led to conflict and violence. Using the Great War as an example of this truth, Riley proclaimed: "There can be no question that the doctrine of 'the survival of the fittest' . . . resulted in an egoism on the part of [Germany] to the effect that those people were the only ones who had real right to remain on the earth and propagate their kind. War, with all its attendant iniquities was the result, and the world's financial and moral bankruptcy were the fruits."[44]

War was bad enough, but if evolutionism was widely accepted as true, then the social costs would be much higher than occasional outbreaks of violence. Those individuals who accepted Darwinism, biological and social, were denying man's divine origins. This meant that they were also denying the moral codes, such as the Ten Commandments, upon which the great modern states rested. If multitudes of people became evolutionists, the result would be that these moral foundations of civilization would "be swept out of their places, gnarled, twisted, torn, and finally flung on the banks of time's tide."[45] As Riley proclaimed in a speech published in 1922, the awful result would be

A godless world that will make unto itself graven images and by bowing itself to them, go back to the heathenism of the past; that will take the name of the Lord God in vain, for the purpose of showing their contempt of such a term; that will trample the Sabbath day under its feet in order to prove its disrespect for any expression of law; that will refuse honor to father and mother on the ground that the family is not a Divine institution and parenthood imposes no obligation; that will kill; that will commit adultery without conscience because the law against the same was only made sacred by Capitalism; that will steal without conviction of sin, since personal property rights were never sacred; and that will take from neighbor house or wife or servant or beast, if he is able, on the sole ground that 'in the struggle for existence' only the stronger have rights that are to be regarded. . . . Is there any longer any doubt as to the relation between Evolution and Anarchy?[46]

Befitting both his combative personality and his belief that truth required an active defense, Riley took to the debate platform in the early 1920s. As outlined in a January–March 1923 issue of *Christian Fundamentals in School and Church*, his terms for debate were rather simple. He was willing "to travel any reasonable distance" to spar with an evolutionist. In addition, if his opponents had not "the courage to debate without the sure backing of admiring students," he would, "if necessary, enter any school building that is adequate for the crowds and meet our opponent on his own ground." (As we will see, Riley was being somewhat disingenuous here.) But there were two conditions. First, the audience, rather than a panel of judges, would decide the victor. Second, his opponent must have "sufficiently high professional standing to qualify as a representative of evolutionary advocates." In other words, Riley felt that the bigger the opponent, the harder the opponent would fall when defeated, and thus the greater the blow to evolutionism.[47]

A good number of hardy souls accepted the challenge, including Maynard Shipley, president of the Science League of America; Edward Adams Cantrell, field secretary for the American Civil Liberties Union; Henry Holmes, chair of the philosophy department at Swarthmore College; and Charles Smith, president of the American Association for the Advancement of Atheism.[48] Whatever their intellectual credentials, Riley's opponents must have found debating the fundamentalist leader a most confounding experience. A practiced speaker and a master of verbal combat, Riley made little attempt to deal in any systematic fashion with the evidence for evolution. Playing to the crowd, he combined anecdotal attacks on natural selection and the stratification theory with quips designed to disarm his opponent. Once, when confronted with parthenogenesis, he replied, "I know only one Genesis and that is good enough for me."[49] Another time he held up drawings of prehistoric men, mockingly mispronounced their names, and ridiculed their looks: "Come up here after the debate and look at these pictures, and I am sure you will see somebody who looks just like them when you get down town." Occasionally Riley's adversary would attempt to match him in the realm of ridicule, an effort that could quite easily backfire. For example, in a New Orleans debate Charles Smith of the American Association for the Advancement of Atheism "appeared on the platform . . . accompanied by a gorilla clad in a full-dress suit, with patent leather shoes and provided with a bottle of liquor." But the quick-witted Riley turned the situation to his advantage, bringing down the house with the remark "I came down here to meet Charles Smith, President of the American Association for the Advancement of Atheism. Since my arrival I find I have to meet the 'Smith Brothers!'" When the laughter died down he continued, "I trust they have brought along plenty of cough drops for they are going to need them."[50]

Riley's debates received wide media coverage. A few were even carried live on the radio. Most resulted in resounding victories for Riley. In 1941 he gloated that he was undefeated in twenty-eight debates, and he pleaded for new opponents: "It has been some years now since the last debate and my Irish humor is getting a bit rusty. I am aching for some fun. Who will accept it?"[51] Riley's memory had dimmed a little; according to his own 1926 report, at the conclusion of a Chicago debate against Joseph McCabe, a slight majority of the audience supported the proposition that "Evolution Is a Proven Fact and Should Be So Taught in Public Schools." But in explaining this defeat Riley revealed one reason why he was usually victorious: "We committed our cause to Rev. L. C. Stumpf, our leader of Fundamentalism in Chicago and Illinois, but he was out of the city, and we had few friends present." Riley regularly used fundamentalist ministers in host cities to pack the crowd with supporters.[52] The fact that Riley was often preaching to the converted, plus his considerable verbal skills, meant it was almost inevitable that postdebate votes would go his way. Of course, whether he convinced many outside of the fundamentalist camp is another matter. Certainly Riley's form of debating did nothing to quell the increasingly popular notion that fundamentalists were obscurantists.

W. B. Riley did not restrict his efforts to the debate platform. He also maneuvered the World's Christian Fundamentals Association into an antievolutionism crusade. This shift in emphasis was reflected at the 1922 convention, where many of the addresses dealt with the unscientific, unscriptural, and socially dangerous theory of evolutionism. In his report of the proceedings Riley explained the reasons behind the WCFA's new focus: "This Fourth Annual Convention gave little attention to eschatology, not because its leaders are weakening at that point, but because *we increasingly realize that the whole menace in modernism exists in its having accepted Darwinism against Moses, and the evolutionary hypothesis against the inspired Word of God.*" (emphasis mine).[53]

Interestingly enough, while Riley's emphasis here was on the negative effects of Darwin's theory on Christian doctrine, he did not feel that it was enough to combat evolutionism in the denominations and their seminaries. The WCFA's crusade had to be much broader, because American culture as a whole had been placed in grave danger by the fact that evolutionists had sown their seeds of untruth in the wide field of public education. Riley announced a few months after the 1922 convention that it was necessary for Christian taxpayers and parents to respond en masse to this threat to the public schools: "When we have found one field infested and its fruitfulness ruined, it is a suggestion, at least, that we had better set a watch against the stealthy sower. That is the exact method of this hour. There are hundreds of teachers whose hands ought to be stayed from this broad-casting, and hundreds of text-books that ought to be excluded before their teachings take root in the garden of the Lord, the Home, or in the greater fields, the Church and the World."[54]

As early as the spring of 1921 Riley was holding antievolution meetings in Kentucky. Two years later Riley had expanded these efforts into a series of WCFA-sponsored campaigns aimed at creating a public sentiment that would force state legislatures to eliminate the teaching of evolution from their educational systems. Riley himself led forays into Texas, Virginia, and Tennessee. Thanks in part to WCFA efforts, in early 1925 the Tennessee legislature passed an antievolutionism statute.[55]

Recognizing the importance of the Tennessee law, and at the prodding of W. B. Riley, the World's Christian Fundamentals Association became involved in defending that state's statute from the legal challenge initiated by John Thomas Scopes and the American Civil Liberties Union. At their 1925 convention in Memphis, the WCFA, "in order to secure for the state law a just and adequate hearing," adopted the following resolution: "We name as our attorney for this trial WILLIAM JENNINGS BRYAN and pledge him whatever support is needful to secure equity and justice and to conserve the righteous law of the Commonwealth of Tennessee."[56] Bryan was a natural choice: he had become the de facto leader of the antievolutionist forces in America, and his very name added a luster to the cause that no one else could provide. Realizing this, Riley had even implored Bryan to accept the presidency of the World's Christian Fundamentals Association.[57] Bryan rejected the WCFA presidency but accepted the WCFA's call to prosecute Scopes. In a sermon given at Bryan's death, Riley described Bryan's acceptance of this task in grandiose terms:

Believing as he did that American homes had been what they were because of their belief in the Bible and God, that American schools enjoyed in that same confidence the greatest single educational inspiration, that American laws had been righteously influenced by the same matchless faith, that American shores had been a haven of safety for the persecuted souls of all the earth in consequence of the exercise of her more Christian faith, Mr. Bryan could do nothing else than see in this battle for the faith the best opportunity that had ever opened before him, for the truest testing of, and the most important employment of his superb talents; and with that abandonment which characterized this man of convictions, he flung himself into this controversy without reserve, asking not even a financial reward while he wrought.[58]

The story of the Scopes trial has often been recounted, and so only a few comments regarding the role of W. B. Riley and the World's Christian Fundamentals Association bear repeating here. Despite the fact that Riley's organization had striven mightily to corral Bryan into serving as prosecuting attorney, the WCFA head was not even at the trial. Bryan wanted him there, but coinciding with the trial in Dayton, Tennessee, was the annual meeting of the Northern Baptist Convention, in Seattle. Because this was a crucial convention for the fundamentalist faction in the NBC, Riley and other fundamentalist Baptists such as J. Frank Norris and T. T. Shields chose Seattle over Dayton.[59] Perhaps if Riley and his colleagues had known how much publicity the Scopes trial would receive and how important this case was for the antievolutionist crusade, then they would have been in attendance. Instead, Riley watched the Scopes trial from afar.

In the memorial address he delivered at Bryan's death, Riley pronounced that "the Great Commoner" had achieved at the Scopes trial a "signal conquest" for the fundamentalist forces: "He not only won his case in the judgment of the Judge, in the judgment of the Jurors, in the judgment of the Tennessee populace attending; he won it in the judgment of an intelligent world." But in this same sermon Riley angrily attacked the sophomoric and "blood-suck[ing]" journalists covering the trial, whose "reports made poor reading for thinking people." And in his official report on the trial he railed at length against Clarence Darrow's "unfair methods." He complained, "Mr. Darrow's questions to the Honorable William Jennings Bryan were unworthy a high-class attorney. They were both captious and conscienceless. Imagine converting the opposing attorney into a witness for the defense by putting snap judgment questions concerning the exact years when a number of heathen religions were born, and then trying to make it appear as if the failure to answer them offhand was a lack of knowledge, if not of intelligence."[60] One wonders if Riley's intense anger at the press and the opposing attorney reflected a deep-seated realization that Bryan's performance at the Scopes trial had indeed made fundamentalists appear ridiculous, thus greatly harming the antievolution crusade.

While Riley might have sensed the damage done at Dayton, in the two years after the Scopes trial he and his WCFA forces actually accelerated their antievolutionist activities. Their greatest effort came in Riley's home state of Minnesota. Riley had created a Minnesota Anti-Evolution League in 1923, but it did little except launch occasional attacks on the presence of "atheistic, rationalistic, and materialistic text books and teachers" at the University of Minnesota. The state crusade began in earnest in 1926. In March of that year the university administration denied Riley the use of campus grounds for an antievolution talk. In response the affronted Riley gave a dramatic speech to a capacity crowd of fifty-five hundred at the Kenwood Armory. After a lengthy attack on the administration and faculty for propagating "this atheistic, immoral and unscientific philosophy," Riley concluded by calling on the enthusiastic crowd to support "those of us who make up the anti-evolution league of Minnesota. . . . Unite in your demands that the university which belongs to us shall not become the personal property of a dozen regents or a hundred Darwinized or Germanized, deceived and faithless professors. Back us up in this fight for a decent respect for the God-believing, God-fearing Minnesota majority."[61]

Aware they had made a tactical mistake, the university administration in November permitted Riley to give a series of talks on university grounds.

But the fundamentalist forces, emboldened by the show of public support, were not mollified. Soon after his speech at the university, Riley drew up a bill which prohibited tax-supported schools from teaching "that mankind either descended or ascended from a lower order of animals." In February 1927 Riley presented this bill to the state legislature. Riley was confident that his law would pass. Not only was Minnesota his home turf, but the state's predominantly rural, theologically conservative (Lutheran) constituency would, in his opinion, enthusiastically rally to the cause. Riley, Gerald B. Winrod, and other "Flying Defenders of fundamentalism" visited over two hundred towns, exhorting the populace to pressure their legislators into voting for the proposed law. Riley himself gave sixty-five addresses, the final one in front of the state legislature. But for all these labors, the fundamentalists encountered strong opposition, not only from the expected quarters. Many rural editors and Lutheran ministers were, as the WCFA leader had surmised, staunch antievolutionists. But they opposed Riley's bill on the grounds that it violated the separation of church and state. Without their support Riley's antievolution law was doomed. On March 9, 1927, the state senate killed the bill by an overwhelming margin of fifty-five to seven.[62]

This humiliating defeat in Riley's home state signaled the imminent demise of the antievolution crusade. Except for a 1928 campaign in Arkansas, the Minnesota debacle was the WCFA's last major effort to ban evolution from the public schools. This is not to say that the antievolution crusade, however short-lived, bore no fruit. By the end of the decade many southern states, including Arkansas, had passed laws or established administrative rulings restricting the teaching of evolution.[63] This regional success notwithstanding, the question remains: Why did the movement fail to fulfill its early promise and not attract a wider base of support? One obvious answer is that the Scopes trial forever linked antievolutionism with the rural South, thus dooming the movement outside the region (and perhaps advancing it inside the South). More than this, as Willard Gatewood perceptively explained, sympathetic conservatives, of whom there were many, became increasingly disenchanted with "the shrill, indiscriminate assaults" of the antievolutionists, as well as with "their inclination to tamper with such hallowed principles as religious liberty and separation of church and state."[64] In light of the Minnesota battle, the latter seems particularly important. Except for some areas in the South, in an increasingly pluralist and secularist America the day for legislating religious beliefs seemed to be long past.

The collapse of the antievolution crusade also meant the collapse of the World's Christian Fundamentals Association. A tiny organization remained to limp along for the next few decades. In essence, interdenominational fundamentalism at the national level had proven to be a bust. Divisions among leaders, the failure to provide an alternative to institutional Protestantism, and the absence of an enduring, unifying purpose all combined to kill Riley's grand dream. But Riley and his fundamentalist forces did not limit themselves to interdenominational efforts. Simultaneously with the interdenominational crusade, fundamentalists worked within the individual denominations in a struggle to capture the reins of power from the modernists.[65] For W. B. Riley, this meant a fundamentalist crusade within the Northern Baptist Convention.

World War I and the cultural alarms it raised moved many conservative evangelicals toward aggressive opposition to modernism. Moreover, the wartime prophetic conferences, which were the precursors of the annual WCFA gatherings, provided conservatives with a militant sense of mission and solidarity. But they faced an aggressive and confident enemy. The close cooperation of the denominations during the war encouraged in Baptist and other liberals the heady belief that this cooperation could be replicated in peacetime, with the eventual result being denominational unification. The most important manifestation of these liberal hopes was the Interchurch World Movement (IWM). Dubbed by opponents as American Protestantism's League of Nations, the Interchurch Movement sought to coordinate all domestic and foreign agencies within Protestantism into a single drive for volunteers and, especially, for money. As the Interchurch general committee announced, the movement was to be "a cooperative effort of evangelical churches . . . to survey unitedly their present common tasks and simultaneously and together to secure the necessary resources . . . required for these tasks." Both proponents and opponents realized that this colossal effort, if successful, would be a major step toward the liberal dream of one Protestant denomination.[66]

At its 1919 convention in Denver the Northern Baptist Convention ratified its support of the Interchurch World Movement. W. B. Riley was horrified. He viewed the Interchurch as a "choice medium of Modernists," because its "very lack of a doctrinal basis" provided its members with "their opportunity for their bloodless, gospelless propaganda." Moreover, while only Protestant bodies were then connected with Interchurch, its lack of doctrine also meant that eventually Unitarians, Catholics, and even "Mohammedans" would be included under the Interchurch umbrella. But more than Interchurch's heterodoxy appalled Riley. In keeping with other biblical literalists, Riley saw in the modernist dream of "one church" a sign of the last days. He viewed the Interchurch as establishing the foundation of the biblically prophesied institution of apostasy. The result would be: "When this super-church is created, spirituality will fare poorly; preaching a pure Gospel may easily be made again a criminal offense; the men who dare to believe in the blood of Christ may once more endanger their own blood thereby. It is a strange procedure, to say the least, that a Protestantism which knows what church hierarchy accomplished in the middle ages . . . should deliberately plan to reintroduce it into the world."[67]

Befitting such apocalyptic concerns, Riley and other ultraconservatives pounded a drumbeat of opposition to Northern Baptist participation in the Interchurch. Aided by revelations of ineptitude among IWM's leaders, the anti-Interchurch campaign succeeded. The NBC withdrew from the movement in 1920. Northern Presbyterian conservatives had similar success that same year. Without Baptist and Presbyterian support, and without the expected extradenominational financial assistance, the Interchurch World Movement collapsed.[68] In an address delivered at the opening of the third annual WCFA convention in Denver, an exultant Riley crowed: "Let not the Liberals forget that the greatest single endeavor ever attempted by them went down to signal if not disgraceful defeat, when the 'Interchurch' came to signal, if not disgraceful disintegration."[69] Riley's exuberance was understandable. In the space of one year he had formed the WCFA, led a nationwide evangelistic campaign, and helped ensure that the first battle within the Northern Baptist Convention was won by the conservatives.

The anti-Interchurch campaign set the stage for the creation of an organization of conservatives within the NBC. In the May 20, 1920, issue of the Baptist periodical *The Watchman-Examiner* the editor, Curtis Lee Laws, along with 154 signatories, suggested that a "General Conference on Fundamentals" be held immediately preceding the next annual meeting of the Northern Baptist Convention.[70] The next month in Buffalo this preconvention conference was indeed held. Its primary purpose was to discuss ways in which to combat modernist influence in the NBC. Conservative luminaries such as Amzi C. Dixon, Cortland Myers, and J. C. Massee were present, but it was W. B. Riley who set the fundamentalist agenda for action. As one observer noted, the Minneapolis minister "threw a bombshell" into the tense gathering. In a lengthy and emotional address entitled "The Menace of Modernism in Baptist Schools," Riley assailed Baptist colleges and seminaries as "hotbeds of skepticism." He vigorously attacked the modernism taught by professors at Chicago, Crozer, Newton, and elsewhere. He proclaimed that, thanks to these teachers, in denominational schools "our distinctive doctrines are being denied; our distinctive mission is being disparaged; our distinctive influence is being destroyed." As a result the Northern Baptist Convention itself was in great peril and would soon collapse if modernist professors and textbooks were not removed from the schools. Riley concluded his address with a desperate, dramatic call to militant action: "The Samson of Modernism, blinded by the theological fumes from Germany, feels for the pillars of the Christian temple and would fain tear this last one away and leave Christianity itself in utter collapse. If, in any measure that ever be accomplished, let it not be said to the shame of Baptists that they were engaged as 'pipers of peace' at the very time when their denomination perished!"[71]

The Fundamentals Conference, an observer noted, responded to Riley's indictment with "profound feeling." The conferees adopted a resolution requesting that the Northern Baptist Convention "appoint a commission of nine members to investigate the teachings in all secondary schools, colleges, and theological seminaries" for the purpose of discovering "whether these schools and individual teachers are still loyal to the great fundamental Baptist truths as held by the denomination in the past." After a tumultuous discussion, and much to the delight of the fundamentalists, the Convention did accept their proposal, albeit a modified and somewhat less militant version.[72] The convention also agreed to name as the investigatory committee the nine Baptist leaders suggested by the fundamentalists, a group which included W. B. Riley. But Riley refused the committee post, in response to criticism that his position as head of a Bible school biased him against the denominational seminaries.[73]

This was a decision he would have good reason to regret. The report of the Committee on Denominational Schools at the 1921 NBC convention in Des Moines was in marked contrast to Riley's fiery speech of the previous year. The committee, chaired by fundamentalist Frank M. Goodchild, announced that their investigation revealed "that for the most part our schools of all grades are doing a work of which the denomination may well be proud." The report did grant that "here and there doubtless is a teacher who has departed from the Baptist faith or has lost the Saviour's spirit." These few teachers who reject traditional Baptist teachings certainly should depart the school; if they do not, "we ought to use persuasive methods to assist [them] in going." But persuasion was the limit of denominational response; the denomination could not force an un-Baptist person to leave, for it had no power to serve as "a court where a man shall be tried for heresy."[74]

It is not surprising that the man who launched the NBC investigation of denominational schools was unhappy with this report. In the October–December 1921 issue of *Christian Fundamentals in School and Church*, Riley complained that the "report made by the committee was unsatisfactory to true Baptists"; when they did talk about the removal of un-Baptist professors, they "practically suggested that this let-down be as easy and comfortable as possible." He then went on to argue that "either the Philadelphia or New Hampshire Confessions should be reaffirmed by Baptists."[75]

This call for a confession was crucial. As disappointed as Riley was with the committee report, he recognized that the only way to give the NBC the power to enforce orthodoxy in the schools was to establish a denominational creed. This matter of a creed was at the heart of the liberal-fundamentalist battle within the NBC, and both sides drew upon an authentic, albeit contradictory, Baptist heritage. Liberals argued that the establishment of a creed would impinge upon the traditional Baptist principle of "soul liberty," the belief that each individual has the freedom to believe as he or she wishes. But to Riley and his fellow fundamentalists, who drew upon the Calvinist side of the Baptist heritage, the adoption of a creed meant simply the codification of what Baptists had believed through the ages. Baptists had always emphasized doctrinal purity, and thus it was nonsense to them to tolerate non-Baptist teaching and preaching within the denomination. They did not see this as intolerance, but simply as intellectual honesty. Ronald Nelson observed in his 1964 thesis that "the real point of the fundamentalists . . . was not that others do not have the right to believe as they wish, but that they do not have the right to do so and maintain membership in a body which traditionally has held other views."[76]

In 1921 the Fundamentalist Fellowship (the name by which the Conference on Fundamentals was now known) adopted a confession of faith that was a combination of several historic Baptist confessions, including the New Hampshire and Philadelphia confessions. In an apparent fit of indecision, the Fundamentalist Fellowship did not ask the 1921 convention at Des Moines to adopt the creed. Riley was chagrined, because he felt that "the temper of the Des Moines Convention was exactly such as would have adopted a straight up and down . . . Baptist confession of faith."[77] The next year at Indianapolis, Fundamentalist Fellowship leaders again betrayed confusion, or perhaps fear of defeat, and again decided not to press the issue. As *The Watchman-Examiner* reported, "it seemed that the question would not come up." But Riley could not wait for his colleagues to muster their resolve. On June 16, 1922, in a packed auditorium, he moved that the NBC adopt the New Hampshire Confession as the official denominational creed. He argued that the adoption of this creed was necessary "in view of the unquestioned defection from that faith that now endangers the good name and the greater progress of our holy cause." Displaying a preparation and solidarity that the fundamentalists could only dream about, Cornelius Woelfkin of the liberals quickly offered a counterproposal: "Resolved that the Northern Baptist Convention affirm that the New Testament is an all-sufficient ground for Baptist faith and practise, and they need no other substitute." It was an ingenious tactic. Not only did it allow for an enormous range of theological positions, but it also presented conservatives with the unpalatable prospect of voting against the New Testament. After a heated three-hour debate that ended with a fervent plea by Riley, Woelfkin's motion won, 1,264 to 637.[78]

It is not known whether this sudden reversal of fundamentalist fortunes in the Northern Baptist Convention contributed to Riley's decision at approximately the same time to shift WCFA efforts from ecclesiastical reform to antievolutionism. Certainly the 1922 defeat awakened Riley to the difficulties facing his denominational crusade. While the large majority of NBC delegates were probably theological conservatives, they were reluctant to join Riley in calling for compulsory theological conformity within the denomination. One observer explained that the moderates situated between the warring factions viewed the program and evangelistic outreach of the denomination as being more important than divisive theological battles. Riley, who of course put great emphasis on doctrinal fundamentals, scorned these "compromisers" as "soft souls, . . . incapable of thinking or unwilling to take the consequences of decision," and unaware that the "vocabulary of Christianity does not contain the word 'compromise'!" Referring to a similar controversy in the NBC, Riley lamented that, for the sake of denominational peace, "the compromiser would not object at all to having the pre-existence and deity of Christ, the infallibility of his teachings, his mediatorial and intercessory work . . . repudiated and derided."[79]

In light of the failure to act at Des Moines and then the crushing defeat at Indianapolis, Riley concluded that this compromising spirit had infected some of the Fundamentalist Fellowship leaders. Certain Fundamentalist Fellowship leaders had "softened under the persuasive voice of their opponents," resulting in indecision and an absence of coherent strategy. More disturbing was that, even after the Indianapolis debacle, certain Fundamentalist Fellowship leaders were calling for complete loyalty to the denomination. In a 1923 article entitled "Whipping Fundamentalist Leaders into Line," Riley "confess[ed] very frankly that appeals now made to us to support the steam-roller machine find no cordiality of response." Moreover, regarding at least one unnamed Fundamentalist Fellowship leader, Riley saw a sellout in this plea for conciliation: "When a Fundamentalist writes to a young minister and takes the position that he cannot commend him to a church unless he supports the denominational policy, that Fundamentalist (?) can no longer be depended upon in our fellowship, and we are sorry to say that it looks very much as tho [sic] his price had been found and paid by the denomination. If he can compromise in this matter, the same man and school under his leadership, can compromise in the matter of doctrine if that seems essential to its financial and numerical success."[80]

After Indianapolis it was quite evident to Riley that if victory "is to be accomplished at all, it cannot be by compromise, connivance or even by conciliation."[81] Triumph required militancy. Toward this end Riley and a company of fellow hard-liners left the Fundamentalist Fellowship and formed a new group, the Baptist Bible Union (BBU). The organizational meeting of the BBU was held in Chicago in late 1922. The executive committee included the leading extremists in Baptist fundamentalism: T. T. Shields (president), Amzi C. Dixon, J. Frank Norris, R. E. Neighbour, and W. B. Riley, who also served as editor of the BBU's official paper, *The Baptist Beacon*. Preachers founded and preachers dominated the BBU; while it claimed to have thirty thousand members in 1925, the organization's historian has acknowledged that there was never any "evidence of large-scale lay participation."[82] What prompted these fundamentalist ministers to create this new organization, and what they hoped it would accomplish, was clearly stated in a resolution passed at the first annual BBU meeting in 1923:

THEREFORE BE IT RESOLVED . . .

That we place on record our conviction that Dr. Cornelius Woelfkin's repudiation of these fundamentals of the Baptist position while at the same time professing adherence to the New Testament furnishes one more example of what, in the nature of the case, Modernism when it is finished, must bring forth; and that Dr. Woelfkin's pronouncement, like a bugle blast from an enemy's camp, should summon all Bible loving Baptists to arms more earnestly than ever to contend for the faith once for all delivered to the saints; and further

That we declare our determination not to withdraw from the various conventions represented by our membership; but on the contrary with renewed vigor to endeavor to purge our beloved denomination from such heresies, which if unchecked must inevitably destroy the foundations upon which Baptist churches rest.[83]

In this determination to eliminate modernism, the purpose of the Baptist Bible Union sounds very similar to the purpose of the Fundamentalist Fellowship. But in a fascinating 1923 article Fellowship leader Frank M. Goodchild accurately outlined the substantive differences between the Baptist Bible Union and the older group: the Union sought to unite sympathetic Northern, Southern, and Canadian Baptists, while the Fellowship concentrated on the Northern Baptist Convention; the Union had an official membership, while the Fellowship did not; the Union was essentially a premillennialist association, while the Fellowship included pre- and post-millenarians; the Union was willing to boycott "modernist-tainted" agencies and start new agencies, while the Fellowship worked to purge the old agencies of modernism.[84] Two years later a less equanimous Goodchild included belligerency vs. moderation as a further, and perhaps more important, distinction: "When at a recent Convention a fundamentalist counselled against a precipitate assault on a modernist in open meeting, an eminent member of the Union gave as his method of procedure Davy Crockett's maxim, 'Whenever you see a head hit it.' The contrast is typical."[85]

In keeping with the frontiersman's advice, at the same time as the national antievolutionism drive, W. B. Riley and the Baptist Bible Union mounted a series of frontal attacks on modernism within the Northern Baptist Convention. Often opposed by moderates as well as modernists, the campaign was an unmitigated disaster. In 1924 Riley suggested that paid employees of the Northern Baptist Convention, whom he viewed as mere lackeys of the denominational leaders, be denied voting privileges at the convention. Opposed by less militant fundamentalists, this proposal died without a serious hearing. The same year the BBU attempted to press heresy charges against an NBC missionary. Supported by the liberals, J. C. Massee of the Fundamentalist Fellowship proposed instead a Commission of Inquiry to ascertain the American Baptist Foreign Mission Society's policy regarding missionaries who did not hold traditional Baptist beliefs. This defused the BBU attack and, in the eyes of Fundamentalist Fellowship leaders, meant a truce in the fundamentalist-modernist battle.[86]

At the 1925 convention the Commission of Inquiry reported that most Baptist missionaries were loyal to the faith. To alleviate any concerns, the commission also suggested that the NBC strive to ensure that its representatives to foreign countries "go out having a warm-hearted, positive, and evangelical message."[87] As might be expected, this did not satisfy the Baptist Bible Union. In response, the BBU attempted to force the NBC, as Riley had suggested the year before, to "declare itself unequivocally on all matters of Christian faith and tell the Foreign Mission Board that it is to send out only [orthodox] men and women." Presented by W. B. Hinson of Oregon, the BBU resolution stipulated that the foreign mission boards would be required "to recall immediately every representative, whether in evangelistic or educational work, who is found on investigation to deny any of the great fundamentals of our faith." This resolution was perhaps the Baptist Bible Union's best chance for success, particularly considering that the convention was being held in Seattle, and the conservative Northwest provided the militants with a good number of supportive delegates. Nevertheless, the Hinson resolution failed by a vote of 742 to 574.[88] Nineteen years later Riley was still furious about liberal maneuvers that he felt were responsible for this outcome: "The Hinson Resolution . . . would have carried four to one, had it been voted on the morning of the report! But by deft political management twenty-four hours were secured in which to whip middle-of-the-roaders and weaklings into line, so that the false count of the day reckoned the Hinson Resolution lost."[89]

Finally, the next year in Washington, D.C., Riley proposed that "the Northern Baptist Convention recognize its constituency as consisting solely of those Baptist churches in which the immersion of believers is recognized and practised as a pre-requisite to membership." While the NBC did pass a resolution recognizing immersion "as the only Scriptural baptism," the vast majority of delegates, including many Fundamentalist Fellowship members, refused to dictate terms for membership, in this way preserving the independence of the local churches. Riley's resolution lost by a two to one margin. This crushing defeat, which occurred just months before the Minnesota antievolutionism debacle, closed the BBU campaign. It would be the last great convention battle over the "fundamentals of the faith" for twenty years.[90]

As this last defeat unfolded, "the fury of the militants was directed," George Marsden has observed, "against those conservatives who had undermined the movement by yielding to compromise." Their anger was well directed, in that Fundamentalist Fellowship opposition doomed whatever chance the Baptist Bible Union had of success. In this regard the moderates had done more than just vote against their militant brethren. Fellowship leader J. Whitcomb Brougher toured the country in 1925 urging NBC members to quit the doctrinal controversy and "Play Ball." The next year in Washington an appreciative convention elected him president. At that convention former Fundamentalist Fellowship president J. C. Massee gave a powerful speech, pleading with NBC members to "agree to hold controversy in abeyance for six months, to put ourselves distinctly and definitely in grace for a service which cannot be accomplished by the direct contentions and the controversial issues."[91]

While most of the war-weary delegates eagerly applauded Massee's message, the BBU leaders were not swayed, viewing this talk as a sign of Massee's apostasy. The argument that it was time to concentrate on soul-winning and evangelism carried no weight with W. B. Riley: "This is not a battle. It is a war from which there is no discharge." Riley's scorn for the Brougher/Massee group did not dim with the years. Reflecting in 1938 upon these "Compromisers," Riley mocked them as individuals who "believe with us on the Nine points, but who have an exalted notion of their own wisdom in matters of controversy, and who conclude that soft-pedaling the truth and outward friendship for its enemies is the way to win this

battle. . . . These men can make themselves comfortable with either side
of the theological conflict. They are the friends of fundamentalism, in
faith, but they have become its foes, in fact."[92]

The phrase "soft-pedaling the truth" is the key to understanding the failure of the crusade Riley led in the Northern Baptist Convention. Certain
of the truth and unwilling to tolerate even minor disagreements with their
positions, BBU leaders were doomed in their quest to take over a denomination that had no machinery to enforce orthodoxy, that harbored a diversity of theological viewpoints, and that was controlled by a leadership un-
sympathetic to the fundamentalist cause. The Baptist Bible Union slowly
disintegrated in the years after 1926, battered not only by denominational
defeat but also by scandal. In 1927 the sagging BBU purchased the bank-
rupt Des Moines University from the Northern Baptist Convention, intend-
ing to create a fundamentalist college. From the beginning problems beset
this ambitious enterprise. Chairman of the board T. T. Shields immediately took steps to create a rigidly orthodox school. He fired a large number of the faculty, imposed a strict declaration of faith on the remaining
professors, and instituted an espionage system to uncover student apostates. Students protested Shields's iron grip, and when the rumor of an
affair between Shields and his secretary hit the campus, a riot ensued. A
humiliated Shields demanded that all employees resign, and he closed the
school. While Des Moines University reopened for awhile, by 1929 the
school was dead and so was the Baptist Bible Union. The only recourse
was separation. In 1932 a remnant of the BBU left the NBC and formed
the General Association of Regular Baptists (GARB). The denominational
title made it clear they viewed those who separated with them as the only
true Baptists.[93]

W. B. Riley, however, ignored the logical conclusion of his theology and
stayed within the modernist-tainted Northern Baptist Convention. As he
also had not converted the World's Christian Fundamentals Association
into a separate denomination, so he did not join the GARB. In fact, Riley's
efforts, including the destruction of thirty thousand pro-separatist pamphlets, probably kept the BBU from becoming a separate fellowship of
churches much earlier than it did. But his decision to stay in the NBC certainly was not the path of least resistance. He lamented in 1936 that "no
man living knows the unpopularity of this course better than the writer."
On one hand, his theology and militancy isolated him from denominational leaders and kept him from attaining any positions of prominence;
on the other, he endured a good deal of criticism from the Regular Baptist
fundamentalists for failing to "come out" from the denomination.[94] He still
endures separatist criticism for his decision: in a 1982 Th.D. dissertation

a fundamentalist student of church history claimed that Riley stayed in the denomination in order to continue receiving funds from wealthy moderates for his Northwestern schools.[95]

Since no evidence has been provided for this accusation, the question remains: Why did W. B. Riley remain within the Northern Baptist Convention? One reason he gave was that to leave the denomination was to abandon the numerous orthodox foreign missionaries and evangelists connected with the NBC. Moreover, ever solicitous of the fate of his own Northwestern-produced pastors, he was afraid to encourage ministers and churches to separate only to have the withdrawal movement collapse, leaving them high and dry. But the most important factor was his firm belief that he and other fundamentalists within the denomination would eventually bring the NBC back to "that Faith [that] has been written into all its history."[96] In 1935 he proclaimed: "No one has grieved the theological drift of the Baptist denomination, a drift which has been deleterious to date, and threatened even the destruction of the denomination itself, more than the writer; but he has not as yet seen fit to withdraw from its fellowship on that account, since he firmly believes that time will correct many of these regrettable results." He was still hopeful in 1943. In an article entitled "Recovering Majority Baptist Rule!" he called on fundamentalists to run the modernists out of the denomination and then concluded: "I am no longer a young man; but believing as I do in the personality and power of the Holy Spirit, I despair not of seeing this desired result ere my days end."[97]

In short, for Riley to leave the denomination would have been an admission that his fundamentalist crusade had failed to turn the Northern Baptist Convention from modernism. Whether he wanted to admit it or not, Riley's national fundamentalist crusade was indeed a failure, inside and outside the Northern Baptist Convention. Divisions among headstrong and inflexible leaders, tactical errors (and opponents' strategic successes), and ill-advised rhetorical flourishes all damaged the fundamentalist cause. Moreover, in an age of religious and intellectual pluralism, and in an increasingly secularized society, the fundamentalist insistence on adherence to a rigidly delineated set of theological doctrines made them in some ways strangers in their own land, and even in their own denominations.

The collapse of his fundamentalist crusade did not silence Riley on national issues. But while he remained adamantly and vocally opposed to modernism and evolutionism, in the 1930s these issues were eclipsed by a new concern. The depth of W. B. Riley's alienation from mainstream American culture was reflected in his new obsession with the international Jewish conspiracy.

3

The Conspiracy

In 1946 journalist Carey McWilliams published an article in *Common Ground* entitled "Minneapolis: The Curious Twin." According to McWilliams, what made Minneapolis curious was its extremely pronounced pattern of anti-Semitism. In this regard, Minneapolis was unusual in contrast not just with St. Paul but with most other American cities. In fact, McWilliams asserted, "One might even say, with a measure of justification, that Minneapolis is the capitol [*sic*] of anti-Semitism in the United States." In 1946 Minneapolis seemed to be the only major American city in which Jews were ineligible for membership in service clubs or the automobile club. Moreover, Jews were refused admittance into the Minneapolis Athletic Club, denied employment by many of the chain stores in Minneapolis, hindered in buying residential property, almost never included on civic boards or in government, and drastically underrepresented in the higher echelons of local business. In keeping with this general pattern of discrimination, McWilliams claimed, "Minneapolis has more than its share of active anti-Semites." Some of the most vocal of the local anti-Semitic leaders were "local pulpit-thumping fundamentalists"; in fact, "a local fundamentalist academy" run by one of these preachers was reputed to be "a training school in anti-Semitism." To be fair, these anti-Semitic leaders did not create the prejudice against Jews in Minneapolis; they just exploited it. At least in part, McWilliams argued, "the activities of these weird prophets is to be accounted for in terms of the maxim 'monkey sees, monkey does.'"[1]

According to McWilliams, one of Minneapolis' "weird prophets" was W. B. Riley. Riley's own Northwestern Bible and Missionary Training School was the reputed anti-Semitic training ground.[2] While it may have been an exaggeration to describe Northwestern in this manner, McWilliams was right on the mark regarding Riley. In the 1930s and 1940s Riley transferred much of his intellectual energies from his failed fundamentalist crusade to the active promotion of an anti-Semitic, conspiratorial interpretation of national and international events. The primary target of Riley's attacks was Franklin Roosevelt's New Deal. But Riley had not always opposed reform. In the early years of the century he had been quite involved in urban reform efforts in Minneapolis. Because of Riley's status as a fundamentalist leader, his journey from progressivism to the fringes of the Far Right sheds some light on the historic connections between one branch of religious fundamentalism and Far Right politics in America.

In 1906 W. B. Riley published a collection of sermons entitled *Messages for the Metropolis.* He dedicated this volume to the cause of "civic righteousness," and he called for an alliance of the "two well defined movements [which] have characterized these first years of the twentieth century"—evangelism and reform.[3] The notion of such an alliance jarringly clashes with the common scholarly perception that the social gospel clergy and the evangelistic clergy were in mutually exclusive camps. But Riley was not a lonely voice in the wilderness. In contrast with the post–World War I years, during the Progressive Era a host of conservative evangelicals were involved in urban uplift programs. To mention only two, future fundamentalists Mark Matthews and John Roach Straton energetically worked both to save souls and to improve their cities.[4]

W. B. Riley also pursued both goals. Of course, for Riley and other future fundamentalists, there was no question of which task was more important. In his sermon "The Moral Redemption of the Metropolis," Riley made clear that the surest way to bring about a moral city was to evangelize the citizenry: "The future of your city, and the future of any city, depends upon how many may be numbered among the redeemed of the Lord. . . . Every time a soul is snatched from the moral sinks of the metropolis, the evil power of those sinks is reduced, and good citizenship is increased." The "voluntary morality" born of "Divine redemption" was best for society, but as long as there were some souls who resisted Christ's call, there would be need of "enforced morality." This was, of course, the function of government. But constantly "cajoled and threatened by the whole vicious crowd who want to Sodomize the city," municipal officials did not always do their duty. As a result, the moral element of the citizenry needed to undertake whatever reform efforts were necessary to clean up their city. Because they were the most moral of citizens, true Christians were *"especially charged with civic reform."* It was up to the converted to ensure that city government restrained evil and promoted virtue.[5]

Riley followed his own advice. In Bloomington, Illinois, he ignored threats to his person and led an attack against gambling in the city, which resulted in 250 convictions. In Chicago he helped organize a Civic Federation which prodded the city government to enforce laws against the sale of liquor after hours.[6] But his greatest reform efforts came in Minneapolis. Riley moved to Minneapolis in 1897. Two years later Amos Alonzo Ames was elected mayor, and he immediately established the political machine described by Lincoln Steffens in a 1903 *McClure's* article entitled "The Shame of Minneapolis."[7] Riley was horrified at the corruption rampant in Ames's administration. He thus delivered a series of blistering sermons attacking the mayor. The agitation on the part of Riley and other reformers succeeded. Ames was defeated at the polls and some of his cronies were sent to prison.[8]

But Riley was not satisfied with Ames's successor, J. C. Haynes, because Haynes seemed rather reluctant to enforce civic virtue, particularly the laws regarding drinking establishments. Riley abhorred bars more than any other "institution of vice"; in his sermon "The Moral Leprosy of the Metropolis," he declared: "The darkest blight on the municipal body is that blood-stained institution you call the saloon! . . . It will convert the fairest child that ever drew sustenance from a mother's breast into the foulest fiend that ever fattened its lust upon the lives of others. I hang my head for very shame that city, or state, or nation, should ever have entered into an alliance with this iniquitous traffic by which it has legalized its murderous and lecherous work."[9]

What Riley truly wanted was the prohibition of liquor, the "mother" of all other vice. Short of prohibition, he wanted to force bar owners to abide by laws regulating their operations, and he dedicated himself to this task. Appalled by the fact that bar owners routinely ignored legally mandated closing times, the newly arrived Baptist minister repeated his Chicago experience and helped form a Civic Federation, which published broadsides and held mass meetings protesting city government's failure to enforce saloon regulations. Riley was selected to be chair of the Committee on Legal Closing. Riley recalled afterward that he and his fellow committee members "wrote to the mayor . . . an open letter, publishing it in all the dailies, and fixed a time on Friday following, for his order to close the saloons at eleven at night and keep them closed on Sunday, as the law prescribed, or take his place in court under impeachment." The law was with Riley; as the minister chortled years later, a reluctant Haynes ordered saloon-keepers to obey the mandated closing times.[10]

While Mayor Haynes did cave in, his reluctance in enforcing the liquor laws irked Riley and his fellow reformers. As a result, the Civic Federation labored to secure the election of a reform candidate for mayor. They succeeded, with the election of David P. Jones. After this election Riley proclaimed in his 1906 book: "We join heartily with that better crowd of citizens who cried 'Bravo' over the closing of saloons on election days and Sundays, the notification of gamblers that their businesses must go, and especially the warrant . . . upon the wretched keepers [of brothels] that they must vacate! It is a noble beginning!"[11]

W. B. Riley the urban reformer concentrated on combating vice and promoting good government. He did, nevertheless, speak out on other issues, particularly the conflict between capital and labor. In fact, he devoted the last four sermons in *Messages for the Metropolis* to this topic. In the first of these sermons Riley attacked the "growing and grasping corporations" and the greedy millionaires who ran them. Despite their unlimited wealth and power, the corporate tycoons continued to cry for protectionist tariffs. Worse, despite their oft-publicized philanthropic efforts, they insisted on employing and overworking "weak women and little children" in a further drive for profits. The sad reality was that the millionaires made their riches by exploiting their workers: "It is impossible to follow the toilers from any one of the great factories of this country to their homes and see their plain appointments, and then go directly into the home of the owner and operator and look upon the luxuries, without feeling that a fair division of the fruits of combined labor and capital has not yet occurred, and that the well-to-do quite often label as their own, that on which ought to be written, 'The spoil of the poor.'"[12]

But while capitalists exploited and misused laborers, W. B. Riley believed that the laborers themselves were not blameless. Many were indolent, and almost all of those who were unemployed were "out of a job because when they had one they did not work at it." Moreover, many of those who were employed but poor were that way not because their wages were too low but because they were imprudent. They squandered their money on bawdy entertainment, frivolous items such as chewing gum and ice cream, and, worst of all, alcohol. The latter not only rendered workers destitute but also left them physically ruined, mentally impaired, and morally degraded.[13]

In short, owners were unjust, workers were unworthy, and each group resented the other for its shortcomings. But as Riley asserted in his sermon entitled "Is There Any Salvation from Social Disorders?" capital and labor were not "hostile forces contending for a common ground which cannot be occupied by both." If each group would cease to be suspicious of and hostile toward the other, and if businesses would implement some form of profit-sharing, then the result would be a spirit of cooperation between employers and employees. Riley went on to assert: "But to make this surrender of groundless suspicions possible, and this sharing of profits in the proper ratio the greatest power for good, *capitalist and laborer should wor-*

ship the same God. The rich and the poor must meet together the Lord
and Maker of them all. When owners and workers worshipped God, 'all
ill-gotten gain will go back again whence it was taken,' all 'poverty will
come to an end,' and all class tensions will cease."[14]

To summarize, W. B. Riley was an antiliquor, "good government," anti-
monopoly progressive who found the solution to capital-labor difficulties
in Christ-centered cooperation. Upon close examination, it is clear that
Riley had an extremely limited vision of social reform.[15] The state should
restrain evils such as graft and vice, particularly the consumption of alcohol. Beyond this, the state should protect the freedom of the individual.
Structural problems such as poverty and class conflict required spiritual,
not governmental, solutions. Riley was not unusual among progressives
in his perception of the state's limited role in righting social wrongs. As
Otis L. Graham, Jr., documented in *An Encore for Reform*, most anti-
monopoly, "good government" progressives emphasized education rather
than governmental coercion. Moreover, these progressives, also in keeping with Riley, saw as their ultimate goal a general spirit of cooperation
that transcended class divisions. Of course, such ideas would prove to be
in stark contrast with the reforms of the New Deal. The New Deal policies
were coercive and were based upon the idea that certain groups in society
had special claims requiring "frank class legislation." Considering these
differences, it was only natural that most progressives of Riley's ilk who
survived to see Franklin Delano Roosevelt take office opposed his New Deal
programs.[16]

In the 1920s Riley's political conservatism, apparent in his efforts at urban reform, was further bolstered by his involvement in the crusade against
modernism. As noted in earlier chapters, religious fundamentalism in the
United States arose out of opposition to the spread of liberal or modernist
theology in American Protestantism. The fundamentalists believed that
the modernists had gutted orthodox Christianity of its traditional dogmas.
In the opening address of the first World Conference on the Fundamentals
of the Faith in 1919 Riley blasted modernists for their lack of a true commitment to the historic Christian faith, a fact manifested by their failure
to affirm a declaration of doctrinal fundamentals. Riley then went on to
assert that instead of doctrinal principles, the modernists had established
"the test of social service" as the defining mark of a true Christian.[17] This
latter accusation was central to the fundamentalist critique. In the eyes of
the fundamentalists, the modernists' subordination of doctrine to social
concern was heresy. The fundamentalists assiduously labored to rid American Protestantism of such notions. But as numerous historians have observed, in so adamantly opposing the social gospel, the fundamentalists

(as well as less militant conservatives) increasingly began to suspect all forms of social concern. Particularly questionable were governmental actions. By the end of the 1920s the evangelical interest in liberal social concerns had all but disappeared, an event referred to by many historians as the Great Reversal. Among American Protestants, theological conservatism had become inextricably linked with political conservatism.[18]

Even in his heyday as an urban reformer Riley felt that the role of government was essentially limited to restraining evil. His involvement in the crusade against modernism strengthened this already-present conservatism; after 1920, for example, he was nearly silent about the evils of greedy capitalists (except as the latter fit into his theory of a Jewish-Bolshevik conspiracy).[19] It is thus no great surprise that in the 1930s W. B. Riley vehemently attacked the relief and reform policies of Franklin Roosevelt's administration. A Democrat from his Kentucky youth, Riley had voted against Al Smith in 1928 because he "was unwilling to have Rome rule at Washington, and a thousandfold less willing to have Rum rule there." But it was the Roosevelt administration that led him to forsake forever the party of his forefathers. The primary reason was not their repeal of prohibition but their economic policies, which Riley believed to be both ignorant and misguided.[20] In a 1937 message entitled "The Social Economy of Jesus Christ," Riley proclaimed that while Democratic "politicians fill their lips with the phrase 'the poor laborer,' 'the under-fed,' 'the ill-clothed and sick,' [and] 'the aged poor,'" the truth was that the poverty-stricken in America were "a mighty minority." Moreover, this minority could blame their poverty on their unwillingness to work and/or their failure to abstain from alcohol: "If the money that is being expended today in the saloons of America, the favored institution of the Party in power, by 'the ill-fed,' 'ill-clothed,' and 'ill-housed,' was put into land and houses, inside of five years nine-tenths of those who are now the subject of our sympathy and tears would be independent of both and chargeable with belonging to 'the capitalist classes.'"[21]

But the "so-called Brain Trust" ignored the obvious facts that prosperity reigned and impoverished individuals had only themselves to blame for their poverty. Worse, the brain trusters, who were products of atheistic universities, also rejected the biblical principle that impoverished individuals were responsible for working themselves out of poverty. Instead, Riley argued, the Roosevelt administration accepted left-wing notions that "ignore individuality, tend to disparage originality and seek to accomplish a social and financial equality on the part of people who are . . . essentially different, both in ability and disposition to work." When put into practice, these misguided ideas were "doomed to defeat."[22]

According to Riley, Roosevelt's doomed policies included oppressive taxes designed to redistribute the wealth and overbearing governmental regulations that denied capitalists rightful control over their own enterprises. Worse were paternalistic efforts to help the poor. Government jobs programs only encouraged sloth. Riley joked in 1937 of the Works Progress Administration: "It is said the disease of horses that puts them to sleep on foot, and finally kills them, is mosquito inoculation from the blood of a W.P.A. employee. There is a sure cure but hard to get in quantities, and that is sweat from a WPA employee!"[23] But at least the pretense of work in part redeemed the jobs programs. What really incensed Riley were reform schemes which indulged man's selfish and lazy impulses. In a 1935 sermon entitled "Shall It Be a Dole or Endeavor?" Riley pronounced that insurance for the unemployed would inevitably be abused by the indolent, while grants to the elderly would allow old drunks to "retire to a continuous round of guzzling and sleep." The latter program would also create a situation "in which ungrateful and godless children shall slip from their solemn responsibility to father and mother, and fling them ruthlessly upon government grants."[24]

While the rhetoric was rather extravagant, these criticisms differed little from what many "old progressives," fundamentalists, and other conservative critics were saying about governmental policies in the 1930s. To put it another way, if the above two paragraphs were the summation of Riley's political views in the 1930s, this would be, in essence, a neat but thoroughly unremarkable account of an old urban reformer and fundamentalist who opposed the New Deal. But the above discussion is somewhat disingenuous, for the most important elements in Riley's political analysis in the Roosevelt years have been excised. The reality is that W. B. Riley went far beyond standard criticisms of the New Deal to an anti-Semitic, conspiratorial explanation of national and international affairs.

Riley's first public anti-Semitic pronouncement came in his 1921 address to the World's Christian Fundamentals Association convention in Denver. Entitled "The Conflict of Christianity with Its Counterfeit," most of this speech involved an attack on modernism. While discussing the devious methods used by modernists to capture power in the major denominations, he used the Jews in Germany and Russia as an analog. To this end, he quoted from *The International Jew:* "As nature encysts the harmful foreign element in the flesh, building a wall around it, so nations have found it expedient to do with the Jew. In modern times, however, the Jew has found a means of knocking down the walls and throwing the whole national house into confusion, and in the darkness and riot that follows, seize the places he has long coveted."[25]

A review of Riley's writings from the 1920s indicates that anti-Semitic remarks like this one were extremely rare. It was not until the 1930s that, in innumerable books, pamphlets, articles, and sermons, Riley developed and propagated his anti-Semitic, conspiratorial theory of world events. Before examining the details of Riley's conspiracy, one question needs to be addressed: Why did W. B. Riley make this intellectual leap to the fringes of the Far Right? To say that he was responding to a general crisis of culture in the 1930s may be true enough, but considering that most Americans in similar straits did not adopt conspiracy theories, other factors must be taken into account. In his 1983 book, *The Old Christian Right*, Leo Ribuffo argued that in the cases of William Dudley Pelley and Gerald L. K. Smith, personal misfortunes were at the heart of their conversion to anti-Semitic conspiratorial theories.[26] It appears that personal failure also played a major role in Riley's Far Right extremism. As the chief leader of American fundamentalists in the 1920s, Riley confidently marshaled his militantly conservative followers into a crusade designed to save America by purging the major denominations of modernist theology and the public schools of evolutionist teaching. He believed that the latter effort was particularly crucial for America's survival; as he observed in 1922, widespread acceptance of Darwin's theory would destroy the "moral foundations" on which the United States rested, thus creating social chaos.[27] But W. B. Riley failed. With the fate of American society hanging in the balance, all of Riley's efforts came to naught. The national fundamentalist crusade was dead by 1930 at the latest. His World's Christian Fundamentals Association was moribund; the modernists had won almost all the denominational battles, including the battles within Riley's beloved Northern Baptist Convention; and the brief flurry of antievolutionist legislation had ceased, with Riley's own state of Minnesota failing to respond. Then, hard on the heels of these defeats came the Great Depression and the collectivism of Franklin Roosevelt's New Deal. Alienated from both mainstream Protestantism and mainstream American culture, Riley needed a scapegoat for what had happened to his world.

Of course, this begs the question of why Riley selected the Jews as his scapegoat. There may have been some personal reasons for his choice. Riley felt that through the years he had endured a large amount of Jewish harassment. In a revealing sermon at the First Baptist Church of Minneapolis in October 1936, he described why he came "to hold the Jew with suspicion." First, Jews were his "most outspoken opponents" when, some years

before, he suggested mandatory Bible reading in the public schools. More
important was Jewish opposition to his antievolution crusade in the 1920s.
Riley was incessantly heckled on his antievolution tours. According to Riley,
his "most annoying hecklers were young atheist Jews," a fact that he "resented." His suspicions about the Jews were then confirmed in the 1930s,
when he noticed that they predominated in Communist parades and demonstrations in Minneapolis.[28]

There is a problem with Riley's portrayal: How did he know that the
hecklers at his antievolution lectures and the marchers in left-wing demonstrations were Jewish? Perhaps he did know for certain; however, it seems
quite likely that he did not know. The simple fact was that he was predisposed to see his opponents as Jews. One reason for this may have been
the unusually high level of anti-Semitism in Minneapolis. Carey McWilliams hypothesized that Minneapolis had been settled by a group of New
England Yankees who from the beginning controlled industry and politics
in Minneapolis and who had used various forms of anti-Semitism to maintain their preferred social standing. Their anti-Semitism had then been imi-
tated by the Scandinavians and others below the top rung of the social
ladder. Whatever the explanation, from the late nineteenth century Minneapolis had an unusually strong pattern of anti-Semitism.[29] As a prominent minister with more than three thousand members in his church, Riley
certainly contributed to the city's general anti-Semitism. Considering that
the pattern had been well established before the 1930s, it seems just as
likely that he also borrowed from the prevailing culture.[30]

Another primary reason for Riley's predisposition to see his opponents
as Jews resided in his dispensational premillennialism. Certain elements
within premillennialism lend themselves to anti-Semitism. According to
the premillennialist interpretation of biblical prophecy, the Jews were God's
chosen people and would someday benefit from the fulfillment of God's
promises to them. But that was in a future age. Having rejected Jesus' offer
to establish the messianic kingdom, the contemporary Jews were in open
rebellion against God and thus under Satan's power. Many had completely
rejected God. Having rebelled against God, the Jews were destined to en-
dure an unending series of persecutions. These anti-Semitic persecutions
would intensify as Christ's Second Coming neared, the "positive" result
being that the harried Jews would flock to Palestine, as prophesied. But
because many of the Jews who return to the Holy Land will be apostates,
they will ally themselves with the Antichrist in the final struggle during
the Tribulation.[31]

While a fully developed anti-Semitism was not inherent in premillennialism, it is obvious that an ambivalence about the Jews was an integral

part of this eschatology. Timothy Weber observed in his excellent study of premillennialism that while the premillennialists were acutely aware of the Jews as God's chosen people, "their fraternal feelings for Jews as co-heirs of the promises of God could not alter the Jews' present position as rejectors of Christ and the eventual tools of the anti-Christ." Most pre-millennialists did remain sympathetic, if ambivalent, toward the Jews. But a few made the not-so-enormous jump from the notion of Jews as rebels against God and allies of the Antichrist to a full-fledged anti-Semitic conspiratorialism. Gerald Winrod did. So did W. B. Riley.[32]

By 1933 or 1934 Riley had latched onto the Jews as his personal and social scapegoat. His guidebook to the machinations of the Jews was the notorious forgery *Protocols of the Learned Elders of Zion*. Written by Russian anti-Semites at the turn of the century, the *Protocols* purportedly provided a detailed explanation of how a secret Jewish cabal had been working since the time of Christ to wreck Gentile civilization and control world affairs. The *Protocols* were popularized in the United States by *The International Jew*, a 1920 collection of articles elaborating upon the *Protocols* which had originally appeared in Henry Ford's *Dearborn Independent*. Within a few years, five hundred thousand copies of this book, as well as various versions of the *Protocols*, had been put into circulation in the United States.[33] In the late 1930s Riley explained how he became converted to the truth of the *Protocols:*

Less than eight years ago we were invited to dine at the Curtis Hotel, Minneapolis, with a noted evangelist and his wife. At the breakfast table he regaled me with "The Protocols," and so excited was he over the subject that no other topic of conversation had a look-in for the hour that we spent together.

When we left the Hotel, my wife, Lillian Riley, remarked: "Dear, isn't it too bad; he is crazy! He has lost his mental balance; he is done for!"

I said: "Dear, you are right. He is gone! . . ."

But, in his enthusiasm, he had thrust the book into my hands enjoining me to read it and retain the same to him. I took it to my room and left it in neglect. . . .

[But a few years later I read it.] Since that time I have read it over and over and over again. Daily I am compelled to institute comparisons between what is taking place in France, in Italy, in Germany, in Austria, in Spain, in the South American Republics, in Mexico, in China, in India, . . . in Russia, and . . . in the United States, with this diabolical plan.[34]

Prior to the 1930s Riley spoke of "history running into the mold of [biblical] prophecy." Perhaps reflecting that premillennialists, having accepted one cosmic conspiracy, are more willing to accept a second, in the 1930s Riley integrated the *Protocols* into his premillennial eschatology, now speaking of "history running into the mold of the *Protocol* program."[35] What was this *Protocol* mold or plan? According to Riley, behind the scenes of world events there operated an international Jewish-Communist conspiracy. (In Riley's later writings the words Jewish, Communist, and Bolshevik are virtually interchangeable.)[36] These plotters sought to manipulate affairs in order to bring wealth and power to themselves and chaos and poverty to the Gentile masses. Riley claimed that World War I was an excellent example of their maneuverings: in a "diabolical procedure" these "unseen counsellors of Presidents and Kings" had maneuvered the nations into a conflict that sent masses of Gentile youth to their graves while at the same time benefiting Jewish bankers and arms merchants.[37] In his 1934 article "The Blood of the Jew vs. the Blood of Jesus," Riley argued that the Jewish cabal had as its ultimate goal "the establishment of a single government headed by what is called the 'king despot of Zion,' whose place and power will be made secure by a reign of terror that will put to the most torturous death any and every opponent; the plan being to exalt a few of Jewish blood to honors and untold opulence, and retain them there at the expense of the world's millions." This "king despot of Zion," who in Riley's writings seems to be synonymous with the Antichrist, would have absolute control of the world's finances, education, press, and courts and would establish a uniform atheistic religion to which all people would be required to adhere.[38]

The Jewish cabal was attempting to execute its Communist plan throughout the world but was further along in some countries than others. The plan had been brought to perfection in Russia; as Riley observed in his article "The Jewish Web for the Gentile Fly," "Every well-informed man who has been sufficiently unprejudiced to study the Russian situation in the light of 'the Protocols by the Learned Elders of Zion' knows full well that there is not a single suggestion in that diabolical book that is not being carried out in Russia today by rulers, 81 per cent of whom are Jews."[39] This "successful mob of atheistic Jews" had enslaved 150,000,000 people. While the Jewish rulers luxuriated in wealth, many of their subjects were starving to death. Those who dared to disagree with the Jewish cabal faced a slow, tortuous death.[40]

In Riley's view, the *Protocol* plan, so perfectly adopted by the Russian rulers, "anticipates the day when the Gentile world will be as absolutely enslaved as is the suffering, native Russian of this hour."[41] Riley argued in his 1934 book, *Protocols and Communism*, that in the United States Jewish-Communist subversives sought to "filch the land of all its gold, take over its cattle and its farms, and possess themselves of all its factories, arts and industries." In fact, they were already a long way toward having economic control of the United States: "Today in our land many of the biggest trusts, banks, and manufacturing interests are controlled by Jews; tobacco, cotton, sugar,— they handle in overwhelming proportions. Many of our journals they edit. Most of our department stores they own. They are the landlords of enormous resident properties. The motion pictures, the most vicious of all immoral, educational and communistic influences, is their creation. Fifty per cent of the meat packing, sixty per cent of the shoe making, a large proportion of men's and women's ready-made clothing . . . they loom in them all." Worst of all, thanks to this economic power, they had managed to take over higher education in America. This meant that evolution was in, and the Bible out.[42]

And with the Franklin Roosevelt administration, Riley believed, the Jews had taken the reins of governmental power. Riley was vague about whether Roosevelt was an active member or an unwitting dupe of the Jewish-Bolshevik conspiracy. Either way, Riley baldly stated in 1935 that "the present Roosevelt regime is a Jewish controlled regime. The man who denies that simply is ignorant of the rulers at Washington." The evidence was plain: Eleanor was "pink," some of the brain trusters were secret Stalinists, and the president himself had Communist sympathies.[43] Thanks to Roosevelt's work, America was coming increasingly close to replicating the Soviet experience, as witnessed by the oppressive taxes and Bolshevik-like alphabet agencies.[44] Most important, Riley divulged in 1935, Roosevelt was rapidly approaching the Jewish conspiracy's primary goal of concentrating "in the hands of one person the interests, yea, even the lives of all the people." As the federal government became more paternalistic, as more people became dependent on the dole, the day came closer when the conspirators behind the throne would be able to enslave all citizens.[45]

Another sign that the Roosevelt administration had been captured by the Jewish-Bolshevik conspiracy was its 1933 recognition of the Soviet Union. In January of 1934 Riley published an article entitled "Why Recognize Russia and Rag Germany?" a title which indicated that the fundamentalist leader was not only anti-Communist but also pro-Nazi. Riley had harbored strong feelings against Germany after World War I, but with the ascension of Adolf Hitler he decided to "be fair toward a once-hated enemy." While Riley applauded Germany's economic success, what he most admired was the way in which, "with help from on high," Hitler had snatched "Germany from the very jaws of atheistic Communism."[46] As the *Protocols* made clear, Jews in Germany and elsewhere were in the forefront of Communist subversion. If Hitler's anticommunism involved oppression of the Jews, so be it. Riley had no patience with critics who were silent about the millions "murdered in Russia" but who began "tearing their hair . . . the moment a Jew-Communist in Germany had his store closed."

The fact was, as Hitler correctly recognized, the Jews had earned their op-
probrium: "Jewry, from the day that she crucified Jesus Christ until the
present time, has given many occasions for her own rejection and for that
opposition which she has politically pronounced persecution. Hear Hitler, who speaks from first-hand knowledge: 'The Jew is the cause and bene-
ficiary of our slavery. The Jew has caused our misery, and today he lives
on our troubles. That is the reason that as Nationalists, we are enemies
of the Jew. He has ruined our race, rotted our morals, corrupted our traditions, and broken our power.'"[47]

Riley made this pronouncement in 1933. But he was no fair-weather
friend of Hitler. Four years later he approvingly quoted from a September 12, 1937, letter to him from fellow fundamentalist Arno Gaebelein,
who was traveling in Germany: "A new Germany has arisen, and I am sorry
to say much of what we read in our American newspapers is nothing but
slander. . . . There is no question in my mind that Hitler was an instrument of God to save Germany and Europe from the Red Beast." In 1939
Riley vigorously argued against the notion that Jews in Germany were being punished for their religion (rather than for their subversive politics).
According to Riley, this was a charge "that the Communists formulate and
put into the mouths of duped defenders of Israel." Only with the advent
of World War II did William Bell Riley cease his defense of Adolf Hitler's
Jewish policies.[48]

Riley also supported his fellow Far Right activists in the United States.
In this regard Riley lavished the most attention on Father Charles Coughlin. In an interesting foreshadowing of recent political alliances of fundamentalists and Catholics, Riley overcame his native anti-Catholicism to
support the Detroit priest. Before Coughlin's slide into open bigotry Riley's
reviews were somewhat mixed. In his 1935 book *The Philosophies of Father Coughlin*, Riley congratulated Coughlin for his blistering attacks on
atheistic Bolsheviks and international bankers. Riley went on, however,
to complain that Coughlin was so harsh in his criticisms of American corporations that it seemed as if he "purposely [wanted] to throw his influence to agitation, strikes, and economic disorder." But after 1938, when
Coughlin, to quote Alan Brinkley, moved from "embittered conservatism"
to "an ugly anti-Semitism," Riley praised him to the heavens.[49] In a March
1940 article, Riley celebrated the Christian Front as a "solid front for democracy and constitutional government." Regarding the Christian Front's
leader, he proclaimed: "We have heard Father Coughlin often; we have
read many of his printed addresses, he represents the Papacy. I represent
its exact opposite — the Baptist denomination . . . yet, I say without apol-

ogy, that of all the men to whom I have listened on the economic questions of the day, I have found more intelligence in this Priest's deliverances,
and more evidence of loyalty to true democracy and to constitutional government . . . than I have received from any other orator of the hour." Riley
remained a staunch supporter of Coughlin through World War II.[50]

It is less surprising, perhaps, that Riley also continued to support his
friend and fellow fundamentalist, Gerald Winrod. Winrod and Riley had
worked together in the fundamentalist crusades of the 1920s: not only had
Winrod served as extension secretary of Riley's World's Christian Fundamentals Association, but he had assisted Riley in the ill-fated campaign
to have the teaching of evolution banned in Minnesota. In keeping with
Riley, in early 1933 Winrod began to promote the idea of a Jewish "world
conspiracy," as outlined in *The Protocols*. Riley aided his friend's efforts,
contributing right-wing articles of his own to Winrod's magazine, *The Defender*.[51] Remaining true to his anti-Semitic and fundamentalist comrade,
during World War II Riley wrote articles blasting the federal government's
prosecution of Winrod, among others.

Riley supported other Far Right spokespersons as well. He published
in *The Pilot* articles by Elizabeth Dilling, author of *The Red Network* and
The Octopus, the latter described by Ralph Lord Roy as perhaps "the most
virulent anti-Semitic tract ever published in the United States." Riley also
published articles by right-wing stalwart Dan Gilbert, whom Riley eventually tapped to be coeditor of *The Pilot*.[52] But as far as authors of the
Far Right are concerned, Riley seems to have been particularly taken with
Elizabeth Knauss, author of *Red Propaganda in the Churches*. Knauss's
Pilot articles included "Communism as Glimpsed behind the Scenes in
Sovietland," "Communism and the Illuminati," "Communism and Protocols," and "Communism and the Jewish Question." In the latter piece Knauss
asserted that while Jews tell Gentiles there is no connection between Judaism and Communism, among themselves and in their publications they
proudly assert that Bolshevism is a Jewish plot. When Joseph Cohn, head
of the American Board of Missions to the Jews, took Riley to task for the
Knauss articles, Riley primly responded: "Our advice to Joseph is to be
silent, and especially not to charge falsehood to a woman who writes as
intelligently and faithfully and truly upon the subject of Communism as
Elizabeth Knauss is doing."[53]

Whether writing articles in their defense, giving them space in *The Pilot*,
or opening his pulpit at First Baptist to them, in the 1930s W. B. Riley
actively supported the activities of fellow anti-Semites in the United States.
Perhaps the best example of this was Riley's support of Far Right leader

William Dudley Pelley and his Silver Shirts. The Silver Shirts was a national organization created by Pelley in 1933, when Adolf Hitler became
chancellor of Germany. According to the American Jewish Committee,
Pelley's group was the most vicious anti-Semitic organization in the United
States. While the national organization never attained a membership of
more than fifteen thousand, Minneapolis was considered to have one of
the stronger chapters.[54]

In response to the activities of the Silver Shirts and other anti-Semites
in Minnesota, the Anti-Defamation Council of Minnesota was informally
organized in 1936. Its primary project was an undercover investigation of
the Minneapolis branch of Pelley's organization. A special target was W. B.
Riley, because he was reputed to have some connections with the local Silver Shirts. As part of the investigation, in October 1936 the council's undercover agent, "S.W.," attended both services at First Baptist Church and
a few classes at Riley's Bible school. According to the final report, "numerous workers in the Christian Party [Silver Shirts] . . . attended Rev. Riley's
sermons." This fact was corroborated by an undercover interview with a
member of the organization.[55]

If S.W.'s summaries of Riley's sermons were accurate, then there is no
mystery in the Silver Shirts' choice of a church. In his October 11 sermon
Riley talked about examples of Jewish agitation, including the activities
of Leon Trotsky, and intimated that he said much less than he would like
about the Jews. That evening Riley preached on the book of Jonah. In a
rather novel interpretation, Riley explained that Jonah pleaded with God
to destroy Nineveh because he was a Jew and Nineveh was filled with six
hundred thousand Gentiles: "And there is one thing that is characteristic
of the Jew: they are loyal to their own." The next week, in his October 18
sermon, Riley explained in detail why he was suspicious of the Jews, in
the process observing that "if the Jews were unpopular in America it was
their own fault."[56]

But in his October 4, 1936, sermon Riley directly confronted the Silver
Shirts question in a message entitled "Why Shiver at the Sight of a Shirt?"
Subsequently published as a pamphlet, this sermon was a response to an
exposé of the Silver Shirts written by the young Eric Sevareid in the *Minneapolis Journal*. Riley began by pointing out that he was not a member of
Pelley's organization, a fact that perhaps said more about the minister's
caution than his sympathies. He then observed that he was not speaking
"in defense of the Silver Shirts," a statement he promptly belied: "[I] speak
because we have noted of late a disposition to attack immediately and almost mercilessly any company of men who are known to stand four-square

for the Constitution of our land, and vigorously against Communism." Communists in America and elsewhere had the jitters about the Silver Shirts, because the Brown Shirts in Germany and the Black Shirts in Italy had so completely "triumphed against Communism." The *Journal* reporter had some "special grudge" against the Silver Shirts and thus attempted to paint them as "jibbering idiot[s]" whose "concern for [their] country is a species of insanity." Riley proclaimed that, the Communists' jitters and Sevareid's antipatriotic smears notwithstanding, it was becoming apparent to American taxpayers that it was better to have their own version of a Brown or Black shirt, if "that shirt represents power and progress," than to be poor and overtaxed. Riley asserted that while he was "not pleading for the adoption of 'The Silver Shirt,'" the reality was that unless certain social trends were reversed, increasing numbers of Americans would be attracted to Pelley's organization: "Whether a shirt of some definite color, representing national loyalty, shall become popular, rests entirely with the Red-shirted company. If there are 52,000 emissaries already at work in America, as propagandists of Communism, Silver Shirts will increase. If the mistaken recognition of Russia is not rectified by our nation, it is sure to favor the Shirtmakers." After threatening disloyal foreigners, particularly Jews, with the prospect of immigration restrictions and deportations, Riley concluded "Why Shiver at the Sight of a Shirt?" with a lengthy diatribe against communism.[57]

Charles I. Cooper of the Anti-Defamation Council wrote in the summary of the 1936 investigation that "Rev. Riley serves to give the Pelleyites a certain amount of standing and moral support." This was a fair assessment, and it can be broadened. Within his church, school, and regional empire Riley gave standing and moral support not just to the Silver Shirts but to a truculent brand of anti-Semitism. In a 1946 article entitled "The Jews of Minneapolis and Their Christian Neighbors," Cooper put it this way: "From the First Baptist Church and the Northwestern Bible Institute there radiated . . . a particularly vicious, reactionary and antisemitic influence which poisoned the minds of thousands of families."[58]

The case should not be overstated. Not all of Riley's church members developed a virulent hatred of Jews, nor did all of his students leave Northwestern as believers in the *Protocol* conspiracy. Certainly a good number of these midwestern fundamentalists held onto the religious doctrine while winnowing out the anti-Semitic conspiratorialism.[59] Nevertheless, it is important to realize that anti-Semitism was not simply a peripheral part of Riley's message in the 1930s and 1940s. The charismatic Riley preached and wrote on the *Protocols* often, in such a way that he made anti-Semitic

conspiratorialism seem a natural part of premillennial eschatology. Moreover, Riley had a peculiarly captive audience, beyond the thousands who
heard him preach Sunday mornings and evenings at First Baptist of Minneapolis. In the upper Midwest Riley had created a tightly knit network
of fundamentalist churches centered around himself and his Northwestern
Bible School. Thousands of church members heard the ministers he trained,
read the written materials he authored, and attended the summer institutes he administered. While one can only speculate on the precise impact
of his message in this region, it is certain that at least some of the fundamentalists in Riley's empire bought the whole package — fundamentalism
and anti-Semitism.

Riley was not just a regional figure. While his national influence may
have waned a little by the 1930s, this organizer of the fundamentalist crusade and founder of the World's Christian Fundamentals Association was
still one of the preeminent fundamentalist leaders of his time. For him to
espouse an anti-Semitic conspiratorialism hence gave the message a certain legitimacy within the national fundamentalist movement that it would
not have had otherwise. This said, it is important to realize that the majority of fundamentalist leaders found Riley's brand of anti-Semitism distasteful. Of course, the aforementioned ambivalence about the Jews was
built into their premillennial eschatology; moreover, early in the 1930s some
fundamentalists, including Arno Gaebelein and James M. Gray, president
of Moody Bible Institute, joined with Riley in proclaiming the truth of
the *Protocols.* By the second half of the 1930s, however, most fundamentalists, including Gaebelein and Gray, had rejected (or at least ceased to
defend) the anti-Semitic conspiratorialism of the *Protocols.*[60]

Some fundamentalists actively combated the spread of anti-Semitism
within their movement. Fifty fundamentalists, including the militant J. Frank
Norris, joined together to sign a manifesto that condemned anti-Semitism
"in whatever form it may take, as . . . unworthy of those who bear the
name of Christian."[61] Leaders of Hebrew Christian organizations attacked
Riley and his compatriots for their stand against Jews.[62] And in a formal
effort to counter the message put out by Winrod, Riley, and company, in
early 1938 a group of fundamentalists organized the American Prophetic
League (APL), which sought to warn "Christians of the nation of the imminent peril to all nations . . . arising in Germany — the Aryan doctrine
with Jew-baiting as its fore-runner."[63]

Riley was stung by the criticisms of his fundamentalist brethren. In July
1936 he even promised to stop selling *Protocols and Communism.* As *The
Pilot* reported, this was not because his views had altered: "He has not

at all changed his opinion that the atheistic and international Jew is a world-menace, but he is entirely unwilling as the Executive-Secretary of the World's Christian Fundamentals Association to press a point on which the Fundamentalists are not agreed."[64] Riley repeatedly claimed that he had "no sympathy with anti-Semitism" and that there was "no race prejudice involved" in his anticommunism. But while he loved "the loyal Jew," he had no choice but to expose the world-conspiracy of the Jewish cabal.[65] Moreover, he felt that some of the opposition to him within fundamentalist circles was due to the fact that he had exposed "racketeering" in Christian missions to the Jews. Riley's chief target was Joseph Cohn, who headed the American Board of Missions to the Jews. In 1934 Cohn attacked Riley for publishing *Protocols and Communism,* to the point, according to Riley, of threatening a lawsuit. Riley spent the next decade charging Cohn with running not a Christian enterprise but a financial racket that skimmed thousands and thousands of dollars from good Christian people. According to an infuriated Riley, Cohn once even had the audacity to slip into the First Baptist pulpit when Riley was out of town and con members of the congregation into giving money to his organization.[66]

As the decade advanced and the nature of Hitler's anti-Jewish policies was becoming apparent, Riley became more extreme in his anti-Semitism. He may have promised in 1936 to cease sales of *Protocols and Communism;* whether or not he kept the promise, it proved to be hollow, for in 1939 he came out with his most stridently anti-Semitic work, *Wanted — A World Leader!* This book was so vicious that Riley had to publish it himself. He noted inside the front cover that the "volume bears the name of no publisher" because the "average Publisher is not sufficiently independent to run the risk of offense."[67] This was 1939. But as American entry into World War II neared, Riley all but stopped making blatantly anti-Semitic remarks in his writings or speeches. He also ended his defense of Hitler. In fact, in 1941 Riley published the pamphlet *Hitlerism; or, The Philosophy of Evolution in Action,* in which he described Hitler as the "BEAST-MAN" who was putting into practice Darwin's doctrine that "might makes right."[68] It is not clear why Riley ceased attacking the Jews and began attacking Hitler. Perhaps his intense nationalism, aroused by the imminence of war, was coming to the fore; perhaps he feared governmental prosecution if he continued his defense of the Nazis.[69] In this regard, it is noteworthy that in *Hitlerism* Riley did not even mention Hitler's persecution of the Jews. Put more baldly, there is no indication here or elsewhere that Riley ceased his public attacks on the Jews because he had undergone an intellectual or moral transformation.

HEAR AMERICA'S GREAT PULPIT STATESMAN
TWICE DAILY !   AT 9 30 A.M. AND 7 30 P.M.
APRIL 1st THROUGH 14th. 1940
'4 GREAT DAYS WITH DR. W.B. RILEY !

William Bell and Marie Acomb Riley (center) in Owensboro, KY, in the spring of 1940

In January 1942 the American Prophetic League published in its news-letter an article entitled "Let's Come Clean!" In this article the author, apparently APL president Keith Brooks, recalled that just a few years before "some of our most prominent Fundamentalists were sold on the Jewish Protocols plot idea and were rushing about the country warning believers that Communist Jews were at the point of taking over our nation as well as the world. They collected thousands of dollars from aged people who were scared nearly to death and poured tons of sensational warning literature on the churches." These fundamentalists criticized and even smeared anyone who spoke out against Hitler and anti-Semitism. But "now that everyone has been forced to recognize that the world's peril is not 'Red Jew' and 'Protocols plotters' but *the pagan Fascist combine*," these people have had to change their tune. According to the author of "Let's Come Clean!" some had courageously apologized for their errors.[70] Questions still remained, however, about some of those who had once advocated hatred of the Jew and who now, since the declaration of war, had "swathed themselves in red, white, and blue":

Have their old animosities been eradicated, or are they scared out of their wits? If they have seen the errors of their ways, they will humbly and publicly acknowledge the fact and promptly convey to the federal authorities their deep regret that they have allowed themselves to be used by the enemy to strengthen the fifth column forces within our borders. . . .

We are still justified as regarding them as potential Quislings who, should Hitler gain a toe-hold on our shores, would again bring out their old weapons. Let us pray for them that God will give them courage to *come clean*, and so to *clear the church at large from the charge laid against it by unbelievers, that it has been a tool of Hitler and the Jew-baiters.*[71]

The APL article did not mention W. B. Riley by name, but there is no question that he was a primary target of the piece. This is confirmed by the fact that the Minnesota Jewish Council, which somehow procured the First Baptist membership list, energetically sought to have a copy of "Let's Come Clean!" sent to every member in Riley's church.[72] But the obstreperous and aged Riley had no intention of "coming clean." During the war years Riley continued to argue that the *Protocol* plan "for world subjugation" was in operation. He was careful, however, not to make too much of the fact that the conspirators were Jews.[73] He also defended, but not too vigorously, those of the Far Right who were prosecuted by the federal government for sedition, a fate Riley managed to avoid. He observed in August 1944 that "we have . . . been amazed that [Col. Sanctuary], Mrs. Dilling, Dr. Winrod, and other Christians should have been included in the indictment net drawn in defense of the Roosevelt New Deal." The next year, when the trial ended in mistrial with the death of the presiding judge, a *Pilot* editorial apparently written by Riley happily proclaimed that "the termination of this trial savors of divine intervention!"[74]

In short, Riley rejected Keith Brooks's call for repentance. The patriarch of fundamentalism never retracted or apologized for his earlier statements. More to the point, he gave no evidence that he had changed his opinion of the Jews or their *Protocol* conspiracy. While one cannot know with certainty the true nature of a person's soul, there is little doubt that when Riley died in December 1947 he died an uncontrite anti-Semite of the first order.

W. B. Riley was born in 1861. He was in his seventies and eighties during the time he was crusading against the Jewish-Communist conspiracy. Granting that his ideas were exceptionally noxious, it is possible to maintain a measure of sympathy by viewing the final two decades of Riley's life as rather pathetic. Here was an old man whose crusades against modernism and evolutionism had been repudiated by his denomination and his country. Bitter, he latched onto the Jews as his personal and social scapegoat. This proved to be a decision that politically stranded him at the Far Right fringe of American society.

It is a mistake, however, to see the post-1920s W. B. Riley as an irrelevant and elderly fundamentalist who lived too long and who was left without influence in the final two decades of his life. While at the national level his fundamentalist crusades had failed and his anti-Semitic conspiratorialism left him isolated, at the regional level Riley ruled over a thriving grass-roots fundamentalist empire that revolved around himself and his Northwestern Bible School. And as Riley got older his empire became increasingly powerful. While Riley might have lost much of his influence at the national level, in the upper Midwest this fundamentalist patriarch was anything but irrelevant. That is the second half of this story.

4

The School

In early 1919 W. B. Riley published in *School and Church* a promotional article for the upcoming World Conference on the Fundamentals of the Faith. In this piece Riley asserted that a modernist confederacy had recently emerged which sought to unify Protestantism around the banner of the social gospel. This confederacy was such a threat that "the life of the true Church is at stake, and the interests of the Kingdom are in the balance." Fortunately for Christendom, the Holy Spirit had inspired Christian leaders like Riley to create a countermovement to fight the modernists. Riley and his fellow antimodernist leaders were as serenely confident of their ultimate victory as had been "the great Generals of the Entente." A primary reason for their confidence was, Riley proclaimed, the fact that this "new fellowship is not at all without its affiliation forces." He then went on to list these powerful allies of the conservative crusade:

Hundreds of the most eminent preachers of the world, eminent because of their confidence in Christ, and their unshaken belief in the Bible, recognize themselves as already members of the new brotherhood. Their churches have followed what they believed to be divinely appointed leadership. Within a very few years, in the Old World and America great Bible Schools have sprung into existence. Almost without exception they are orthodox, evangelical, premillennial. And in the wake of these schools even the most wonderful movement of modern times, the Bible Conference, has walked. The world is being stirred by it now as it has never been stirred by any single spiritual force. . . .

[Finally,] a veritable flood of evangelical and premillennialist literature is pouring from the present-day press; and the magnitude of it is giving much annoyance to the Confederacy company; and the popularity of it, with the true people of God, is proving at once its spiritual power and the promise of victory for the cause of our Christ.[1]

Despite the promise of victory, within a decade the fundamentalist crusade was dead. Nevertheless, the "affiliation forces" remained. Fundamentalist churches, Bible conferences, publishing houses, and mission boards flourished despite the collapse of the national movement. Most important were the Bible schools. More than any other institution in this interdenominational network of antimodernist institutions, the Bible schools promoted grass-roots fundamentalism.

One of the most successful of these schools was W. B. Riley's own Northwestern Bible and Missionary Training School of Minneapolis. Riley returned from the crusade to a thriving institution at the center of an emerging regional fundamentalist empire. While Northwestern was too successful to be labeled typical, a close examination of Northwestern reveals much about both the nature of Bible school education and the ways in which Bible schools contributed to the advance of fundamentalism. This examination of life at Riley's school in its heyday (1917–1947) concentrates on the following questions: How was Northwestern administered and financed? What was the school's purpose, and how did this shape the sort of education offered at Northwestern? Who attended Northwestern, and why? Northwestern was, in every sense, "Riley's school." Its mission was to prepare students for careers as Christian warriors, combating modernism and spreading the truth in an indifferent and sometimes hostile world. The Bible school succeeded, and at the same time it provided the "nontraditional" students in attendance with the opportunity to build better lives for themselves in that same unfriendly world.

Most Bible schools had modest beginnings. Northwestern was no exception. Riley began the school in 1902, with seven students meeting in a little classroom off the First Baptist chapel. By 1917 eighty-one students were attending classes in a nearby building unflatteringly described by the school newspaper as being less than sanitary. But in 1923 Jackson Hall was erected. Adjoining the First Baptist Church, where Riley continued to serve as minister, the new building was used by the church for its Sunday School program and by the Bible school for classes, offices, and chapel services. The school now also owned four dormitories.[2] Bible school enrollment continued to rise, reaching 388 in 1935. In that year Riley founded a second school, Northwestern Evangelical Theological Seminary. Northwestern College of Liberal Arts was added in 1944. In the autumn of 1946 seven hundred students attended the combined Northwestern schools, and this number does not include the one thousand individuals who took advantage of the evening offerings. Riley died the following year, while guiding another building program designed to meet the expanding enrollment at his schools.[3]

Because only a few administrative records remain, the precise nature

Northwestern Bible and Missionary Training School Board of Directors, mid-1930s. Seated, left to right: S.E. Robb, school treasurer; Archer Young, businessman, Faribault, MN; W. H. Schmelzel, businessman, Jacksonville, FL; W. B. Riley; Peter MacFarlane, superintendent, Union Gospel Mission, St. Paul; G. G. Vallentyne, pastor, Park Avenue Methodist Church, Minneapolis; E. A. Crosby, treasurer (retired), Minneapolis Street Railway Company; John R. Siemens, pastor, First Baptist Church, Hastings, MN. Standing, left to right: C. K. Ingersoll, cashier, Van Dusen Harrington Elevator Co.; U. J. Bisbee, accountant, Hallet and Carey Grain Co.; A. A. Bjorklund, attorney, Soo Line Railway Co.; N. T. Mears, presisdent, Buckbee-Mears Engraving Co.; and, C. T. Shoop, instructor, University of Minnesota. Board members not in the picture: Colgate Buckbee and Earle V. Pierce.

of Northwestern's organizational structure is rather hazy. An interdenominational board of fifteen directors existed from the school's inception. According to Marie Riley, the board's primary function was to rule on major financial matters, such as the purchase of properties.[4] But administration of the institute was left to its founder, who served as superintendent until the 1930s, when he became president of the board. Change in titles notwithstanding, Riley's role at Northwestern varied little in his forty-five years there. Among other responsibilities, he set educational policy and spearheaded fund-raising efforts. In short, Riley ran Northwestern.

In the early years Riley, a man of prodigious energy, had little problem fulfilling his administrative duties. What assistance he needed was given by fellow millenarian leader A. J. Frost, who served as dean for the first decade of Northwestern's existence. But the aged Frost relinquished his post in the early 1910s.⁵ The school continued to expand; as Marie Riley observed, the work became "heavier and larger." Considering that he was simultaneously serving as minister of First Baptist Church and superintendent of the school, Riley needed someone to share the load. According to his biographer, Riley "conceived the idea that [adding] another Superintendent (who would also be a financial man) might enable the school to meet its ever-increasing cost."⁶ While retaining the title General Superintendent, Northwestern's founder in late 1916 voluntarily relinquished some of his power to Myron W. Haynes, a specialist in college fund-raising. It was one of Riley's rare administrative mistakes. Marie Riley later charged that in his one-year term Haynes "raised no money; the school went into debt $9,000.00, and all its property was in danger." By the end of the next year Haynes resigned, perhaps under duress. Riley reassumed his former powers and brought his school back from the brink of disaster.⁷

Riley still needed someone to assist him in administering the school. The onset of the fundamentalist crusade exacerbated this need, for the superintendent's national commitments meant he had little time to spend nurturing his school. Northwestern's magazine, *The Pilot*, lamented in March 1921 that while students "rejoice[d] in the fact that the Lord is using him [Riley] in the great Bible Conference work," they would "never be reconciled . . . to having him away."⁸ This time, however, Riley was able to delegate his responsibilities to more effective lieutenants. H. B. O. Phillpotts ably served as First Baptist's assistant pastor and dean of Northwestern Bible School from 1918 to 1926. He was succeeded in both posts by the talented Moody Bible Institute graduate Robert L. Moyer. In 1926 Riley made his final major national effort, and soon thereafter the WCFA leader turned more of his attention to the upper Midwest. Together Riley and Moyer effectively guided Northwestern's destiny.⁹

A primary task of Riley and his assistants was the raising of sufficient outside support to keep the school going. A 1917 plea for support in *School and Church* observed that "many of our professors in the school have taught from its beginning without salary, and will continue to do so for the present; but when it is remembered that the students are, as a rule, without means, working their way through, it will be seen that to aid such as are not quite able to accomplish this . . . some thousands of dollars are absolutely demanded during the school year." Little money was ever raised from tuition fees: no tuition was charged in the early years, and only thirty to thirty-five dollars per annum was required in the 1940s.¹⁰ When all fees are included, it appears that in the years Riley headed Northwestern students never contributed more than 33 percent of the cost of maintaining the school. This is reflected in a 1932 report on Northwestern's financial

The Northwestern troika in 1941: Dean of Men Robert Moyer, Dean of Women Marie Acomb Riley, and President William Bell Riley.

situation: "The entire cost of educating these 400 and more students per annum is about $40,000. Nearly one-third of this comes from the small registration fee of the students and from payments on board and room. The remainder has been the gift of God's people as directed by His Spirit. In other words, from the first, it has been a work of faith."[11]

It appears that Riley and company had the requisite faith. Over the years Northwestern's administration consistently succeeded in overcoming this perennial shortfall, keeping the school afloat. Northwestern's performance in the 1930s provides an instructive illustration of the school's financial stability during the Riley years. Virginia Brereton has noted that "for most Bible schools the onset of the Great Depression in 1929 meant sharp curtailment of their efforts."[12] In contrast, Northwestern operations suffered only minor cutbacks in the 1930s. In some instances the school even expanded its operations, as in the establishment of a theological seminary in 1935. Moreover, total enrollment (day and evening school) increased from 446 in 1928 to 525 in 1934 and 815 in 1938.[13] This does not mean that Northwestern did not feel a financial pinch. Adjusted for price fluctuations, particularly price deflation, contributions to Northwestern in the years 1932–1936 were 80 percent of what they had been in the years 1927–1931. Contributions to Northwestern and Riley's First Baptist Church together in 1932–1936 were 77 percent of what they had been in 1922–1926. But during the next five years (1937–1941), giving to the school was 5 percent greater than it had been a decade earlier.[14] So healthy was Northwestern's financial state that its indebtedness on buildings was reduced from $100,000 to $23,375 in the years 1936 to 1939, and the debt was completely paid off by 1941.[15]

In 1937 fellow fundamentalist F. S. Groner exclaimed that "the way Dr. Riley has financed the combined [Northwestern] institutions is a marvel."[16] Although the shallow level of data makes this a speculative enterprise, Northwestern's financial health deserves explanation, particularly in light of the difficulties other Bible schools were having in the Depression decade. Groner's reference to the "way Dr. Riley has financed" Northwestern points to one obvious reason for the Bible school's ability to stay on course in the Depression – the president's administrative talents. William Bell Riley was the one great administrator in the galaxy of fundamentalist leaders. In his book, *Voices of American Fundamentalism*, C. Allyn Russell even entitled his chapter on Riley "The Organizational Fundamentalist." Northwestern was Riley's school, and it appears that his administrative acumen kept Northwestern from overextending itself in the prosperous 1920s, unlike, say, the Bible Institute of Los Angeles. In contrast with the desperately strapped BIOLA, the onset of the Depression did not force Northwestern to make drastic cuts.[17]

In this regard, Riley and his colleagues also displayed a talent for running clever fund-raising campaigns. One example of this skill was a series of advertisements published in the early 1930s in the school's nationally circulated magazine, *The Pilot*. The ads played upon the Depression-induced fears of the readers. One 1930 notice advertising Northwestern annuities pronounced that "in recent months millions of dollars have been lost in speculation. Literally thousands of people have been stripped of their last cent. Many Christian losers now grieve that they didn't invest for the Lord. Let the men of the world gamble if they will, but Christian men and women should be content with a FAIR AND CERTAIN EARN-ING and happy to be able at the same time to invest for Christ." Another ad featured a beleaguered individual standing outside a closed bank wailing "I wish I had invested my money in a [Northwestern] annuity!" While the absence of sympathy for those individuals in financial straits may seem unkind, it is not hard to see the potential effect of such advertisements in the first years of the Depression.[18]

Finally, despite First Baptist's numerous working-class and lower-middle-class members and Northwestern's predominantly working- and lower-middle-class student body, Rev. and Pres. W. B. Riley moved in well-heeled circles.[19] Hence, it is quite possible that his Bible school attracted an unusual number of wealthy contributors, contributors who would be relatively unaffected by the Great Depression. While no Northwestern financial records remain from the 1930s, the smattering of information remaining from the 1920s is instructive. These records reveal that, as Riley was wont to boast, a large number of five- and ten-dollar gifts were made to Northwestern. For example, according to the spring 1921 quarterly report, 339 contributors gave $6043.69, for an average of $17.83 per person. But the same report also noted that Charles Stimson of Los Angeles had donated $23,000.00. Over the years numerous contributions ranging from $1,000.00 to $85,000.00 were made to the school, beginning with a $20,000.00 gift written into the will of Minneapolis scion Augusta Russell at the time the school was founded.[20] Notwithstanding Riley's protestations that fundamentalism had no wealthy contributors,[21] and despite the school's role as the headquarters of a grass-roots movement, it is doubtful that Northwestern Bible and Missionary Training School would have enjoyed such financial health, especially during the Depression, without the intercession of Riley's wealthy acquaintances and admirers.

It is only fair to note that the Northwestern leaders attributed their schools' prosperity during the Depression to supernatural forces. In her 1938 biography Marie Riley discussed the difficulties of raising funds in the 1930s, concluding with the observation that "we have a prayer-answering God, and my husband's trust in Him was more than justified." The Bible school president was so confident in the effectuality of prayer that at times he marshaled the students in massive pleas for divine assistance. For example, Anna Rieger (from the class of 1935) recalled: "Once when in [the] library stacks, the librarian announced: 'Dr. Riley calls every[one] to get

on your knees where you are — pray for money needed by [a specific time].'
A few days later he came to chapel, and held high a *check* just received
to cover [the] need!"[22]

This anecdote perhaps reveals less about Northwestern's dependence upon
prayer and more about the school's dependence upon its president, as both
boss ("Riley calls every[one] to get on your knees") and hero ("[he] held
high a *check* just received to cover [the] need!"). The reality is that the
towering figure of W. B. Riley overshadowed all aspects of life at Northwestern Bible and Missionary Training School. This is not to say that he
was always there. Even after the demise of his national crusade Riley spent
a good amount of his time on the road, preaching and raising money for
the school and evaluating the work of pastors who were Northwestern
alumni. Sometimes upon Riley's return to campus Robert Moyer or some
other Northwestern official would facetiously introduce him to the chapel
audience as a guest at the school. But as one alumnus recalled, even when
Riley was not at Northwestern, all of the students could feel his "dominat-
ing presence."[23]

Certainly he dominated when he was present. The tall, striking, well-
dressed Riley cut a commanding figure on campus, an impression heightened in class and chapel by his verbal polish and resounding voice. Add
to this his national reputation as the patriarch of fundamentalism, and
it is easy to see why, a half-century or more after they were at Northwestern, alumni often used the word *awe* in describing how, as students, they
had felt about Riley. One referred to Riley as "my hero," a man who "inspired, awed, and gently led" the students. Another said, "I was very young
while at Northwestern (16–18), and I stood in awe of Dr. Riley. To me,
he was a great leader of people, a very strong pulpiteer, and a commanding presence on any platform." David Hammar, a student at Northwestern
in the 1930s, summarized well the feelings many students had for their
esteemed leader: "For a young (19) fellow from a farming community of
southwest Minnesota, Dr. Riley was awesome. He was tall, well-dressed,
very articulate, and a great preacher! I can recall sitting in the BIG auditorium of First Baptist Church of Minneapolis and thinking to myself that
I could never be a preacher or pastor like Dr. Riley. However, his great-
ness did not overwhelm me but instead, was an inspiration."[24]

For some students, William Bell Riley remained a distant hero, one who
never took the time "to mingle with the students outside his classes."[25] But
for others, Riley served as a father figure, personally encouraging, coax-
ing, and advising them. To some degree, there was a pecking order among
the students for Riley's affections. At the top were "his boys," young men

he had targetted as sterling prospects for pastoral success. Raymond Anderson, class of 1940, is a good example. He recounted in a 1986 interview, "From the beginning Riley saw me as one of 'his boys.'" This meant that Riley frequently called Anderson into his office for chats about such matters as "which pastors in the region I had to watch out for — particularly, who the modernists were." Riley also invited Anderson to his house, ostensibly to have him chop wood or perform some other task; instead, the job often ended up being "to listen to Riley tell about Baptist convention battles, his life as a fundamentalist leader, etc." In short, Riley saw Anderson as a protégé. This was all too apparent to one of Anderson's classmates, who in another interview ruefully observed: "I wasn't one of Riley's boys, like Ray Anderson was. I learned much from Riley, but I wasn't close to him, like Ray."[26]

This last sentence is telling. While not all Northwestern students were close to Riley or fell under the sway of his overwhelming personality, Riley had an impact on all of them. He was Northwestern's founder and chief administrator for forty-five years, and hence his vision of what a Bible school should be shaped life at Northwestern. Not that he envisioned his school as being radically different from other Bible schools. In fact, it appears that when W. B. Riley created Northwestern, he looked to Moody Bible Institute as a model. Although his second wife stoutly asserted that "the Moody Bible Institute never entered [Riley's] mind by way of example,"[27] Riley had a good deal of contact with Dwight L. Moody before and during his years at Chicago's Calvary Baptist Church, and he was deeply impressed with the famous evangelist. Moreover, the Moody Bible Institute was coming into prominence when Riley was in Chicago. It is inconceivable that this school left no impression on the young minister. In a 1915 plea for contributions to Northwestern, the anonymous author, almost certainly Riley himself, proclaimed that the Moody institute and church were "one of the most conspicuous monuments to Christ in all the world." This was a daunting example, but Northwestern now had "every opportunity" to become a "kindred monument to the King of kings, and Lord of Glory!" Twenty years later, with Northwestern well established, Riley observed in an address at the Moody church that the institute had acted "like *a grain of wheat cast into the ground*,'" multiplying itself "thirty, sixty, yea, even a hundred-fold." The obvious implication was that Riley's own school was one of the hundred.[28]

Like Dwight L. Moody and other Bible school founders, Riley wanted his school to be a training ground for laypersons to become religious teachers, evangelists, and missionaries. The Minneapolis minister felt that preparing individuals to teach and preach the gospel was an absolute necessity in light of spiritual conditions in the upper Midwest. The region was, Marie Riley noted, in "dire need" of Bible knowledge. The predominance of Catholics and Lutherans meant an ignorance of certain biblical truths. For instance, Riley's wife observed that when Riley "arrived in Minneapolis in 1897, he found among the city pastors but one single confrere in his premillenarian faith." Men and women educated in this and other fundamentals and trained in "more efficient Christian service" could provide the "Bible indoctrination" the upper Midwest so desperately needed.[29]

Preparing Christians to spread the true gospel was Northwestern's raison d'être throughout the Riley years. This was in keeping with other Bible schools. But unlike Moody and other Bible school founders of the time who avoided competing with seminaries and concentrated on training church workers and evangelists, Riley felt from the beginning that it was most important to train pastors for the task of spreading truth. His initial reason for choosing this strategy was simple: there was a ministerial shortage in the upper Midwest. Riley later reminisced that "at the time when [I] established this school there were ninety-three Baptist churches in the state of Minnesota alone, and one hundred and fifty-two in the state of Iowa, without a pastor."[30] Churches of other denominations suffered similar problems. As was the case across the nation, most of these were small rural churches that found it difficult to attract ministers because of their isolation and their lack of financial resources.[31] Riley claimed that many of the ministers who did come to Minnesota actually made the situation worse: "[Every year we had] an agent go east and search through the graduates of defunct theological seminaries to see if some could be had for Minnesota. Those secured were naturally the leftovers, and their success in Minnesota was never marked. On the contrary, when two or three of them had come one after another for a few months to one of these little churches, the local constituency concluded that it [the church] could not be saved and were ready to vote to sell the property and turn in to the State Convention the financial result."[32]

Riley saw all of this firsthand. As a member of the Minnesota State Missions Board in the years at the end of the century he was "called upon almost monthly to vote to sell another building, and wind up another Christian center." Wearying of this state of affairs, Riley decided to provide struggling churches in the upper Midwest with an alternative to the reliance on eastern seminary graduates who seemed to lack the necessary spiritual commitment to preach the gospel in difficult circumstances. As noted in a 1943 retrospective, "he envisioned . . . a school that would prepare western men to take these western churches. He conceived that if they were properly educated, they could be brought to a complete willingness to start with a bare living and trust God for increase, both in church membership and remuneration."[33]

Training ministers and other religious workers for service in isolated and nearly defunct country and small-town churches in the upper Midwest remained an important part of Northwestern's mission throughout the Riley years. By the late 1910s, however, Northwestern's purpose had expanded. A dangerous new enemy had appeared on the scene — modernism. Riley recalled in 1933:

"This work was scarcely begun, when another and far more important proposition had to have consideration. The defection from the Faith on the part of men trained in our present-day universities, and later in our theological seminaries, rendered hundreds of [prospective ministers] unfit for the pastorate. Certainly to give out personal skepticism and excite the same in the hearts of hearers, skepticism that questions the authority of the Bible, the Deity of Christ, the Blood Atonement, the necessity of regeneration, and every other fundamental of the Christian Faith, was not the objective of the Christian ministry."[34]

At the national level Riley responded to the modernist advance by organizing a fundamentalist crusade. At the local level Riley responded by gearing his Bible school toward the preparation of Christian warriors — ministers, church workers, evangelists, and missionaries who would, upon graduation, join the fight against the modernist traitors to the faith. The dangers posed by the modernist menace meant that it was now not enough simply to prepare pastors for rural pulpits. Riley thus broadened his vision, seeking to train ministers also capable of serving urban churches, and in regions beyond the upper Midwest if necessary.[35]

To enable his graduates to compete successfully with graduates of traditional seminaries for these posts, in 1917 Riley stiffened Northwestern graduation requirements from two years to three years of courses. Similar motives also compelled him in 1935 to found Northwestern Evangelical Theological Seminary, which provided a more in-depth theological training than did the Bible school. Riley was not alone in his decision to compete directly with the established seminaries. Unlike Riley, most Bible school executives had resisted incorporating the formal training of pastors into their curricula. The modernist threat induced them to change their policy. Virginia Brereton has documented that by the early 1920s Moody Bible Institute's leaders, appalled at the spread of modernist theology, had quite self-consciously moved beyond laity training and "entered into competition with the American theological seminaries."[36]

As Riley saw it, the first task in preparing students for lives as full-time Christian warriors was to educate them in the truth. Toward this end the curriculum at Northwestern was quite different from the curriculum at a typical Protestant seminary. A key reason for this difference was Riley's disillusionment with his own seminary training: "Notwithstanding the fact that [I] had sat at the feet of some of the greatest of the then living professors, [I] graduated with very little knowledge of the Bible. . . . [My] teachers were great scholars, but not a one of them had been a prominent pastor, and in their instruction had majored upon Greek, Hebrew, Biblical Introduction, Church History, and a score of other studies, leaving altogether too little time with, and information upon, the content of the Sacred Book."[37]

In contrast, Riley proclaimed, the "pivotal point" of a Northwestern student's education was Bible study. As an early Bible school catalogue noted, this meant that Northwestern "students study the Bible instead of studying about the Bible." This battle cry of the Bible school movement referred to the study of the English Bible without reference to commentaries and without specialized knowledge of archaeology, history, and ancient languages. This emphasis on the Bible, in and of itself, was in line with the fundamentalist view of the Bible as God's inerrant and infallible word. But there were also pedagogical reasons for this approach. It was in keeping with the educational level of Northwestern's student body; moreover, as Virginia Brereton has pointed out in her study of Bible schools, concentration on the English Bible per se allowed students at Northwestern and other Bible schools "to gain familiarity with the whole sweep of the scriptures in a relatively short time."[38]

By the third decade of the school's existence Northwestern administrators had followed the lead of Moody Bible Institute and established a systematic course of Bible study. First-year students took a general class which involved reading the entire Bible and outlining certain books therein. In their second and third years they examined in detail selected books or groups of books. Students also took classes designed to aid this textual analysis, including Bible Doctrine, Bible History, and Bible Study Principles.[39] The result was that the students were, in the words of one alumnus, "saturated with Bible teaching." There was little concern about the possibility of scriptural overkill; in 1924 one administrator proclaimed, "We have discovered that the Bible is an exhaustless store house, and during the 3 years about all we can do for the student is to give him a start."[40]

There was a variety of Bible courses at Northwestern, but there was not a variety of biblical interpretations. One mildly disillusioned graduate observed, "The primary emphasis at Northwestern was an indoctrination" in the fundamentalist view of the Bible. A more disgruntled graduate substituted the word "brainwashing" for "indoctrination."[41] While Riley would

Reverend C. W. Foley teaching a class at Northwestern Bible School, 1930

have rejected the implication that he was brainwashing students, he readily conceded that biblical teaching at Northwestern was not an open-ended affair. As he noted in his address given at the ninth annual 1927 WCFA convention in Atlanta, biblical "doctrines are not individual opinions that can be bandied about at pleasure," but "are forever settled in heaven."[42] Fundamentalism was but the affirmation of these obvious biblical truths; to teach a fundamentalist interpretation of Scripture was to teach the true interpretation of Scripture. Why permit the teaching of untruth when truth is known?

Riley thus permitted as teachers only those individuals who would sign a statement affirming the nine-point WCFA creed (see Appendix A). This ensured that Bible study at Northwestern would instill students with a staunch fundamentalism. Thus instilled, Northwesterners could, as one student thankfully observed, resist "the rationalists of today" as well as "all the false religions."[43] Riley bragged, almost certainly with exaggeration, that as of 1929 "not one of the [Northwestern] graduates has ever turned to modernism," a testimony to "the soundness and thoroughness of the school's courses." He even established a one-year Bible course for students who were going to attend a secular college; this set of classes was designed, the publicity notice proclaimed, to inoculate students against "hav[ing] their faith destroyed by the modernistic teaching" so prevalent in higher education.[44]

Antimodernism involved more than correct belief. Hence, education at Riley's Northwestern included not only indoctrination in fundamentalist theology but also practical training designed to prepare students for ser-

Typing class, Northwestern Bible School, 1936.

vice in the cause of militant orthodoxy. Toward this end students had the
choice of several "courses," or majors, dependent on their chosen profes-
sions. Riley was most interested in training ministers, and the Bible course
was tailored for them. It included not only Bible classes but also classes
in homiletics (the art of preaching), public speaking, evangelism, and church
history. The Missions course included missionary biographies, history of
missions, and comparative religions, besides the required Bible classes.[45]
The Secretarial course was aimed at training pastor's assistants, and its
classes prepared students to "teach the Word, do pastoral visitation, [as
well as perform] shorthand and typewriting." Majors added in the 1940s
included Medical Missions and Music Ministry.[46]

Northwestern's most exotic training program was the Russian course.
Throughout the 1930s Riley had frequently, almost obsessively, published
articles on the dreadful conditions within Russia.[47] Then came the alliance
of the United States and the Soviet Union in World War II, and Riley and
other fundamentalists permitted themselves the hope that after the war
the Soviet Union would permit the preaching of the gospel. Riley did not
believe this would happen immediately, but he felt it would come eventually, and fundamentalists needed to prepare for the opportunity. Hence,

in January 1944 he established the Northwestern Russian department. The department offered classes in Russian grammar, literature, missions, and culture, in addition to the requisite Bible work. According to Dean Vaclav Vojta, it was the only department "in America which is presenting this unequaled opportunity for young men and women to prepare themselves for future missionary work in Russia."[48] The optimistic Vojta was confident that their opportunity would come, and he bristled at criticisms that his Russian missions students were wasting their time. In a December 1945 rebuttal entitled "Justifying My Opinion," Vojta proclaimed that the day for preaching the gospel in the Soviet Union was at hand: "Russian people are writing to us, 'We are free.' Churches are open; native Russian missionaries are able to travel and preach; the Greek Orthodox church has opened eight seminaries; and all denominations have equal freedom. It is true that the freedom is not what we have in the United States, but the evangelical church in Russia is more free now than it was under the Czar's regime. . . . Are we too optimistic? No!" By the end of 1946, however, reality had started to seep in. The Russian department then turned its efforts toward training missionaries to minister to Russian and other Slavic immigrants.[49]

The most important addition to the Northwestern program in these years was the establishment of the Evangelical Theological Seminary. Riley founded the seminary in 1935 in order to provide prospective pastors the academic training that would help them compete with modernist seminarians and that increasing numbers of congregations were demanding of their ministers. In doing so, Riley instituted a two-year program of classes akin to the classes he had unhappily endured at Louisville, including Greek, Hebrew, French, Christian philosophy, archaeology, and hermeneutics.[50]

As might be expected, Riley was sensitive to the charge that the founding of the seminary marked a shift in Northwestern's mission. In a July 1935 article heralding the new school's formation Riley firmly asserted:

This is not the end of the Northwestern Bible School. It will continue to exist; the seminary is simply a further development; and, inasmuch as the denominations seem enamored of the name SEMINARY, we will meet that demand. But we announce to all the world that there will be no change whatever in the theological attitude of Northwestern. THE NORTHWESTERN EVANGELICAL SEMINARY will stand as strictly for the fundamentals of the Christian faith as has the Northwestern Bible and Missionary Training School. . . . In other words, no 'new Gospel' is to be expected from the lips of the graduates of the Northwestern Evangelical Seminary; and no compromises with modernism, the so-called social gospel, or even postmillennialism, will be permitted."[51]

Riley was correct in arguing that the establishment of the seminary did not mark a change in mission. Northwestern still educated students in fun-

damentalist theology and prepared them to serve as crusaders in the cause
of militant orthodoxy. Nevertheless, the establishment of the seminary in
1935 illustrated an increasing emphasis on academics at Northwestern. This
shift began in 1917 with the addition of a third year of studies and continued in 1925 with the requirement that students without a high-school
education take a year of preparatory classes at the school before embark-
ing on the regular Bible school program. The seminary and, a decade later,
the liberal arts college furthered the trend.

The pages of the school magazines reflected this change of emphasis from
piety to academics and professionalism. Before the mid-1920s both administrators and pupils frequently exhorted Northwestern students to recognize that their spiritual life was much more important than their classroom
training. One student succinctly observed, "The greatest task for the Bible
student is not in mastering his studies, but it is in walking before Him
daily." Sometimes this call for spirituality bordered on the mystical. In
a 1916 article Dean of Women Jessie Van Booskirk held up the Northwestern students of 1915–1916 as a shining example: "Instead of becoming
mechanical and formal in their study of God's Word, as is too often the
case in theological schools, the spiritual life of the student was constantly
deepened while the flame of their devotion rose higher and higher, until
chapel service, prayer meetings, and the very class room itself, became
the scenes of sacred intercourse with the Lord."[52]

With this emphasis on a passionate devotion to God, it is no wonder
that some students looked somewhat askance on the whole process of academic training. For example, in 1921 one Northwesterner wrote to *The
Pilot* with the observation that "in our anxiety to enter Christian service
we are very apt to overlook the thing most essential to our preparation."
The "greatest task for the Bible student is not in mastering his studies, but
it is in walking before Him daily"; dedication, zeal, or "intellectual training is of no value aside from the gifts of the Holy Spirit."[53]

This observation was perhaps a response to the increasing emphasis on
academics already evident in 1921. By the late 1920s it was rare to find
in *The Pilot* warnings not to overemphasize intellectual training or observations that daily devotions and openness to the Holy Spirit were more
important than opening the books. Much more common were admoni-
tions for students to "toil and study and sacrifice," in this way preparing
for a lifetime of fruitful Christian service.[54] Some contributors even made
frontal attacks on the older notions. One administrator complained in
1932 that "some of the would-be wise of the church" disparage academic
training for ministers as "just a waste of time"; however, the truth was that
"there cannot be too much preparation for this most important calling in

the world," and so all prospective pastors should get the best education possible.[55]

During the years of Riley's presidency academic study and professionalism assumed an ever-increasing importance. Nevertheless, Northwestern's mission remained essentially the same — to educate students in fundamentalist theology and to train them for full-time service in the cause of militant orthodoxy. Admittedly, the addition of the liberal arts college in 1944 marked the beginnings of a shift from this mission. While the college had a required component of Bible classes, it did not limit itself to training individuals for full-time Christian service. But the college did not graduate its first class until 1948, so its impact was not truly felt until after Riley's death. It is thus fair to say that in the Riley years there was an essential continuity in Northwestern's fundamentalist educational philosophy, despite a gradual movement toward a greater emphasis on academic study.

One sign of this continuity was the fact that Riley and the administrators under him never surrendered the notion that education involved more than book-work. It was not enough to inculcate students with correct doctrine; the goal was to train Christian activists. Toward this end, like students at other Bible schools, each student at Riley's Northwestern had to spend some time every semester performing a definite Christian service. In this way, the dean of women noted, students familiarized themselves with services "which they may in future be called upon to render." This requirement also provided students a convenient outlet for religious zeal acquired in the classroom and gave Northwestern instructors an opportunity to evaluate and correct evangelistic techniques.[56]

Under the guidance of the practical work department Northwestern students were sent out to perform a whole array of tasks, all of which had soul-winning as their primary focus. Some made weekly visits to present the gospel message to the residents of jails, hospitals, nursing homes, and orphanages. Other students organized in teams to conduct daily church services at city rescue missions. Alumnus Henry Van Kommer's participation in such work was typical: "I played an instrument and with 10 others made up an orchestra which played for each service at the St. James Mission where the jobless found shelter. . . . At noon I made myself available to preach at one or the other Missions for a Street meeting. We did personal work on the street or in restaurants or wherever a soul needed the Saviour."[57]

Other Northwesterners organized neighborhood Bible study groups. Sometimes these groups were established among recent immigrants and in connection with the Christian Americanization Society. While soul-winning was primary, these Northwesterners were not hesitant to supplement the Bible teaching with efforts to upgrade the morality of their listeners. For example, at a Bible class conducted in a Minneapolis home by Northwestern students "the temperance pledge is recited, temperance songs are sung and the evils of nicotine and alcohol are forcefully portrayed. One interesting phase is the 'cigarette count' taken each Tuesday. The children are asked to count the number of cigarette and cigar 'butts' they stamp out each week. They are very enthusiastic about this work and eagerly demonstrate how they grind into the dirt the loathsome 'butts' which many derelicts and young boys would otherwise pick up and smoke, thus spreading disease."[58]

Much of the students' practical work aided fundamentalist churches in the area. In 1942, for instance, forty-six Northwesterners taught Sunday School classes and a host of others spoke at youth meetings, conducted evangelistic campaigns, and taught in weekday church schools. This does not include the numerous Northwestern-sponsored choirs, quartets, trios, duets, and instrumental groups that toured the circuit of local fundamentalist churches. The demand for Northwestern students was so great that the practical work department maintained a Daily Flying Squadron. As described in a 1934 *Pilot* article, the squadron was "divided into daily groups, and it is their duty to respond to any emergency call that may come throughout the week" from churches in desperate need of a teacher, musician, or evangelist.[59]

Some students held pastorates in churches unable to retain the services of a full-time minister. Often the church was a hundred miles or more into the country, a distance which could result in all-night train trips on the weekend and Monday morning exhaustion. As a general rule, Northwestern administrators permitted only second- and third-year students to hold a pastorate.[60] Occasionally, however, promising and/or insistent freshmen were granted this privilege. Francis Tarrant, class of 1935, was one such individual: "I had preached in many churches in southern Minn. before going to Northwestern. . . . Soon after coming to school, I was called into the Dean's office, for preaching in various missions and churches. Dr. Moyer said, 'Don't you know freshmen are not allowed to preach?' I answered, 'I have been preaching for many months, and the Holy Spirit has used my message. Are you going to stop my preaching?' He answered, 'Go ahead and preach!'"[61]

Aiding fundamentalist churches in the region did not stop with the end of the school year. Northwestern's largest evangelistic enterprise came in the summer, when hundreds of students fanned out into Minnesota, the Dakotas, Montana, Nebraska, Iowa, and Wisconsin to run daily Vacation

In the summer of 1930 Northwestern's Glad Tidings Male Quartette, pictured here, toured the upper Midwest in this Gospel Patrol Car. As the Quartette reported in the August, 1930 *Pilot:* "Our machine is, of course, a cause of attraction. We do not have any difficulty attracting a crowd."

Bible Schools. When Northwestern began sending out these summer missionaries in 1922, Vacation Bible Schools were novelties in the upper Midwest.[62] In the first few years administrators sent letters to various churches offering students as teachers, only stipulating that the churches pay transportation costs and provide room and board. The head of the practical work department reflected in 1942 that it was not long before "pastors, rural missionaries, laymen, and laywomen, who nurtured a concern over the spiritual welfare of neighborhood and community churches, began to reverse the operation and write to *us.*" Many of those requesting student workers were Northwestern alumni who sought to carry out a more extensive evangelistic work than would have been possible had they relied solely on their own church labors. Those making requests must have been satisfied with the results, for by the 1940s over four hundred students went forth annually to conduct daily Vacation Bible Schools. As a result of their labors thousands of "saved" individuals and hundreds of churches were brought into contact with Northwestern. Some of the converts actually became Northwestern students. In 1942, for example, there were "19 full-course students who stood in a recent chapel service to testify to conversion in a daily vacation Bible school, seventeen of which were conducted by our volunteer teachers."[63]

It is probable that many or most of the nineteen students who rose in that chapel service were different from typical college or seminary students, not simply because of their conversion experience in a fundamentalist daily Vacation Bible School. In keeping with other Bible schools, Northwestern attracted a very large number of "non-traditional" students, students whose age, gender, lack of schooling, and, perhaps most important, class would generally have kept them from pursuing higher education.[64] It is important to understand what Northwestern had to offer these working- and lower-middle-class men and women. Not only did the school provide them with a thorough grounding in the fundamentalist faith and inspire them to serve as crusaders in the cause of militant orthodoxy, but Northwestern also gave them a professional preparation that would allow many of them to move up in the world. Of course, the ministry, evangelism, or missions work as a profession were often quite poor-paying and not inordinately high in status, particularly for Bible school graduates. Nevertheless, for a good number of the individuals who chose to attend Northwestern, full-time Christian service signified a chance to fulfill personal ambitions and improve their standing in life, as well as being a sacred calling.

One indication that Northwestern provided an opportunity for students to move up the social ladder is seen by looking at the jobs that students left to begin attending Northwestern. Many of the students at Northwestern were in their twenties or older, and according to a 1935 survey, over half of them had worked elsewhere before deciding to return to school to prepare for religious work. The survey also revealed that most of the men and many of the women had left blue-collar, laborer, or service positions to come to Bible school. To note the nine most popular pre-Northwestern occupations — the students had been farmers, teachers, clerks and salesmen, housemaids and cooks, stenographers, nurses, cattle and sheep ranchers, bus and truck drivers, and mechanics.[65]

As might be expected, many of these students had not received much in the way of formal education prior to attending Northwestern. The

Bible school made provision for them with lax admission requirements. Students with only a grammar-school education were permitted into Northwestern, although after 1925 they were required to take an extra year of courses. College graduates could finish in two years, high school graduates in three years, and those without a high-school education could complete their work in four years.[66]

Northwestern also sought to help its students by charging very little for room, board, and tuition. Despite low school fees, however, many of the working- and lower-middle-class individuals attending Northwestern found it difficult to pay for this opportunity for social advancement. A 1918 *School and Church* article observed that "for a man or woman to arrive at the school with as much as $50.00 is an event; many of them have arrived with less than $5.00."[67] The economic standing of the student body did not seem to change drastically over time. According to reports in the 1930s and 1940s most students were "without means" and thus needed to work their way through school.[68]

The school's administrators responded to their students' needs by establishing an employment department. This remarkably successful service placed women in restaurants as waitresses and cooks and, more often, in homes as maids and governesses. Administrators viewed the students' work in homes as valuable training; as noted in a 1939 article, "they go into the best of homes; they learn the technique of neat and competent housekeeping, and cooking; and, consequently, [they] receive one of the most essential features of a woman's education." This same reporter went on to observe that finding jobs for men was a much more difficult task. Nevertheless, thanks to "divine help," the employment department was also able to place men, as chimney sweeps, dishwashers, night watchmen, janitors, chauffeurs, and even undertakers.[69]

The employment department did not confine itself to placement efforts. In a particularly inspired moment in the 1930s this office devised a product that students could both make and sell — the SCRAPE-EZ, a tool somewhat akin to a putty knife. Students made them for a nickel and sold them for a dime. The product was popular. Students sold five thousand scrapers between November 1938 and January 1939. The employment department had apparently discovered a consumer need. As one ad in *The Pilot* raved, the SCRAPE-EZ was ideal for cooks and homemakers; a special attraction was that "[it was] slick to get raisins off the floor that have been stepped on!"[70]

Combined with the school's low fees, Northwestern's official and unofficial efforts to find jobs for students ensured that even the poorest of the poor who desired a Northwestern education could gain one: "The boys and girls who come to us with . . . enough to pay for registration fees, buy books, and get comfortably located for a week — and are in health, and willing to work, can be assured they can work their way through the three years of school."[71]

This blandly cheerful assessment masks the fact that the outside work could entail forty or more hours of labor per week; moreover, the students often worked two or even three jobs, one of which probably involved working all night. One student at Northwestern in the 1930s was painfully aware of the costs of juggling school and work: "What was it [school] like? I don't think I know — I was relief clerk at a nearby hotel 3 nights a week, and washed dishes at a cafe for my noon meal, which, with classes from 7:30 to about 12:30, kept me busy from 11:00 P.M. until 2:30 P.M. the following day. I'm sure I wasn't even a very good auditor in classes some days, and I know I relied heavily on notes taken by my sisters in earlier years in the same subjects." But Glenn Erickson, who also attended Northwestern in the 1930s, remembered these challenges as simply serving to make him a better person: "As a student I had to pay my way by washing dishes in restaurants [and working as] night watchman of an oil burner company, answering distress night calls of 'No Heat!!' It was worth it all and gave me valuable lessons of God's care and direction in those depression years."[72]

If completed questionnaires and letters from and interviews with over seventy alumni are any indication, most Northwestern graduates agreed with Glenn Erickson in viewing the high costs of balancing work and school as well compensated by the Bible instruction and professional preparation they received at Northwestern. This positive perspective on Northwestern was particularly true of one non-traditional group well represented at the Bible school — women.[73] This is not terribly surprising. Even more than for working- and lower-middle-class males, the Bible school offered women of all classes escape from vocational limitations. Many women trained at Northwestern to become not only pastors' wives or church secretaries but also missionaries at home and abroad, pastors, and evangelists. Northwestern women graduates served with such missions agencies as Wisconsin Rural Mission, Northern Gospel Mission, and China Inland Mission. Perhaps more surprising, Riley's school prepared women to pastor churches in towns throughout the Midwest, including Granby and Frazee, Minnesota, and Swaledale and Rockwell, Iowa.[74] Minnie S. Nelson was one of these women. She recounted her efforts in a 1948 article: "Thief River Falls and Clearbrook, Minnesota, Great Falls, Montana, and Iron River, Michigan, were my pastorates during fourteen years. I also supplied Henning and Cook, Minnesota, each for three months. God has opened many other doors of service for me too. . . . Resurrecting dead churches, uniting divided ones, repairing church property, paying old church debts, strenuous travel and speaking engagements—these do not make for an easy program, but thank God for the Ebenezer stone!"[75]

Northwestern also prepared women to serve as traveling evangelists. Perhaps the most renowned evangelistic team to come out of Northwestern, male or female, was the twosome of Alma Reiber and Irene Murray. Beginning in the 1910s, Reiber the preacher and Murray the song leader spent at least thirty years touring churches in the upper Midwest, at times staying in one church as long as six months. Their work in country and city churches often received rave reviews; for example, in 1923 the *Antigo* (Wisconsin) *Journal* reported: "The Misses Reiber and Murray, who have been the human instruments in this work, leave Antigo for other fields of labor carrying with them the highest endorsement of the pastor and people. . . . [Through] these consecrated young women God has bestowed upon the First Baptist Church the greatest spiritual blessing that it has ever received."[76]

In Northwestern's early years the administration encouraged or at least tolerated Bible school women who sought to be ministers and evangelists. But by 1930 Northwestern administrators were speaking out against women serving in the "public ministry." The pages of *The Pilot* reflect that in the 1930s and 1940s Northwestern administrators and teachers instructed women that they could not hold positions of authority within the church. They were not to serve as preachers, evangelists, or even (some argued) missionaries. In the September 1931 issue of *The Pilot*, longtime Northwestern professor C. W. Foley responded to a reader's question on this topic:

Q. In I Cor. 14:33–35 is it inferred [*sic*] that women are not to express themselves on any occasion in the church? If so, what part can women have in Christian service?

A. I Tim. 2:12 throws light on the question: 'But I permit not a woman to teach, nor to have dominion over man, but to be in quietness.' The whole passage relates to the public worship of the church; the context plainly limits the word 'teach,' as used here, to teaching or preaching in the public assembly. The words 'nor to usurp authority (have dominion)' give a reason for the preceding prohibition. The position of teacher or preacher, in the public congregation, in itself implies superiority or authority over those who are taught; and the functions of this office are, therefore, forbidden a woman, as inconsistent with the subordinate position that God assigned her. . . . This does not bar her from the Sunday School class, daily Vacation Bible School, etc., but certainly closes the door of the public ministry of the church. It is as plain as anything could possibly be, that a woman is not to take the oversight of the church, or publicly teach or preach in the man's appointed place.[77]

Northwestern Bible School students and faculty, 1915. Note W. B. Riley in the center and the large number of women students.

As strained as was his distinction between private and public ministry, Foley summarized well Northwestern's later teachings regarding the role of women in the church. For example, while in earlier years W. B. Riley had not spoken out against (and apparently had even encouraged) Bible school women serving in the ministry, by 1935 Riley (or a subordinate presumably writing with Riley's approval) observed that there were "no women pastors mentioned in the New Testament" and thus "it is not our purpose" in the new Northwestern seminary "to prepare women for that particular office."[78]

Riley and his fellow Northwestern administrators were not alone in modifying their views regarding the proper training and role of women. As Janette Hassey has documented, between the world wars "a significant reversal among Evangelicals took place," and the result was a "gradual decline of public ministry opportunities for Evangelical women." This shift was, in great part, due to the emergence of the fundamentalist movement in the 1920s. The fundamentalists not only (as part of their cultural anti-modernism) militantly opposed the changing social values regarding women, but their emphasis on literalist interpretations of Scripture meant, to quote Hassey, "less flexibility in interpreting a topic like women in ministry." Moreover, as fundamentalism became institutionalized, the resultant emphasis on professionalism and specialization resulted in women being pushed to the lower rungs of the full-time Christian service ladder.[79] Northwestern's establishment of a seminary in 1935, with its "men only" pastoral training program, is a classic example of this process.

Still, the fundamentalist advance required numerous workers in the public ministry, and not nearly enough men were willing to make the oft-necessary sacrifices in time and creature comforts to fill these positions. Probably because of this need for Christian service personnel, even after 1930 Northwestern officials closed their eyes to the fact that they had trained and were training women who would violate their biblically defined limitations by serving as pastors and evangelists. At times the contrast between official doctrine and actual practice was particularly jarring. Throughout the 1930s *Pilot* subscribers were told by Northwestern teachers that, as W. F. McMillan put it, it "is not scriptural for women to preach and teach . . . [or] put themselves forward in the assembly of saints," because "as Eve was deceived and Adam was not, so woman is liable to draw conclusions which are not according to God." But in January 1937 these same readers learned that Northwestern was conducting an evangelistic sweep through the upper Midwest, and two of the *school-sponsored* evangelists were the "eminently successful soul-winners — Miss Alma Reiber, and Miss Irene Murray, singer"; churches "desiring their services can reach them in care of *The Pilot*."[80]

Perhaps she was violating fundamentalist doctrine regarding the proper role of women, but Alma Reiber was a wonderful example of the graduates Northwestern Bible School produced at its most successful. Northwestern inculcated Reiber and her comrades with a burning desire to serve as Christian warriors who would advance the cause of truth in an unfriendly world. Riley's school instructed these prospective crusaders for God in a militant orthodoxy and trained them in a religious vocation. Thus prepared, many Northwesterners followed Alma Reiber's lead and graduated to pastorates or other posts to serve the fundamentalist cause. The result was a cadre of fundamentalist ministers in the upper Midwest who were loyal to the fundamentalist faith, loyal to the school that taught them this faith, and loyal to their school's founder and hero of the faith.

5

The Empire

In his path-breaking study of fundamentalism Ernest Sandeen argued that a "great deal of confusion which has existed over the nature of the fundamentalist movement" could be resolved if attention was paid to the role of the Bible school. According to Sandeen, "by failing to examine the manner in which the Bible institutes provided a form of social structure for Fundamentalism," scholars had "lost one key to understanding" this movement. The Bible institute provided a host of services to the fundamentalist community in its region, in the process becoming the institution of "primary allegiance" for the local ultraconservatives. In short, Bible institutes served as denominational surrogates.[1]

Except for a one-paragraph discussion of Moody Bible Institute, Sandeen provided no evidence for his claim. Nevertheless, regarding the upper Midwest his insights were on the mark. The story of fundamentalism in this region is the story of Northwestern's expanding web of influence. Numerous Northwestern-trained ministers aggressively promoted the fundamentalist cause throughout the Dakotas, Iowa, Minnesota, Nebraska, and Wisconsin. Indoctrinated in the notion that the major denominations were becoming increasingly apostate, they relied upon their alma mater to provide support in the form of evangelists, laity training, and educational material. Overseeing, influencing, and at times controlling the alumni efforts was the ruler of this expanding empire, W. B. Riley.

In discussing Riley's empire, it is important to remember that this vibrant fundamentalist network was expanding its influence at the time when, according to a once-fashionable historical interpretation, fundamentalism was dead and Protestantism was mired in a "spiritual depression." Such notions arose from the erroneous assumption that the history of American Protestantism is, in essence, the history of its major denominations. Northwestern's vibrant empire is evidence that to concentrate on the national level is to misunderstand the nature of religion in America.

Northwestern flooded the upper Midwest with fundamentalist workers; more than two hundred served the area in the 1940s.[2] Other regions, such as the West Coast and the Ozarks, also recieved their share of Northwestern graduates. The following table documents the spread of Northwestern-trained pastors, missionaries, and evangelists in the United States:

Dispersion of Northwestern Pastors and Missionaries

Location	1920	1925	1930	1935	1940	1945
Upper Midwest	18	69	113	155	224	215
Iowa	*1*	*7*	*9*	*19*	*37*	*50*
Minnesota	*15*	*49*	*89*	*101*	*128*	*92*
Nebraska	*0*	*1*	*4*	*12*	*12*	*27*
North Dakota	*2*	*9*	*4*	*11*	*8*	*8*
South Dakota	*0*	*0*	*3*	*5*	*14*	*7*
Wisconsin	*0*	*3*	*4*	*7*	*25*	*31*
Northwest (ID, MT, OR, WA, WY)	2	2	7	16	28	35
South Central (AR, KS, MO, OK, TX)	0	1	4	13	31	35
Southwest (AZ, CA, CO, NV, NM, UT)	0	1	5	7	14	27
Mideast (IL, IN, KY, MI, OH)	2	6	6	17	25	23
Other U.S.	1	2	6	6	17	11
Total	23	81	141	214	339	346

While the raw numbers may not seem remarkable, one should remember that Northwestern was never a large school. At its height of enrollment the number of full-time students at Riley's school never reached more than seven hundred and that number was attained in 1946. Moreover, this table does not include the innumerable Northwestern graduates, most often women, who served as lay workers in fundamentalist churches. Finally, the 1945 totals in the table above are misleadingly low. Because of World War II, many established and would-be pastors were serving with the armed forces; many did not return to the ministry until 1946 or even 1947.

Another way in which this table masks the extent of Northwestern influence is that it does not include alumni working in other lands. At Northwestern, missionary training was second in importance only to pastoral preparation, and by 1943 at least 130 alumni were serving the fundamentalist cause in foreign countries.[3] But the focus here is on how and to what degree Northwestern extended its influence in the United States, particularly in the upper Midwest. This is not to say, however, that the fundamentalist cause in the homeland did not require missions work. Numer-

The Missions' Band, Northwestern Bible School, 1940. According to *The Pilot*, January 1942, "Each Monday the Missions' Band . . . promotes keener interest (in foreign missions) by bringing a speaker before the students, generally a returned missionary."

ous Northwesterners served as missionaries to the hill folk of the Ozarks and Appalachians and to the Indians of Oklahoma. Others served with the American Sunday School Union in Montana and North Dakota, establishing churches and overseeing the summer daily Vacation Bible School effort.

Referring to these efforts in home missions, W. B. Riley boasted that "we have made it our business to undertake the hardest and most difficult of fields."[4] Riley did not exaggerate: missionaries reporting back to Northwestern noted the constant travel over harsh terrain, the poverty and isolation, and the often inhospitable host populations. But what Riley did not say was that the large majority of the missionaries enduring these difficulties were women. For example, all nine Northwestern alumni working in eastern Kentucky in the 1930s and 1940s were women, as were seventeen of the nineteen who served in the South Central states with the Gospel Missionary Union. The reason for this predominance of females is not hard to find. While Northwestern men had the opportunity of securing a regular pastorate, fundamentalist teachings kept most women (although not all) from attaining such posts. Hence, the majority of female graduates serving as full-time workers was relegated to the most difficult positions in the fundamentalist cause.

The Minneapolis-based Bible school made its greatest home missionary effort in northern Minnesota. Most of this work was done under the auspices of the Northern Gospel Mission, an independent evangelistic agency. Dozens of alumni served stints with Northern Gospel. This count does not include the numerous Northwestern students who spent their summer vacations in this soul-winning effort. While some graduates stayed there permanently, many used their time in northern Minnesota as preparation for missions work abroad. According to some participants, the "missionary conditions" there were "equal to those in any land."[5] From nine mission stations scattered throughout the region Northern Gospel missionaries took the gospel to the residing lumbermen, miners, and Indians. Each group provided its own special challenge. A disgusted Hazel Gardner reported back to Northwestern that "floating lumbermen contribute much toward making Northern Minnesota a real mission field. . . . Most of these men are single and have no other aim in life than to make a living and satisfy natural desires." The iron range miners were also a difficult challenge, for they were generally southern Europeans who tenaciously clung to their Roman Catholicism and their native languages. They were easier to reach than their Finnish counterparts, however, who were often described as atheistic Bolsheviks. An anonymous missionary noted in a 1930 article on the Northern Gospel Mission that in one community Finnish "children are taught to ridicule the existence of a God," while their parents "meet together weekly to discuss the orders they receive from Russia." But perhaps the toughest group was the Indians. Missionary William Shillingsburg commented that the Chippewas on the Red Lake Reservation "definitely reject the Gospel, and had their leaders power to do so, they would drive out the missionaries."[6]

For all the labor expended, one would be hard pressed to demonstrate that W. B. Riley's expanding fundamentalist empire included more than a handful of the immigrants and Indians of northern Minnesota. In a letter to her fellow Northwesterners Margaret Hendrickson sadly noted: "Our work here at Orr is chiefly among the Finnish people, a people noted for their unbelief and rebellion. It is very difficult and discouraging at times to bring them the Gospel when we see how they mock at and ridicule the idea of a God. . . . When we see the precious seed fall seemingly to the ground, we are almost ready to give up in despair." While Northwestern professors such as A. H. Norum could claim that "marvelous fruitage is to be found . . . in missionary work among the Red men," a 1933 report from Red Lake Reservation observed that "after years of effort in this field, there is now only one convert."[7] Whether other, more theologically liberal missionaries met similar rebuffs from these groups is uncertain. It seems likely, however, that the inflexible fundamentalism of the young Northwesterners hindered their efforts to proselytize people so different from themselves.

The mining communities and Indian reservations of northern Minnesota notwithstanding, Riley's Northwestern enjoyed ever-increasing influence in the upper Midwest. This was primarily due to the school's success in placing its alumni in pastorates throughout the region. In 1930 at least 85 Northwestern-trained ministers served in the Dakotas, Iowa, Minnesota, Nebraska, and Wisconsin. This total rose to 118 in 1935, and 178 in 1940.[8]

Most of Riley's ministers presented fundamentalism to the upper Midwest from Baptist pulpits. In 1925 approximately 65 percent of Northwestern pastors were in Baptist churches; by 1945 that percentage had escalated to 72 percent.[9] As might be expected from the founder of the interdenominational World's Christian Fundamentals Association, this had not been Riley's intention in founding his Bible school. He observed in a 1947 article that "from the very first" he had "conceived the idea of lending aid to all" denominations. He worked hard to promote Northwestern as truly an interdenominational training ground for pastors. He was more than a little frustrated by the fact that his fundamentalist empire increasingly became a Baptist concern.[10]

But Riley was partially to blame for this situation. His prominence in state and national Baptist circles attracted Baptists to Northwestern. Moreover, he played a crucial role in the placement of many of his graduates. It was only natural that he would be more likely to find jobs for them in Baptist churches. The primary reason, however, that his empire was Baptist was that Baptist churches were extremely lenient in the educational qualifications they demanded from ministerial candidates. In contrast with most other major denominations, the Northern Baptist Convention did not force local church bodies to adopt standards which would prevent Bible school graduates from serving as ministers. The door ajar, Northwesterners flooded through. A study sponsored by the Northern Baptist Convention in 1944 concluded that nearly 40 percent of all NBC pastors in the upper Midwest were Bible school graduates, with the large majority of these presumed to be from Northwestern.[11] Of course, Riley and the Northwestern instructors had inculcated these Bible school graduates with an antagonism to the modernism supposedly espoused by the Northern Baptist leadership. This large number of Northwestern graduates in NBC pulpits would have serious repercussions for the national organization, as we will see in chapter 6.

Riley's empire was consistently Baptist, but it was an empire in motion. The length of a Northwestern-trained pastor's stay at a church averaged 3.67 years.[12] In a 1936 article entitled "Our Marching Clergymen" *The Pilot* decried this state of affairs while also offering a shining example of stability: "While there may be many reasons for pastors to be constantly moving from one church to another, we wonder if that persistent changing of pastorates is not one factor in promoting the weakness and frigidity of our churches. A church that is a great lighthouse and is witnessing for the Master is usually one that has been shepherded for years by the same servant of God. Dr. W. B. Riley has been pastor of the First Baptist Church of Minneapolis for thirty-eight years, nearly thirty-nine, and the work of that church cannot be measured."[13]

Besides the fact that this pronouncement ignored Riley's own mobility in his early years, this was an unfair comparison. Northwestern alumni were not leaving large, thriving churches in metropolitan areas, such as First Baptist of Minneapolis. Often they were leaving churches in small towns and rural communities that offered few material benefits and little hope for a large membership roll. While these Northwesterners would have been loathe to admit it, it seems likely that many alumni were afflicted with a yen for upward mobility. As one graduate ruefully observed in a 1986 interview, natural desires for financial security and increased status moved many of them along from church to church, and sometimes they ended up in an urban pulpit.[14] While his motives are unknown, the career of alumnus Paul Williams suggests this sort of upward mobility. Pastoring in St. Francis, Minnesota, while a student, he served at Baptist churches in the tiny Iowa hamlets of Lorimor from 1931 to 1935 and Corwith from 1936 to 1938. From Corwith he moved to the markedly larger town of Humboldt, where he pastored from 1939 to 1942. From Iowa he went to Central City, Nebraska, for a brief stay; then, in 1945, he accepted "a unanimous call from the McKinley Park Baptist Church in Omaha, Nebraska."[15]

Like Williams, as the years went by an increasing number of Northwesterners landed urban pulpits.[16] Nevertheless, Riley's empire was always strongest in the rural reaches of the upper Midwest. This fact suggests the need for modification of current interpretations of fundamentalism. In an effort to counter previous descriptions of fundamentalism as a strictly rural phenomenon, both Ernest Sandeen and George Marsden strongly emphasized that, in its early years, the fundamentalist movement had much of its strength, to quote Sandeen, "in the cities and in the churches supported by the urban middle classes."[17] In one sense Riley's empire supports this thesis, since Northwestern Bible School and its pastor/founder were based in Minneapolis. On the other hand, most Northwestern students were from the country, and after graduation most Bible school–trained pastors served in country or small-town churches in the upper Midwest. Riley's empire is a powerful reminder that from the beginning American fundamentalism had a rural as well as an urban constituency.

Given the frequent hardships attendant to rural pastorates, Riley was justifed in claiming that he had infused his ministerial candidates with a willingness "to start with a bare living and trust God for increase, both in church membership and remuneration." Because many of these churches were not able to pay ministers supporting salaries, many Northwesterners served two, three, or more churches at once; one energetic soul in North Dakota pastored five. Others worked second jobs during the week. One alumnus cheerfully noted that such employment provided special opportunities for evangelism: "I worked with them in the shop, painted stores and homes alongside of them, and preached to them on Sundays, while all through the week it was my privilege to witness before them." This graduate concluded by noting that "Northwestern men do not work for salaries. They preach because they can do naught else."[18]

This commitment to bring the gospel to the rural reaches of the upper Midwest resulted in the opening of churches that had been shut down. When W. B. Riley came to the Twin Cities in the 1890s he was appalled by the number of rural churches that had permanently closed their doors; their isolation and lack of financial resources made it impossible to attract a minister. Riley instilled in his ministers a desire to reverse this trend. After his 1937 tour of Minnesota churches pastored by Northwestern graduates, Henry Van Kommer claimed that almost all the ministers he visited "spoke of the possibility of opening another closed church somewhere in the vicinity."[19] In his *Pilot* column entitled "Dr. Riley and His Boys," the Bible school president proudly recounted the work of one alumnus:

"Now for a rehearsal of Allan Williams' undertakings: At *Hardwick*, Minn., he found a closed church, vacated by the Presbyterians. The Nordeens [Northwestern alumni] now live there and hold Sunday school, morning preaching services, and midweek prayer meetings. At *Springwater* there was a closed M. E. Church. That Williams has opened, and Sunday school and morning preaching services are held. At *Adrian*, once a Baptist church, but later Unitarian — now thirteen families with a Baptist preference are found, and a Baptist work is hoped for. . . . At *Hills* a prayer group holds a weekly prayer meeting and Bible study. Williams has preached in all these towns and could use another assistant.[20]

This drive to open closed country and village churches was at odds with the policy of the major denominations, which had responded to the population shift to urban areas with a call for consolidation of the rural churches. The ultimate goal was the establishment of federated, or interdenominational, churches. In theory, these churches would neutralize potential conflict within their diverse congregations by de-emphasizing doctrine, focusing instead on social service.[21]

The policy of consolidating weaker rural churches made bureaucratic sense. But it did not display a sensitivity to rural people. Consolidation forced many churchgoers to travel much further to attend services. More important, shutting down the smaller churches stripped from residents an institution important in maintaining a sense of local community. Finally, as a 1916 survey revealed, many rural people did not want federated churches that watered down doctrine for the sake of unity.[22] By seeking to reopen these churches and by promoting a militantly orthodox faith, Riley's fundamentalists were much more in touch with the needs and desires of the grass-roots populace. Such sensitivity was unquestionably a key factor in the expansion of Northwestern influence in the upper Midwest.

Also crucial was the aggressive manner in which Northwestern-trained ministers promoted their fundamentalist faith. Convinced that they knew the truth, they were not content simply to present a militantly orthodox sermon on Sunday morning. Their zeal was in keeping with that of their fundamentalist colleagues across the nation. In a fascinating study of Northern Baptist Convention churches and seminaries, Hugh Hartshorne and Milton Froyd documented that fundamentalist ministers in the denomination had a markedly different perception of the role of the local church than did their liberal colleagues. While the latter were more concerned with social issues, fundamentalist ministers emphasized evangelizing the unsaved, training the laity in evangelization techniques, and supporting missionary efforts in foreign lands. One product of these different concerns was that fundamentalist congregations met much more often than liberal congregations, to the extent that, as Donald Tinder observed, "a check of the present meeting times of a congregation is the simplest way to guess its conservative or liberal stance." Sunday included lengthy Sunday School classes, sermons in the morning and evening, and a youth meeting either before or after the evening service. Prayer meetings were held on Wednesday or Thursday nights, and these meetings sometimes included additional Bible teaching. Often there was a monthly visitation night, when laypersons went into the community to call upon the unsaved or unchurched. Finally, the specialized groups — choir, women's missionary association, children's clubs, business and other committees — held numerous meetings. Tinder concluded, "In light of all these meetings, it is easy to see how much of a per-

son's energies . . . could be taken up by activities of the local congregation and its evangelistic outreach."[23]

An examination of alumni reports in *School and Church* and *The Pilot*
reveals that Northwestern-trained ministers instituted similarly extensive
programs in their churches. After a tour of Minnesota churches alumnus
Henry Van Kommer reported that "from my observation . . . it seems apparent that where a church is open on Sunday night it is because there
is a Northwestern graduate as pastor in that place." But for many alumni,
their burning desire to advance the fundamentalist cause went beyond holding frequent services. They also conducted weekly preaching services at
various points in the region, sometimes many miles into the countryside.
Some ministers even hired full-time missionary assistants, usually women,
who visited homes in the region.[24] For a few Northwestern alumni, this
passion for converts resulted in a full-scale evangelism agency. For example, in the early 1930s Wisconsin minister and Northwestern graduate
Lawrence Oman launched Wisconsin Rural Mission. In the words of one
of its workers, this project sought "to reach the unreached, those who hun-
ger for — they know not what" before they "drift into Catholicism, Pentecostalism, Russellism, indifference, or atheism." By 1940 Oman's agency
employed eight full-time pastors who preached and established churches
throughout northern Wisconsin.[25] In the summer, Wisconsin Rural Mission directed a massive daily Vacation Bible School effort. Dozens of
teachers toured the region: "Two of them spent six weeks in a camp trailer
while others camped out in tents, vacant rooms, old houses, schoolhouses,
or churches."[26]

Most of the ministers and Vacation Bible School volunteers who worked
for Wisconsin Rural Mission were Northwestern alumni or students. This
was not unusual. Another reason for the strength of Riley's fundamentalist empire was that it was not simply a collection of committed individuals.
Instead, it consisted of numerous cooperative ventures scattered throughout the upper Midwest. Northwesterners sought out other Northwesterners as natural partners in the campaign to propagate fundamentalism. They
joined together in local alumni associations or ministerial organizations,
not for the purpose of socializing but in order to engage in specific evangelistic ventures. Often they conducted Bible conferences in fundamentalist churches in the area; at these meetings Northwesterners instructed
ministers and laypersons in techniques of soul-winning and biblical instruction.[27] Northwestern alumni groups even established summer camps, such
as Camp Chetek in northwestern Wisconsin. Here adults and youth were
fed a steady diet of gospel messages; the central purpose was to challenge
them to upgrade their commitment to Christ.[28]

Aggressively, apparently unceasingly, Riley's young fundamentalists disseminated the militant orthodoxy and cultural separatism in which they had been steeped. The result was the creation of explicitly fundamentalist congregations where before there had been moderate, folk evangelical, or liberal congregations, or even no churches at all. Fundamentalism was on the march at the grass-roots level throughout the upper Midwest, and leading the advance were the men and women graduates of Northwestern Bible and Missionary Training School.

In October 1944 *The Northwestern Pilot* reported: "The World Missionary Convention was held in Waverly, Iowa, under the leadership of Rev. Donald Wagner and Rev. Robert G. Gardner, in combination with [four other ministers]. . . . All these men are graduates of our Alma Mater, *to which they are very much devoted*" (emphasis mine).[29] This quote is not simply another example of the range of activities in which aggressive Bible school graduates were engaged. Hyperbolic though it may be, the final passage also reflects the unusually close relationship many alumni maintained with Northwestern. Indoctrinated in the belief that the major denominations were infested with an anti-Christian modernism, Riley's ministers relied upon their alma mater to provide the support structure for alumni efforts at promoting fundamentalism. Northwestern served as a denominational surrogate for its graduates in the upper Midwest.

One way the Minneapolis school supported its alumni ministers was by sending students to work in their churches. The practical work director observed in 1942 that alumni pastors "came back to their *Alma Mater* for that assistance which would enable the carrying out of a more thorough soul-winning work than [if they had] used their own lay workers."[30] This assistance included child evangelism leaders, music groups, and in the summer, daily Vacation Bible School workers. Northwestern also sent out teams of speakers to aid ministers in their evangelistic work. In the early years these groups often consisted of Bible school professors who spent their summers touring fundamentalist churches in the Dakotas, Iowa, Minnesota, Nebraska, and Wisconsin.[31] As the school grew, however, it employed full-time evangelists to perform this work, including the ubiquitous team of Alma Reiber and Irene Murray. In the course of each revival campaign the evangelist often gave one lecture on the virtues of the Northwestern Bible School and seminary, which concluded with the collection of an offering for Northwestern.[32]

Northwestern's most important work as a denominational surrogate involved the indoctrination and training of laypersons through the Northwestern Bible Conference, the evening school, and *The Pilot*. By the 1930s

Student evangelists, Northwestern Bible School, 1910s. Churches pastored by North-western alumni were particularly eager for the assistance of these preachers and musicians.

thirty thousand people were attending the two-week Bible conference meet-ings held each August at Medicine Lake, just outside Minneapolis. While some commuted to the meetings from the Twin Cities, many stayed the whole time on the conference grounds, which had a hotel, dormitories, "tepees, igloos, lodges, wigwams, [and] cottages."[33] Many Northwestern-trained ministers in the upper Midwest brought large contingents from their churches, thus allowing the alumni a chance to renew old friendships while their congregations received further indoctrination in fundamentalism. While some time was allowed for recreation, instruction and inspiration were the primary emphases. In 1933, for example, the daily program in-cluded "a careful and consecutive Bible study; a discussion of Sunday-school methods and plans; a presentation of children's and young people's work; a questionnaire dealing with popular problems; a setting forth of the Fun-damentals of the Christian Faith, and above all, popular evangelistic ser-vices."[34] By the late 1930s the conference was offering courses in Christian education designed to aid both professionals and laypersons in running Sunday Schools, child evangelism classes, and Vacation Bible Schools. So no one would forget who was sponsoring the conference, every evening one to two hours were devoted to alumni testimonies. Graduates talked about such topics as "The N.W.B.S. as It Inspires Evangelism," "The N.W.B.S. and Its Spiritual Impact," "The N.W.B.S. and the Pastoral Office," "The N.W.B.S. and the Foreign Field," "The N.W.B.S. and Its Summer Vacation Work." One alumnus reminisced that these talks so moved Riley that he would often "forget he had an evening speaker lined up."[35]

Northwestern's evening school reached fewer people than the Bible conference but provided more intensive training. While in the early years of its existence the school occasionally held classes at night, a formal evening school was not started until the late 1920s. By 1937 the demand became so great that the Bible school began to offer extension classes in Northwestern-pastored churches throughout the region, a practice which of course tightened the school's grip on these fundamentalist congregations. Courses were offered one or two nights a week, with a diploma awarded after four years of attendance. As an administrator noted in 1927, the purpose was to create an "indoctrinized" and "trained and efficient" laity.[36] The Bible teachers taught the same courses they taught in the day school: Bible Exegesis, Bible Doctrine, Bible Study, Missions, Bible Geography, and Bible Chapter Summary. Sometimes Riley himself taught a class. He was determined as ever to instill in his charges a virulent antimodernism, and his 1935 class centered on "debatable questions": "This latter class is intended to answer all of the false teaching that comes from such sources as the Minneapolis Church Federation, the State University, and other institutions committed to modern skepticism."[37]

While the indoctrination in the evening school varied little from what one would get in the day offerings, the training aspect was necessarily quite different, because the focus at night was on the lay worker. Nevertheless, the underlying message was that, just like ministers and missionaries, the truly up-to-date church worker needed specialized training. In this regard Northwestern was cultivating a demand for its services. A wide range of classes was designed to assist Sunday School teachers, youth leaders, and other lay workers. These courses gave an aura of professionalism to church education, as this 1938 description of a Sunday School methods class demonstrates: "Our Pedagogy unit explains the purpose of Sunday School teaching, the principles of teaching, aims and methods in teaching, the use of questions, illustrations; and, how to prepare and present the Bible lesson to the class most effectively. Having learned in Child Study the characteristics, interests, needs and capacities of each period of childhood and adolescence, the next thing is to select the most suitable methods for using the graded materials of learning to successfully build Christian lives." An Evangelical Teacher Training Association certificate was even awarded after

Registration for evening classes, Northwestern Bible School, 1938

a certain number of classes, which presumably certified recipients to instruct inexperienced teachers in their home churches.[38]

Perhaps Northwestern's most important quasi-denominational service
was *The Pilot*. This monthly magazine began in 1920 as a small student
periodical designed to allow students an opportunity to develop their
writing skills. Gradually, faculty members began to contribute articles, and
with this came an increase in both size and circulation of the magazine.
These increases were accelerated by the 1932 merger with Riley's *Christian
Fundamentalist*, which he shut down as a final admission of the demise

of the World's Christian Fundamentals Association. In 1934 Marie Acomb Riley became the official managing editor of *The Pilot*, a move which signified that the magazine had evolved from a student periodical into the official organ of an expanding fundamentalist empire in the upper Midwest.[39] By the late 1940s thirty-five thousand people subscribed to this monthly magazine, which was renamed *The Northwestern Pilot* in January 1944. *The Pilot* provided Northwestern's ministers with sermon outlines as well as lengthy articles which expounded upon biblical passages and themes. Moreover, *Pilot* contributors gave the ministers detailed suggestions on administering their churches, including how to advertise, how to impose restrictions to keep moviegoers and smokers from being admitted to membership, and how to keep all the members busy in the Lord's work. Finally, the magazine provided laypersons with inspirational stories, detailed Sunday School lessons, and suggestions for youth and music workers.[40]

Northwestern itself was the focus of much attention in *The Pilot*. Interspersed with the theology and the suggestions for lay workers were reports on Bible school happenings, advertisements encouraging prospective students to consider enrollment in the program, and pleas for contributions. Moreover, *The Pilot* kept remarkably close tabs on graduates who were involved in church-related vocations, frequently imploring them to "keep in touch with the home base."[41] Many did, and the alumni pages were filled with information about their activities and movements. This publicity and support probably helped keep many Northwesterners at their isolated, low-paying posts.

In essence, *The Pilot* served as a detailed map of Northwestern's growing web of influence in the upper Midwest. This network consisted of an ever-increasing number of fundamentalist churches that were dependent upon Northwestern for ministers, evangelists, lay training, and written materials. In this role as denominational surrogate, Northwestern itself gained in influence, contributions, and enrollment. Northwestern administrators readily conceded that they expected such benefits from their efforts. In 1929 Extension Director J. W. Welsh candidly observed that in providing assistance to Bible conferences and evangelistic campaigns Northwestern had "these objectives: to save souls, [to] instruct laymen in the Word of God, to revive churches, to present the Northwestern Bible School as a possible place of training for Christian young people, and to afford churches and individuals an opportunity to contribute toward the needs of the school."[42] In contrast with much of modern televangelism, there is no reason to see Northwestern's evangelistic and educational work as a cynical cover for base motives. Northwesterners genuinely believed in the

fundamentalist cause, and they genuinely believed that their school provided the best hope for the advancement of this cause. To them, there was
no difference between promoting fundamentalism and promoting Northwestern.

And promote Northwestern they did. As Bible school administrators
had hoped, alumni pastors worked hard to convince their congregations
to become active supporters of the school. These ministers encouraged
members to contribute funds to Riley's school; some churches even included
Northwestern in their annual budgets. These ministers also did everything
possible to ensure that many of the young people in their churches attended
the "lighthouse of the Northwest." For example, in 1917 *School and Church*
reported that many midwestern pastors were "sending [to the school] the
names of promising young men and women" so that administrators could
join the ministers in "counselling [these individuals] to become students
in this institution." Other ministers from Riley's school took groups from
their churches to tour the school and meet with Northwestern representatives. By the 1940s many were holding Northwestern Days in their
churches, when they would proclaim the school's virtues, encourage the
youth to consider attending Northwestern, and ask for cash contributions
from the parents.[43] All this work seems to have paid off. A 1936 survey
revealed that "most of the students have come to school under some agency
of Northwestern"; one-third of the students were there due to the influence
of an alumnus, and it is safe to assume that often this person was the
hometown pastor.[44]

The ministers were as loyal to W. B. Riley as they were to the school
itself. But they were tied to Riley by more than loyalty, for this truly was
an empire with an emperor. Riley exerted a good deal of influence in the
lives of Northwestern graduates, beyond the fact that he had indoctrinated
them in militant orthodoxy and continued to preside over an institution
which served as the support structure for their evangelistic efforts. Riley
was often directly responsible for the positions the young pastors held.
Particularly after the mid-1920s, when he turned his attention from the
failed national crusade to the local scene, Riley served as a one-man placement office. *The Pilot* noted in 1933: "Those churches that need a pastor
and are looking for a fine young man, would do well to write to Dr. W. B.
Riley, president of Northwestern. . . . He is ready on a moment's notice
to render service to a church looking for a good preacher who is at the
same time a dependable man and destined to prove a successful pastor.
He renders this service without charge to anybody." As Northwestern's
influence expanded, the demand for its ministers accelerated. According
to Riley, by the early 1940s he was receiving as "many as three to five [re-

quests] a day" for Northwestern-trained ministers, with most of the requests coming from "the Central States and the Northwest."[45] In fact, Riley became so inundated with requests that, in an effort "to save us the multitude of personal letters" in response to inquirers, he had a brochure printed — *Looking for a Pastor? Perhaps We Can Help You.*[46]

The Pilot commented in 1943 that "there are more calls for pastors than he [Riley] has men who would be adapted to the places open." This statement indicates the degree to which Riley was involved both in controlling the careers of his ministers and in shaping the emergent fundamentalist empire. He was not simply sending out names of available graduates but was choosing certain individuals for certain posts. Actively fulfilling his role as head of Northwestern's fundamentalist empire, on occasion he even controlled a graduate's move from one church to another: "I have a request today from a church in the South, in a very attractive city, desiring a man of considerable experience, preferring such to any new graduate. That puts upon me the necessity of moving some Northwestern graduate from his present field. . . . I become a party to such removals reluctantly, but in this case I happen to know an excellent man who will fit in and shall immediately recommend him."[47]

Riley's involvement in the life of his boys also included what might be called troop inspections. He frequently visited and preached in churches in the upper Midwest that were pastored by Northwesterners; since Riley was an avid pheasant hunter, these visits often meant that, to quote one alumnus, "we hunted during the day and he preached to our people at night."[48] Moreover, most years, especially in the last decade of his life, Riley and his wife, Marie, would make a formal tour of churches run by Northwestern-trained ministers. Sometimes this trip was limited to the upper Midwest. More often the Rileys combined their visits of alumni with a vacation to the West Coast or the South. Their visits were always big events in the lives of the alumni. Not only would the alumni show the Rileys their church buildings and discuss with them the status of their work but they would also, if possible, schedule Riley to speak at a special service. At least once in their circuit the Rileys would be feted at banquet or picnic hosted by a group of alumni in the area.[49] For all of the socializing, however, W. B. Riley had some deeper motives in making these visits. According to Riley's associate Richard V. Clearwaters, Riley was also checking to make sure that his boys were still true to the fundamentals of the faith and devoted to their alma mater. Whether he ever found a straying alumnus is unknown.[50]

A good example of these tours is a 1937 visit to an area Northwestern administrators considered a mission field, the Pacific Northwest. Engaged to serve in a Portland church for the month of July, the Rileys spent much of their free time visiting alumni in the region. Riley recounted, "In order that there might be a gathering of the Northwestern clan," Portland alumni "arranged a picnic for us" which was attended by a good number of resident Northwestern graduates. In the second week the Rileys began their visits of "our 'old grads' on their respective fields." First they went to Hillsboro to visit the church of Ortiz Weniger. Then they participated in two days of meetings at Arno Weniger's Calvary Baptist Church in Salem. From there it was to Eugene and a dinner in honor of the Rileys. Alumnus Alfred Danielson drove 125 miles from Bend to be there, and afterward he led the Rileys back to his church, where W. B. Riley spoke once again. The Rileys then returned to Portland for a final sermon and some socializing with former First Baptist folks and then went up to Seattle, Washington. There Riley conducted a meeting at the Union City Gospel Mission, run by graduate Francis Peterson. Riley noted that "at this meeting, as at other occasions, several Northwesterners were present — some of whom gave their testimonies before the message." It is probable that these testimonies were essentially tributes to the visitors. Then the Rileys went to Wenatchee to meet alumnus George Kehoe, and then to Cashmere to see alumnus Stanley E. Anderson, where the Northwestern president once again spoke. Then they finally headed homeward. Satisfied with his inspection, the exuberant Riley concluded: "It is impossible to adequately express the pleasure of these visits! The *loyalty* of our Northwestern boys and girls, together with the success that is everywhere attending their endeavors, is a joy unspeakable" (emphasis mine).[51]

Northwestern Bible and Missionary Training School thus served as a denominational surrogate for a tightly knit network of fundamentalist churches in the upper Midwest; moreover, the school's president, William Bell Riley, actively oversaw and at times controlled the workings of this network. The perspective so far has been from the top down, from the throne's perspective, so to speak. But how did the empire look from the bottom up? At bottom were hundreds of fundamentalist churches scattered throughout the upper Midwest. How did they fit within the empire? How and to what degree did they interact with Riley and his Bible school? Did Northwestern serve as a denominational surrogate for these individual churches?

In one sense, these questions are impossible to answer, for it is impossible to examine each of the fundamentalist churches and its relationship with Riley and Northwestern. But even one church's perspective will help us to understand better the detailed workings of Riley's empire. The church examined here is the First Baptist Church of Granite Falls, Minnesota. This church was chosen as the case study because it had been pastored by a series of Northwestern graduates in the Riley years (as had many churches); as a small-town church far from a large city, it was representative of churches pastored by Northwesterners; the remaining records are extensive and accessible; and some of the individuals who pastored the Granite Falls church in the Riley era were still alive and were willing to be interviewed.[52]

Granite Falls is a small town at the falls in the Minnesota River, approximately 120 miles due west of Minneapolis. The first settlement was established there in 1868, and Granite Falls was incorporated as a town in 1879. The state legislature also designated Granite Falls as the seat of Yellow Medicine County. Settlers were attracted to the town by the abundant water power afforded by the waterfalls. By the late nineteenth century Granite Falls was serving area farmers with four flour mills, a sawmill, and a cording mill. In 1892 the power of the falls was harnessed for electricity. The town's role as a provider of electricity for towns and farms in the region was expanded in the early 1930s, when Northern States Power Company built a large generator just downriver from the town. Reflecting the importance of this enterprise to Granite Falls, the high-school athletic teams were and are known as the Kilowatts.[53]

Through the efforts of a Baptist missionary to southwestern Minnesota, the First Baptist Church of Granite Falls was established in 1878. There were nine charter members. For the first few years the nascent church teetered on the brink of extinction, and at one point in 1881 the church actually had no members. But thanks to a loan from the Minnesota State Baptist Convention, the church building was completed in the autumn of 1882, and the church eventually stabilized at about fifty members. While the church survived, it proved to be a revolving door for ministers. Between 1881 and 1906 the First Baptist Church had sixteen different pastors, although during a period in the 1890s, because of the economic depression, the church could not afford a minister. At least two of the pastors in these years seem to have been hired directly from Baptist schools in the East, but neither tarried long in Granite Falls. The revolving door finally stopped revolving in 1906 with the hiring of Rev. G. Melby as minister. Melby served the Granite Falls church until 1920.[54]

On September 20, 1913, a representative from the Granite Falls Congregational Church presented to the Baptist church a proposal that Melby preach alternate Sundays at the Baptist and Congregational churches, with the two churches splitting Melby's salary. For reasons that are not clear, the Baptists, who at this time numbered forty-seven, agreed to this proposal. Six years later the Sunday Schools of the two churches also combined. Finally, in 1920, the already-united churches made their federation official.

In keeping with Northern Baptist Convention optimism for federated churches, the Baptist-Congregational combination in Granite Falls at first seemed to be a big success. The clerk of the Baptist church reported in 1915 that "the work of our church has been blessed during the past year. Since we sustained a federation with the congregational church we have had larger attendance for morning services. New members have been added to both the churches during the past year."[55] But during the next decade Baptist membership slowly declined to just twelve members in 1926. In that year the Baptists shut down their church building. All meetings were then held in the Congregational church. In the winter of 1927 the minister and at least one Baptist church member traveled to Minneapolis to meet with Minnesota Baptist Convention officials regarding the possibility of selling the church property and ending the Baptist work in Granite Falls. The state convention, which held a mortgage on the church property, agreed to this proposal. Word got out that the Baptists were selling; the *Granite Falls Tribune* reported on March 23, 1927, that "one offer has already been made by another congregation in this city, and there is also a movement on foot among the members of the Masonic lodge to buy this property and change it into a meeting place for their order."[56] All that remained was for the few remaining church members to agree to dispose of the property.

Much to the surprise of the Granite Falls community, the *Granite Falls Tribune* reported on April 13, 1927, that "the members of the Baptist congregation of this city decided by a vote of 8 to 1 last evening to retain their church property." The church was hanging on, but the long-term survival of the Baptist work in Granite Falls was still greatly in doubt. In the summer of 1927 a representative from the Sparta Baptist Church, a country church seven miles west of Granite Falls, paid a visit to Granite Falls Baptist. The visitor from Sparta suggested that if the Granite Falls church wanted to survive and grow, it should join the country congregation in hiring Roy Boldt, a dynamic young Northwestern Bible School student who already had been holding Sunday morning services in the Sparta church.[57] Convinced by this presentation, the Baptists voted to sever their federation with the Congregational church and to hire Boldt to a second pastorate in Granite Falls. Traveling out from Minneapolis on weekends, Boldt served Granite Falls for two years. Under his leadership and released from federation with the Congregationalists, the Baptist membership rose from twelve to twenty-eight.[58] Pleased with Boldt's performance, at his departure in the spring of 1929 the Granite Falls and Sparta congregations turned once again to Northwestern. With some direct financial assistance from Riley's First Baptist Church of Minneapolis, the two churches hired Arthur LeMaster, a Northwesterner who had been serving in North Dakota. LeMaster started his pastorates in June 1929.[59]

The Northwestern era had begun at the First Baptist Church of Granite Falls.[60] In a 1986 interview a long-time church member recalled that "our church relied totally on William Bell Riley for pastors, because we felt we had nowhere else to go. And Riley sent us one pastor after another." After Boldt (1927–1929) and LeMaster (1929–1934), Riley sent to Granite Falls Harvey Hill (1934–1939), Fred Julius (1942–1943), Raymond Anderson (1944–1946), and Alf Skognes (1946–1949). Even after Riley's death in 1947, the Granite Falls church continued to hire Northwesterners into the 1950s. The only exception was Nelson Crow (1939–1941), and even he had a Northwestern connection. In the summer of 1937 Crow brought some students from Alabama to attend Riley's school; while at Northwestern he met and impressed a former member of the Granite Falls church, who brought Crow out to Granite Falls to candidate for the post recently vacated by Harvey Hill. The congregation hired Crow. But according to the official and surprisingly candid history of the church, "being Southern born and reared in a predominantly Baptist country, he [Crow] had difficulty in adjusting himself to this community where our denomination is very much in the minority." On the other hand, Northwestern students were trained to serve in the upper Midwest; as the aforequoted church member observed: "After Crow we learned our lesson. From then on we hired 'Riley's boys.'"[61]

The average stay of a Northwesterner at the Granite Falls church was 3.1 years, eight months less than the length of the average ministerial stay in Riley's empire. This is not terribly surprising, considering that Granite Falls was a small and somewhat isolated town and thus was an early step in the career of these Northwestern alumni. But the brevity of the ministers' stays did not dissuade the Baptists of Granite Falls from continuing to hire Bible school graduates.[62] The reason was that, as one member reminisced, the Northwesterners brought in "the glory years." Under the tutelage of Riley's boys, the church jumped from 12 members in 1927 to 104 in 1937 and 121 in 1947.[63] These numbers are even more impressive when one realizes that the fundamentalist ministers continually strove to purge the church rolls of inactive members.

Prehaps one reason for the success of the Bible school alumni was that they did not open the church doors only on Sunday mornings. In keeping

with their fundamentalist colleagues across the nation and in contrast with
the other churches in town, the First Baptist Church of Granite Falls maintained a remarkably busy schedule.[64] The August 31, 1932, issue of the
local newspaper outlined a typical week in the life of the Baptist church:
"The Mission Circle will meet with Mrs. Foley Tuesday afternoon at
2:30 P.M. All women and girls are invited to be present. Bible study and
prayer meeting will be held Thursday evening at 8 o'clock . . . Sunday,
Bible school, 9:30 A.M. . . . Morning worship, 10:15 A.M. Park service,
3 P.M. B.Y.P.U., 7 P.M. Gospel service, 8 P.M. Subject: 'The Inspiration of
the Scriptures: Proofs from Fulfilled Prophecy.'—A. A. LeMaster, pastor."[65]

This array of worship services, Bible studies, youth meetings, and missions meetings were all part of the normal weekly schedule Riley's boys
instituted at the First Baptist Church of Granite Falls. Each year the church
also sponsored a host of special activities. For these activities the Granite
Falls ministers turned to their alma mater for assistance. Northwestern certainly came through: in the words of a former minister, Raymond Anderson, the Bible school "continually funnelled folks out to help us in our
work." Every summer Northwestern provided staff workers for the annual
daily Vacation Bible School, which involved Bible lessons and memoriza-
tion, missionary stories, singing, handiwork, and games.[66] Riley's school
also sent music groups: "Those who attended the Baptist church last Sunday evening were greatly pleased by the service which was conducted by
the Ambassador Trio from the Northwestern Bible and Missionary Training School. The trio is making a tour of the western and northern states
in the interest of the Bible school, which affords them an opportunity of
presenting the claims of Christ to a needy world." Moreover, Northwestern-
trained foreign missionaries occasionally stopped in to hold meetings and
raise money.[67]

Northwestern also supplied the Granite Falls church with evangelistic
speakers. Sometimes these evangelists were directly sponsored by the Bible
school; sometimes they were alumni who were recommended by Bible
school administrators. The meetings could last from one day to two weeks
and often resulted in large crowds packing the church building. At times
so many people turned out for these meetings that the services had to be
held in the city auditorium.[68] The messages were standard revival fare,
although some of the evangelists did their best to personalize and sensa-
tionalize their messages. For example, in the spring of 1933 the First Baptist Church announced that Northwestern alumnus E. C. Stauffer would
be delivering the following series of addresses: "Royalty in the Pig's Sty,"
"Hell's Highway Runs through Granite Falls," "Unpardonable Sins," "Seven
Things in Granite Falls That Damns [sic] a Man's Soul," "God's Heart Turned

Inside Out," "The Devil's Payroll," "Who Is the Biggest Fool in Granite Falls?" "The Only Earthly Possession We Can Take to Heaven," "Will Christ Come in 1933?" and "A Message from a Lost Soul in Hell." Stauffer's messages succeeded; on the Easter Sunday after he concluded his revival, twenty-nine people were baptized at the Baptist church.[69]

Riley's school did not just send evangelists, Vacation Bible School workers, and music groups. Northwestern also sent to Granite Falls individuals whose primary purpose was selling the school itself. Over the years the head of the practical work department, the head of the Russian missions department, and President Riley himself, among others, made promotional presentations at the Baptist church. For example, the church minutes record that on December 26, 1943, Northwestern business manager (and former member of the Granite Falls church) George Wilson "showed moving pictures . . . of activities of Northwestern and a talkie reel [of] a sermon by Dr. Riley."[70]

All of this salesmanship was effective. From 1930 on, the First Baptist Church of Granite Falls wrote Northwestern into its annual budget, giving the school from $10 to more than $150 yearly.[71] This does not include the annual gifts to Northwestern-trained missionaries. But the Granite Falls church did not just send money. More important, the church sent people. In the 1930 annual report the church clerk joyously commented that "two of our Y.P. [young people] are preparing for the Lord's Service at Northwestern Bible School this last year, and many more expect to go next fall. It is wonderful how our young people are growing in grace and knowledge of Him." By 1932 eight or nine of the sixty-one members of the Granite Falls church were attending Northwestern. First Baptist's role as a feeder for Northwestern was quite evident at the church's special sixtieth anniversary celebration on November 25, 1938. At this service, "special recognition was given to all those who had attended Bible School in preparation for Christian work. These all gathered on the platform and sang 'I Will Sing of My Redeemer.' Members and former members who are graduates of N.W. Bible School are as follows: Rev. Carl Knutson, Rev. George Knutson, . . . Helen Barber Bowersfield, Virginia Stratton, Howard Knutson, Harold Barber [missionary to Columbia], Rev. George Wilson, Marcella Wilson, and Lois Martenson [missionary to Brazil], [as well as four others] who have attended the Bible School and who were present."[72]

Overseeing the relationship between Northwestern Bible and Missionary Training School and the First Baptist Church of Granite Falls was Northwestern's president, W. B. Riley. Riley personally helped choose the pastors to serve at Granite Falls, and at times he also advised Granite Falls' ministers to move on to another church. For instance, while at Granite Falls

Raymond Anderson was invited to succeed another Northwesterner at a church in St. Cloud, Minnesota; unsure whether he should leave Granite Falls after being there only two years, he went to Riley for advice. Riley responded, "Well, I wonder who I should get for Granite Falls."[73]

But Riley's involvement in the Granite Falls church was not limited to long-distance control. He also made personal appearances. Occasionally he came out to the southwestern Minnesota town to participate in revival services or to raise money for Northwestern. He also preached the ordination sermon for at least two of the ministers who were ordained while pastoring the Granite Falls church.[74] An appearance by Riley was, of course, a major event in the life of the church; it was also a big moment in the life of the Granite Falls community. On August 7, 1929, the *Granite Falls Tribune* reported that "ordination services were held at the Baptist church last evening for Reverend A. LeMaster. . . . Pastors from all over the state were present at the service and the Baptist church was packed with eager auditors who had come to seize the opportunity to hear Dr. W. B. Riley. . . . Besides being pastor of the Minneapolis Baptist church Dr. Riley founded the Northwestern Bible School and has been an institution there for many years. He is noted far and wide, and having a chance to hear him deliver a sermon is no small opportunity."[75]

It is obvious that W. B. Riley played a central, sometimes dominant, role in the life of the First Baptist Church of Granite Falls. In effect, his Bible school served as a denominational surrogate, taking the place of the denomination with which the church was nominally affiliated, the Northern Baptist Convention. This was not simply happenstance. Riley's boys had been inculcated with a great distrust of the major denominations, and thus at Granite Falls it was only natural that Boldt and the other Northwestern-trained ministers turned to Northwestern instead of the NBC. According to Harvey Hill, the denomination did not equably accept this state of affairs at Granite Falls. When denominational officials heard that First Baptist planned to hire Hill, its third consecutive Northwestern-trained minister, they met with the pulpit committee to protest the employing of yet another graduate of Riley's interdenominational Bible school. Then, after it was clear that the church was going to stick with Hill, a denominational official offered Hill a "salary supplement"; Hill understood this as an effort to obligate or bribe him into toeing the denominational line, and he thus rejected the offer.[76]

Hill was affronted by these maneuvers, but it seems that denominational officials were right to be concerned. When the fundamentalists captured control of the state convention from the denominational loyalists in the mid-1930s, Granite Falls pastor Harvey Hill gave his full support to the rebels.[77] In the late 1940s Granite Falls Baptist Church joined with other Baptist churches in Riley's empire in gradually breaking with the NBC and joining the Conservative Baptist Association. At the same time the church borrowed funds to pay off the mortgage against the church property held by the denomination, thus ensuring that Granite Falls Baptist would not be in "debt bondage" to the modernist-infected Northern Baptist Convention.[78]

This revolt on the part of Granite Falls and other fundamentalist churches in the region marked the apex of Riley's empire. Riley died in 1947, and within a decade the empire had split between separatist fundamentalists and moderate evangelicals. The First Baptist Church of Granite Falls landed in the separatist wing. In 1966 the church left the less militant Conservative Baptist Association and joined the separatist General Association of Regular Baptists.[79] Since 1984 Thorin Anderson has pastored the church. Anderson is a graduate of Pillsbury Baptist Bible College and Central Baptist Seminary, the ultrafundamentalist schools which arose out of the collapse of Riley's Bible school. While the 1986 membership totaled only forty-four, Anderson is determined to revive the evangelistic fervor of "the glory days." In his sermons Anderson emphasizes that the true Christian holds to the fundamentals of the faith, "abstains from worldliness, and refuses to cooperate with those who are perpetuating error or heresy." Forty years after the death of W. B. Riley, one part of his legacy lives on at the First Baptist Church of Granite Falls.[80]

The Granite Falls story depicts, in microcosm, the Riley empire at work. While also pastoring a small country church, an aggressive Northwestern graduate rescued the dying Granite Falls Baptist Church from a federated death and remade it into a fundamentalist institution. Following in his footsteps came a series of similarly aggressive Bible school graduates. Each stayed three years or so and then moved on to a larger pastorate. During their brief stints, however, each of these ministers preached the fundamentalist faith while also maintaining a remarkably extensive program of services. Allowing them to maintain this very active schedule were the evangelists, Vacation Bible School teachers, musicians, and other church workers sent to the fundamentalist outpost by Northwestern. In response, Granite Falls Baptist Church sent the Minneapolis school not only monetary gifts but also prospective ministers and missionaries.

All of this is further evidence that in the upper Midwest the Northwestern Bible School and its alumni joined to build a tight, powerful network of fundamentalist churches. And as the Granite Falls experience also indicates, at the center of this network was the dominant personality of William Bell Riley. The high degree of influence of W. B. Riley and Northwestern in the affairs of fundamentalist churches in the region received its clearest expression in the rebellion of the Minnesota Baptist Convention against its national officers.

6

The Revolt

IN the summer of 1937 Northwestern alumnus and St. Paul minister Henry Van Kommer made an extensive tour of Minnesota. He wanted to visit "as many . . . Northwestern graduates as possible." One purpose of his travels was to gauge the Bible school's impact on Minnesota religious life. Writing for the October issue of *The Pilot*, Van Kommer asserted that "though there be many other Bible institutes," few could match Northwestern's achievements. In Minnesota "the largest pulpits are filled" by Northwesterners, and "many new buildings are being erected under their supervision." The success of the Bible school alumni challenged the pastors who were not Northwestern graduates "to a more vigorous Bible preaching," and in consequence "the preaching of Minnesota churches is purified." Van Kommer explained that "the reason for this effective work of Northwestern lies in the fact that school and its graduates are closely connected. The school, and especially its President, is vitally interested in each individual." As a result of this close partnership among alumni, school, and Riley, "Northwestern has spread a closely woven web over the State of Minnesota."[1]

Van Kommer accurately portrayed the extent of Northwestern's influence in Minnesota. Riley's home state truly was the seat of his expanding empire. His school's influence was strongest within the Minnesota Baptist Convention, and Northwesterners gradually came to dominate the state organization. But this takeover resulted in a conflict between Northwestern's grass-roots empire and the Northern Baptist hierarchy. In the 1940s the parent body attempted to rein in the increasingly emboldened grass-roots fundamentalists. In keeping with Samuel Hays's observations regarding political conflicts, the major battle between the cosmopolitans and the locals took place at the state level, within the Minnesota Baptist Convention.[2] The grass-roots empire of W. B. Riley ensured a fundamentalist victory.

One reason for Riley's success in filling the pulpits of the Minnesota Baptist Convention lay in his successful fight to keep the national denomination from adopting uniform standards for admission to the ministry. Baptists traditionally allowed local congregations to ordain any candidate for the ministry, regardless of training. The result was that, according to a 1945 denominational report, only 38.3 percent of Northern Baptist ministers had graduated from a Baptist seminary. And 21.6 percent completed their educational training in a Bible institute.[3] Twenty-one percent were graduates of non-Baptist seminaries; this group included alumni of Riley's Northwestern Evangelical Theological Seminary. Only 9.3 percent of Northern Baptist ministers were college graduates, and 9.8 percent had at most a high-school education.[4]

Throughout the twentieth century many in the denominational hierarchy sought to require of Northern Baptist Convention ministers either seminary training or at least completion of an NBC-prescribed reading course. These Baptist leaders argued that an increasingly educated public required increasingly educated ministers. In a 1916 call for the creation of a special committee to deal with this issue, the NBC Committee on Resolutions observed: "While we fully recognize that spiritual qualifications are the prime essentials, we nevertheless believe that a high standard of intellectual training is most desirable in order that the minister may be able to command a proper hearing for his message and maintain his rightful place as a religious leader."[5]

Over the next few years, however, it became increasingly apparent that the hierarchy's push for uniform standards was not just an effort to control how much education its ministers received but also an effort to control how its ministers were educated. Primary targets were the nondenominational Bible institutes and their growing crop of fundamentalist pastors. For instance, in a 1935 call for the creation of yet another committee to deal with this problem, the NBC Committee of State Conventions asserted that this was "the day of 'isms,'" a fact that posed problems for the denomination because "too many men are coming out of certain institutions who can be anything else as well as Baptists, but they turn to the Baptist ministry because our democratic form of government offers easy access to the Baptist church. All they need do is to 'sell themselves' to the leadership of the local congregation and the 'trick is done.'"[6]

Considering that many of his boys would have been out of a job, it is hardly surprising that W. B. Riley fought these efforts to standardize ministerial requirements. While Riley's rhetoric became more inflamed over the years, his arguments against standardization remained essentially the same. His starting point was the claim "that the ascended Lord is the only

One who has a right to put any Christian" into the ministry. He liked to point out that most of the apostles surely would have failed to meet ordination standards.[7] To demonstrate further that formal educational requirements had little to do with the making of an effective minister, Riley often referred to his alumni; in a 1918 article he wrote: "We would be glad to have some man point out to us little fields that are flourishing under the hands of theological seminary graduates as compared with fields we can mention which are now growing under the leadership of Bible Training School graduates. We challenge comparison!"[8] He also charged that efforts to create a standardized ministry deviated from traditional Baptist polity, which provided for, to quote from a 1935 speech, "the autonomy and inviolability of the rights of the local church in the matter." Finally, in a claim he made with increasing vehemence, he asserted that these standards were a "bolsheviki" effort by those in power to impose modernism upon the multitude of conservative ministers in the NBC.[9]

The latter must be considered the primary reason for Riley's opposition. For all of his talk about divine call and the autonomy of the local church, his own failed efforts to establish creedal requirements in the Northern Baptist Convention demonstrate that he was quite willing to have a standardized ministry, as long as his group set the standards. Since the convention refused to accept fundamentalist standards, Riley worked hard to ensure that liberal restrictions were similarly rejected. In 1916 the convention created a Committee on the Standardization of the Baptist Ministry to establish minimum educational requirements for those seeking to enter the ministry. The committee returned with the recommendation that a two-year course of theological studies be required and suggested that "ordination be postponed till [the candidate] has satisfactorily completed his required studies."[10] The vigilant Riley vitiated this resolution by successfully attaching to it the amendment "save in that exceptional instance where the members of the examining committee are convinced that the man is so equipped by nature and otherwise that he had great promise of success."[11]

But the standardization committee had also established a suggested reading course for ministerial candidates who were educationally deficient. Riley was unhappy with the modernist bent of the readings; when it became apparent that several state conventions had begun recommending this reading course to their prospective pastors, the Minneapolis minister responded by suggesting an alternative list. Riley convinced the delegates at the 1924 convention to accept the following resolution: "We agree upon the principle that an alternate course be printed, as alternate to and together with the original course in the minutes of the Northern Baptist Con-

vention, and that copies be provided each State Secretary; and, further-
more, that any one having read this [Riley's] course may be regarded as
having wholly met the reading course requirements involved in the thought
of the Committee on Standardization."[12]

While throughout the 1920s and 1930s various denominational committees discussed ways to standardize and raise ordination standards for
ministers, no substantial changes were achieved.[13] Without denomination-
ally mandated ordination standards NBC leaders were faced with a situation in which they held the reins of national power and yet had little control over local congregations. They were concerned about a potential crisis.
In a cogent and fascinating report, the NBC Board of Education in 1938
summarized some of the concerns of denominational leaders regarding the
lack of a standardized ministry. Board members worriedly observed that
"in the central and western states . . . the ministry of our churches is rapidly filling up with graduates of the Bible schools and other short-course
institutions." While many "of these men are most earnest and devoted Christians," they were not sufficiently educated to meet the needs of modern
congregations. But this was definitely not the most critical problem: "In
addition . . . , many of these Bible school graduates have been trained away
from loyalty to our denomination, and due to their lack of knowledge and
to their misinformation they are constantly leading away from the denomination many of our churches that heretofore have been loyal members of our fellowship. We do not believe that it is possible to overstate
the seriousness of this situation. *Unless this strong tendency be checked,
nothing but disaster faces our denomination"* (Emphasis mine).[14]

It is quite possible that when the Board of Education members penned
these words Minnesota was the chief "central state" they had in mind. By
1930 at least 35 percent of the Northern Baptist ministers in the state were
Northwesterners, and this percentage escalated over the next two decades.[15]
These were Riley's boys, and there was no doubt that Riley served as their
commanding general. He exerted a good deal of control over his alumni
ministers and worked diligently to ensure their continued loyalty. As might
be expected, this influence was magnified greatly within Riley's own state
convention. A colleague of Riley's at Northwestern, Richard V. Clearwaters,
observed in a recent interview that within the Minnesota Baptist Convention Riley maintained a phalanx of Northwestern-trained pastors under
his leadership. He put them to good use: by the mid-1930s he and his fundamentalist followers had managed to take control of the state organization from the liberals.[16]

For a good part of the 1920s Riley was preoccupied with the national
fundamentalist crusade. It was not until the collapse of that ill-fated effort

that he began to concentrate his energies at the state level. His first target was Carleton College in Northfield, Minnesota, which was affiliated with the Minnesota Baptist Convention. Basing a good part of his case on lecture notes taken by a freshman student, at the 1926 state convention Riley presented a resolution that began with the charge that Carleton "no longer is an orthodox institution, but is rankly liberal, with a tendency to Unitarianism." The resolution then called for termination of the affiliation between the Minnesota Baptist Convention and the college.[17] The liberal-dominated hierarchy kept this motion bottled in committee for two years while at the same time mounting, in the state Baptist periodical, a publicity campaign designed to convince Minnesotans of Carleton's "high moral standards and spiritual atmosphere." In 1928 the Riley squadron forced a vote on the motion. In a 172 to 135 vote the fundamentalists won. *The Pilot* exulted in the victory, thanking the numerous Northwestern graduates who were at the convention for their "beneficial influence." Riley's boys were beginning to show some muscle.[18]

Another sign of the growing fundamentalist strength came in 1930, with a change in the constitution of the Minnesota Baptist Convention. Prior to that year delegate representation was based on a system allowing one representative for each church with an additional representative for each fifty members, up to a maximum of twenty-five delegates. Riley pushed through an amendment which eliminated the maximum limit, establishing that whenever "any church shall reach a membership entitling it to twenty-five delegates, the basis of representation thereafter shall be one for each additional two hundred and fifty members." The only church affected by this change was Riley's own First Baptist, which had a membership of 3,304 in 1930. Certainly it was only fair to provide some sort of representation to the previously unrepresented 2,054 First Baptist members. Nevertheless, this amendment aided the fundamentalists in future battles within the Minnesota Baptist Convention. Not only liberals engaged in political maneuvers.[19]

One final indication of the growing strength of Northwesterners in the Minnesota Baptist Convention was their influence in the local associations. In his superb work on the distribution of power in the Baptist denomination Paul M. Harrison defined "association" as a grouping of local churches designed "to operate as [a] center of stimulation and organization for state and national organizational work." While they had no official power in the state convention, Baptist associations, Harrison observed, quite often exerted a great deal of control over the churches in their regions. It is not clear how powerful the various Minnesota Baptist associations were. But it is noteworthy that by 1935 Northwestern graduates controlled the leader-

ship positions in three of the six Minnesota associations, and in a fourth
a Northwestern alumnus held a position of authority. Whatever else it
demonstrates, this provides further evidence that in their zeal for fundamentalism Northwesterners were grass-roots activists.[20]

Northwestern's expanding influence in Minnesota and Riley's ability to
control his ministers meant that it was but a matter of time before the fundamentalists wrested control of the state Baptist organization from the
liberals. One alumnus who was pastoring a Minnesota Baptist Convention church at the time recalled that the "conservative takeover was no big
deal, because we waited until we knew we had the numbers to win, and
then we made our move."[21] The revolution, as the militant Riley termed
it, came at the 1936 annual convention. Auspiciously for the fundamentalists, this meeting was held at Anoka Baptist Church, which was pastored by Northwestern alumnus Dudley Thimsen. One of the major tasks
at these annual meetings was the selection of officers for the upcoming
year. Normally the nominations committee prepared a slate of officers which
the convention as a whole would routinely accept. As had been the practice for years, the 1936 nominations committee constructed a liberal-
dominated slate of officers. But this year, the fundamentalist minority on
the nominations committee decided, with Riley's active encouragement,
to come up with its own slate of officers. When on the morning of October 7 the nominations committee presented its suggested slate, Northwestern graduate S. P. Anderson "offered a substitute ballot as a minority
report of the Nominating Committee." The delegates accepted Riley's motion "to distribute copies of both ballots to each delegate." The fundamentalist ballot was victorious by a vote of 144 to 118. Riley's boys were in
charge of the Minnesota Baptist Convention.[22]

Riley crowed years later that this election of officers ended "modernist
control of the Convention."[23] From that moment in 1936 Minnesota fundamentalists dominated leadership positions in the convention. This meant
that W. B. Riley, while not officially elected president until 1944, was the
de facto head of the state convention. Riley's power was such that, according to one Northwesterner, the night before the annual meetings of the
Minnesota Baptist Convention Riley would "gather his boys in his room
and plan the next day's events."[24]

To those in the state organization who were outside Riley's circle of loyal
fundamentalists, Riley's role in the state convention could look quite sin-
ister. In the mid-1940s an unnamed individual, self-described as a long-
time member of the Minnesota Baptist Convention who had served on
the Board of Trustees, wrote a scathing report chronicling the labors of
W. B. Riley as "boss" of the state's Baptists. In the eyes of this individual,

Riley was not a "religious leader" but a "religious politician": "Not even [Riley's] thoughtful friends could rate well his powers of reflection or analytical thinking, or his concern for accuracy of factual statements; but, he is a shrewd and aggressive manipulator. He has the cunning and resourcefulness and uses the recognized methods of the practical politician. . . . His efforts are directed, ruthlessly, in a self-centered contest for political success, for enhancement of personal power and control." According to this observer, Riley had achieved success, in that he had maintained "an autocratic and unprincipled tyranny" over the Minnesota Baptist Convention for a "long duration." But while Riley was devious and ruthless, his personal skills were not the only reason that he succeeded. Most important was the fact that he had a power base: "Through placing graduates of his school, Northwestern Bible and Missionary Training School, in Baptist churches throughout Minnesota, his political control is steadily made more secure."[25]

It is interesting that this unnamed correspondent's rhetoric mirrors Riley's rhetoric concerning the "modernist autocrats" who ran the Northern Baptist Convention. To some degree the language of both men reveals a "sour grapes" attitude. But regarding the assertions made by Riley's detractor, it was true that Riley had enormous influence in the Minnesota Baptist Convention and that his influence was due in great part to the fact that numerous Northwesterners held Minnesota Baptist pastorates. It should be noted, however, that Riley had one problem with his boys (and other fundamentalists) in the Minnesota Baptist Convention—he had to keep them from bolting the denomination. To some degree, this threat to his power base was Riley's own fault. At Northwestern prospective ministers were taught that the major denominations, including the Northern Baptist Convention, were infested with an anti-Christian modernism. When they became pastors of their own churches, the Northwesterners were naturally inclined to lead their congregations out of the denomination.

Riley assiduously worked to convince his graduates and other fundamentalists, as one alumnus put it, to "stay in and clean it up."[26] To those who felt compelled to ignore his pleadings and bolt the denomination, Riley could be merciless. For example, in 1939 the Baptist church in Canby pulled out of the convention. According to the Northwestern alumnus who was the Canby pastor prior to the separation, his successor (apparently not a Bible school alumnus) convinced the congregation that the Minnesota Baptist Convention was not militant enough in its fundamentalism. Riley exploded in the pages of *The Pilot:* "Think, will you, of a church fostered by the Convention itself from the Convention, annual grants toward his own salary up almost to the day when he would secure a vote of that church to quit the Minnesota Baptist Convention . . . and that, mark you, when Conservatism controlled. . . . In other words, fifteen to twenty loyal pastors had sought to build this church, and each of them had found, in the Convention, a satisfactory fellowship; but when one comes who does not so think, he takes the work of the other fifteen, throws it to the winds, that he may have his own sweet way."[27]

While Riley was not able to persuade every ultraconservative Baptist in the state to remain affiliated with the denomination, a large proportion did stay, thus ensuring fundamentalist control of the Minnesota Baptist Convention.[28] A noteworthy example of fundamentalist strength occurred at the 1942 convention in Worthington. Prior to that meeting Richard V. Clearwaters, fundamentalist pastor of a Minneapolis church, asked Riley about the possibility of removing the state body from the Federal Council of Churches of Christ in America (FCCC). As it stood, a percentage of the annual Minnesota Baptist financial contribution sent to the national convention was automatically appropriated for this ecumenical organization. Riley had for years opposed the Federal Council, viewing it as "the executive headquarters for Modernism." He told Clearwaters that "if you do make such a motion, I will back you in the endeavor to be rid of this Modernist incubus." With Riley's influential and active support, the motion carried. Henceforth state churches that wanted some of their contributions to the national convention to go to the FCCC had to designate it thusly.[29]

Not surprisingly, Northern Baptist Convention leaders were displeased with Minnesota's action. In a 1943 article Riley claimed that these officials found it so "distasteful" that they were even threatening "that an effort might be made to have it rescinded." Riley sarcastically observed that it was "*unfortunate* to be sure, to have top-officials dissatisfied." Nevertheless, it was "not at all likely that Minnesota Baptists" would give up their autonomy or their antimodernism just "to satisfy these superior officials": "On the contrary, we are giving notice to these same officials that this is to be looked upon as a first step, rather than a final one, in the recovery of true Baptist principles and the emphasis of established Baptist Polity."[30]

While Riley sounded militant, his remark should not be read as a threat to separate from the denomination, for there is no evidence that Riley had any such intention in the early 1940s. Nevertheless, the fundamentalist leader's statements are telling. He and his army of supporters were in firm control of the Minnesota Baptist Convention, and they had no intention of surrendering their prerogatives or their principles to the liberals in charge of the denomination. And the Northern Baptist Convention was prepared to grant them freedom of action, up to a point. Writing in 1959, Paul M.

Harrison noted that it is "the desire of the policy-makers" of the NBC "to minimize theological cleavage and to placate churches which will contribute to the financial health of the denomination." In the 1940s the latter was particularly important, considering that the denomination had just suffered through a decade of marked financial and numerical losses. Leaders in the denominational hierarchy had no intention of unnecessarily alienating the entire Minnesota state convention. But as Harrison noted, when theological disagreements became heated to the point of disrupting the denominational program, especially regarding financial contributions, the organization men would take steps designed to defuse the threat.[31] This is precisely what happened in the 1940s, and W. B. Riley and his Minnesota fundamentalists were directly involved.

The conflict in Minnesota must be placed within its national context. At the same time that Minnesota fundamentalists were fighting for autonomy within the Northern Baptist Convention, fundamentalism was enjoying a remarkable resurgence throughout America. Thanks in great part to radio ministries such as Charles Fuller's "Old-Fashioned Revival Hour," in the late 1930s and early 1940s there were unmistakable signs of evangelistic awakening throughout America.[32] Seeking to turn these impulses into a full-scale national revival, a new generation of fundamentalist leaders de-emphasized divisions within their ranks and joined together to create a number of national organizations. The most important of these new institutions was the National Association of Evangelicals, formed in 1942. Designed as the headquarters of the conservative Protestant renewal, the NAE reached out to evangelicals outside the fundamentalist tradition, such as Pentecostals. By 1947 this new organization had a membership of approximately one and one-third million.[33] But while the NAE was perhaps the most significant symbol of fundamentalist vitality and unity in the 1940s, most remarkable were the newly created evangelistic associations that aimed at converting youth—Young Life, Inter-Varsity, and Youth for Christ. While all three interdenominational groups enjoyed great success, Youth for Christ was the most sensational. The association was established in the early 1940s, and in 1945 five hundred thousand youth were attending weekly YFC rallies across the country. From the ranks of Youth for Christ workers came a number of prominent evangelists, including Billy Graham, who began his spectacular career as a revivalist during these years.[34]

Another example of fundamentalist vitality in the 1940s was the marked increase in foreign missions interest and commitment. World War II contributed to this concern; as one historian has noted, with the war "evangelical Christians in the armed forces and at home saw new opportunities and new means to proclaim their gospel around the world." A number of interdenominational agencies were founded, including World Vision International and Greater Europe Mission.[35] But this increased fundamentalist interest in foreign missions also manifested itself within the mainline denominations, particularly the Northern Baptist Convention. The result was an intense battle over foreign missions. Most important for our study, the struggle between the Northern Baptist Convention and the Minnesota Baptist Convention had its roots in this larger conflict within the denomination.

From the early 1920s NBC fundamentalists had been concerned with what they perceived as an American Baptist Foreign Mission Society practice of sending out modernist missionaries. In 1924 Frederick Anderson, the chair of the denomination's foreign mission board, announced that the society would "appoint only suitable evangelical men and women." This statement became the official statement of board policy for the next two decades. But as Anderson granted, there were great differences of opinion regarding who was or was not a suitable evangelical; so, within certain limits, the board continued to appoint missionaries from the various constituencies within the NBC.[36] The fundamentalists, who believed that a raft of modernists was under the Northern Baptist umbrella, were horrified at this inclusiveness. In a *Pilot* article entitled "The 'Inclusive Policy' Illustrated, and Disowned," W. B. Riley snidely defined the inclusive policy thusly: "It takes in the people who are supposed, at least, to believe in the deity of Christ, and it takes in the people who flatly deny that deity; it takes in the people who believe a soul can be lost; it takes in the people who repudiate the idea; it takes in the people who by historic descent should hold that the Bible is the final authority in matters of faith; it takes in the people who deny that proposition."[37]

While the division within the denomination regarding missions had existed for two decades, the issue came to a head in 1943 with a controversial appointment. In February of that year the board of the American Baptist Foreign Mission Society, in a decision that displayed insensitivity to fundamentalist concerns, appointed an outspoken social activist, Elmer A. Fridell, to be its executive secretary. An outraged Riley exploded, "Never in the history of the Baptist denomination has Modernism dared so brazen a step." Riley and his fellow fundamentalists viewed Fridell as not only an extreme modernist but also a radical leftist. What infuriated ultraconservatives was that the board had seemingly ignored the large fundamentalist constituency within the NBC. With this choice, Riley fumed, "the Board evidently thinks that it needs no further cover for its unitarian tendencies." Like other fundamentalist leaders, Riley advised pastors not to have their churches send any money to Northern Baptist foreign missions until the missions secretary was "neither Fridell nor any other man who would turn from the Gospel of the Shed Blood to a Social Gospel."[38]

Baptist fundamentalists tried to force the Foreign Mission Society to rescind its appointment of Fridell. Perhaps feeling that the damage was already done, the agency refused. Then the fundamentalists tried to convince the Foreign Mission Society to require of its missionaries a belief in certain doctrines, including the Virgin Birth and bodily Resurrection of Christ. The fundamentalists had failed in a similar attempt two decades earlier, and it was not surprising that they failed again. This time the fundamentalists, believing that a missions organization that would appoint Fridell as secretary was a lost cause, established the Conservative Baptist Foreign Mission Society (CBFMS).[39] By December 1943 this new organization was sending out its own missionaries. A pleased W. B. Riley proclaimed that in "the selection of Fridell, sleeping conservatism was at last aroused, and this new organization was the justified result." He called upon Baptists to withhold their support of the Northern Baptist Convention's official mission society and instead to give their "instant and permanent cooperation" to this new organization.[40] Toward this end his Minnesota Baptists, who had already sent an angry petition protesting the selection of Fridell, passed a resolution establishing a special account "to receive monies contributed by churches, organizations or individuals to the Conservative Baptist Foreign Mission Society."[41]

Even outside of Northwestern-dominated Minnesota the new foreign mission society received a good deal of support. Within a little more than four months of the organization's founding, more than two hundred churches had contributed more than forty-two thousand dollars. But as the organization's historian noted, a major question about the CBFMS remained: "What was its relation to the Northern Baptist Convention?"[42] In the preceding two decades the denomination had allowed the formation of fundamentalist seminaries under the umbrella of the denomination. The founders of the new organization hoped they would receive similar treatment. Even the fiery Riley suggested that a "joint office" be established, in which "thorough-going conservatives as secretaries would handle all the money intended for thorough-going conservatives on foreign fields; and thorough-going modernists would be privileged to administer all modernist moneys, missionaries, and fields." Leaders of the CBFMS worked throughout 1944 and 1945 to establish the society as a recognized NBC missions agency which would work "in comity" with the denomination's American Baptist Foreign Mission Society.[43]

Fundamentalists may have controlled the Minnesota Baptist Conven-

tion, but they did not control the NBC. And the NBC leaders had no intention of recognizing the Conservative Baptist Foreign Mission Society
as an official agency of the denomination. Whatever the parallel with the
fundamentalist seminaries, the addition of a fundamentalist missions board
would, in effect, split the denomination in twain. Such division was anathema to the organization's leadership. Moreover, these leaders probably
viewed the popularity of the new society as a potential threat to the already-
established missions organization. In 1945 the General Council of the Northern Baptist Convention ruled that the "Fundamentalist Foreign Mission
Society . . . is competitive with the ABFMS and in its promotional efforts
it tends to undermine confidence in all Convention agencies and in the NBC
itself." The denomination would not recognize the CBFMS as "another society within the framework of the NBC."[44]

Putting some teeth into their exclusion of the new agency, the NBC hierarchy also ruled that any minister who accepted an appointment under
the Conservative Baptist Foreign Mission Society would be immediately
excluded from the NBC pension program. But a more portentous decision
came at a General Council meeting two years earlier, in December 1943.
There it was ruled that a cooperating church—a church considered part
of the Northern Baptist Convention—be defined as one that cooperated
"in the program of the Northern Baptist Convention and [maintained] reasonable participation in the financial goals of the Convention." Traditionally, the level of financial contribution to the denomination had not been
a factor in determining which churches could participate in running the
NBC. While this was but a general policy statement, it would become clear
that in the requirement of reasonable financial contribution the denominational hierarchy had a weapon that it could use against supporters of the
rebel mission society.[45]

The Minnesota Baptist Convention had wholeheartedly supported the
Conservative Baptist Foreign Mission Society from the agency's inception.
The NBC's maneuvers against the CBFMS heightened Minnesota's opposition to the policies of the national organization. This intransigence was
increased by William Bell Riley's accession to the presidency of the Minnesota Baptist Convention in 1944. Within a year of taking this post Riley,
unhappy with the drift of the denomination, put into motion a plan which
marked a radical break with the Northern Baptist Convention. In the same
month that the NBC decided not to recognize the Conservative Baptist
Foreign Mission Society, Riley pushed through the state convention's board
of managers a resolution that withdrew Minnesota's support of the unified
budget of the NBC. Under the unified system states sent all monies to the

national convention, where national leaders then decided how the money should be spent. States had no say about how much money came back for local work. Under Riley's "Minnesota plan" the state organization would retain 50 percent of the receipts from state churches and would send the remaining half to the national convention. As Robert McBirnie noted in his dissertation on Riley, by this act "the Minnesota Convention severed the financial control of the New York office and at the same time increased the amount of money made available for its own work."[46]

In the same vein, Riley and company decided that the Minnesota Baptist Convention did not need to obtain approval from the denominational hierarchy before hiring salaried officials. In 1945 E. P. Fosmark was elected state executive secretary. Riley primly observed in a 1946 article that Fosmark was "brought into office without asking leave for the action of the Administrative Committee of the Council on Finance and Promotion of the Northern Baptist Convention."[47]

With these moves, Riley proclaimed, Minnesota Baptists demonstrated that they "prefer freedom to further enforced Unitarian fellowship and will exercise it against all would-be BOSSES."[48] But this bravado did not frighten denominational officials into accepting the Minnesota plan. While they were willing to consider increasing Minnesota's allotment, they rejected the notion that Minnesota officials should automatically retain half the monies collected in the state. The argument set forth in numerous letters to and meetings with Riley in 1945 and 1946 by NBC finance officials was a simple one, perhaps deceptively so. The officials granted that donors had the right to designate their gifts; if they designated that their money go to Baptist work in the state, such requests should be honored. But donors who did not specify where they wanted their funds to go were, by implication, designating that their money go for the general use of all the denominational programs. Budget Advisor E. H. Rhoades, Jr., wrote Riley in February 1946 that the problem with the Minnesota plan was that it "violates the basic principle involved": "Under it Minnesota, frankly, says that it will forward to New York gifts especially designated, and that for each dollar so sent, it intends to keep, for it's [sic] own use, an equal amount of money contributed by those who make their contributions for the use of all the work of all the organizations. The direction given by a donor for the general use of all the organizations, as set forth in the Budget, is to be dishonored."[49]

In short, NBC officials felt that they and not state leaders should have financial authority. They were determined not to allow such a visible state organization to establish control over monies. They feared that Minnesota would become a model for other state organizations. Their fears were justified; as Director of Finance and Promotion Reuben E. Nelson noted to E. H. Rhoades, Jr., in a letter written in the spring of 1946: "I have just come back from an emergency trip to Portland, Oregon. . . . Some of the brethren there have made up their minds that they ought to do what Minnesota has done. I tried to do my best to explain the entire situation to them to keep them from any such action."[50]

Afraid the plague would spread, the NBC leaders refused to give back to Minnesota its designated allotment, arguing that the Minnesota Baptist Convention had unilaterally terminated its "existing financial cooperation."[51] The denomination also refused to accept E. P. Fosmark as the Minnesota executive secretary. But these steps did nothing to change the Minnesota Baptist Convention's position. For a year after the establishment of the Minnesota plan Riley and the NBC leaders carried on fruitless negotiations.[52]

The MBC-NBC struggle was not simply, or even primarily, a struggle over money. It was, in essence, a battle between the ideologues and the bureaucrats. In a revealing May 1946 letter to Reuben E. Nelson, an aging Riley downplayed the money issue, frankly admitting, "My chief difficulty, Dr. Nelson, in coming into fellowship with you to the full is the fact that we are so widely separated on the whole subject of the 'Inclusive Policy.' That's the point of division, and it is no use to deny or even debate it. It's a settled question."[53] Riley was saying that there was no hope for reconciliation because he could no longer accept the NBC tolerance for liberals as missionaries. Nelson sent the letter along to his colleague who was working on the Minnesota case, E. H. Rhoades, Jr. In a naive but telling response, Rhoades wrote back to Nelson: "Do you have any idea that if we could reach some working agreement as to this matter of the 'Inclusive Policy,' all our other sins would be forgiven and we could really work together, especially during this year which lies just ahead?"[54] Riley the ideologue had bluntly stated that he was giving up on the denomination because of its doctrinal laxity; not understanding Riley's ideological passions, Rhoades the bureaucrat saw the "Inclusive Policy" as a technical issue to be negotiated so that the work of the organization could continue.

While some of the Northern Baptist officials might not have understood the ideological passions of a W. B. Riley, they did know how to neutralize a divisive element in the denomination. This is precisely what they did at the 1946 NBC convention at Grand Rapids, Michigan. That the denominational officials would succeed in this enterprise was not at all clear before the convention. The fundamentalists had looked to Grand Rapids as the place where they would roust the modernists from their positions of power. They came to Grand Rapids on a wave of optimism. Not only were they buoyed by the success of their new missions agency, but the Fundamentalist Fellowship had conducted a massive preconvention campaign designed to swell its numbers at Grand Rapids. Even some of their opponents predicted that this would be the year that the fundamentalists would capture control of the denomination.[55]

Eschewing a gradualist approach, the fundamentalists went for complete victory at Grand Rapids. They offered four proposals: the removal of voting privileges from paid officials of the NBC; the establishment of a doctrinal requirement for denominational officials; the removal of NBC support from the Federal Council of Churches of Christ in America; and the substitution of a fundamentalist slate of delegates. The second was the most important; it would have required that no convention agency employ any missionaries or secretaries who refused to affirm the Virgin Birth, miracles, and Resurrection of Jesus and "that the New Testament is inspired of God in all its contents." As in Indianapolis twenty-four years before, the nonfundamentalists offered a substitute resolution: "We reaffirm our faith in the New Testament as a divinely inspired record and therefore a trustworthy, authoritative, and all sufficient rule of our faith and practice. We rededicate ourselves to Jesus Christ as Lord and Saviour and call our entire denomination to the common task of sharing the whole gospel with the whole world." Also in keeping with the 1920s, Riley and the fundamentalists had again overestimated their strength within the denomination. By a large majority this resolution was accepted, and the fundamentalist resolution rejected. The other three fundamentalist proposals met a similar fate.[56]

While the rejection of these proposals was certainly disappointing, this was essentially the same defeat Baptist fundamentalists had incurred twenty years before. What most damaged the fundamentalist cause within the NBC was a surprise amendment offered by the liberals. Completing a course started three years earlier in the NBC General Council, this amendment would establish that the number of delegates a church could send to the annual meeting was contingent upon the percentage of that church's "benevolence giving" that went to the NBC. If a church of nine hundred members gave 100 percent of its benevolence funds through the denomination, it would have ten delegates; 80 percent, eight delegates; 20 percent, two delegates.[57] To the point, if an NBC church gave most of its mission money to the Conservative Baptist Foreign Mission Society, then the number of delegates it could send would be drastically reduced. In one sense this was a fair rule; why should churches not financially supporting the denominational program have the right to vote on denominational policy?

But as Paul M. Harrison noted, "the amendment was eminently just in everything but intention, which was clearly to weaken the forces of the fundamentalists without joining in serious theological debate." The NBC leaders got their wish. The amendment carried by a vote of 2298 to 585.[58]

Fundamentalist Baptists were furious. W. B. Riley charged: "In the meeting at Grand Rapids last May a few of the top officers of the Northern Convention, in secret session, received with favor the statement that it was better to forfeit, if need be, 2,000 more churches than to compromise the convention's liberal policy." Notwithstanding his conspiratorial tone, Riley's observation was on the mark. Now that they had been rendered powerless, what choice did churches have who felt compelled to support the Conservative Baptist Foreign Mission Society, except to leave the NBC?[59]

Certainly the Grand Rapids meeting ensured the withdrawal of Riley's Minnesota Baptist Convention from the parent organization. This final break did not come in 1946. Delegates at that meeting merely affirmed the status quo. They regretted that "a mutually agreeable basis for cooperation could not be reached between the Northern Baptist Convention and the Minnesota Baptist Convention," and they urged "all the churches of our State to give a proper proportionate financial support to our Minnesota Baptist Convention."[60] But in early 1947 Riley called on all Baptist conservatives to withdraw from the NBC and join the Conservative Baptist Association, the fledgling denomination organized by Baptist fundamentalists (including Riley) in response to their devastating defeat at Grand Rapids.[61] Finally, in a May 1947 letter to the denominational president, which was published in *The Northwestern Pilot*, the ailing Riley personally withdrew from his once-beloved Northern Baptist Convention. Sadly noting that he had been part of the NBC for sixty years and had attended perhaps fifty convention meetings, Riley concluded, "I am no longer a young man, having seen my eighty-sixth birthday, and I should be ashamed to die in a fellowship that seemed to me so un-Biblical, and consequently un-Baptistic."[62]

Riley died that December. Delegates at the 1948 meeting of the Minnesota Baptist Convention, many of whom were Northwesterners, followed the example of their fallen leader: "The Minnesota Baptist Convention serve[s] notice on the General Council of the Northern Baptist Convention that it has severed its relationship of affiliation." In Minnesota at least, the fundamentalist empire was now a separate entity.[63]

This story of the Minnesota Baptist rebellion is, at heart, the account of a grass-roots religious enterprise at war with an unresponsive national denomination. The cosmopolitans in charge of the Northern Baptist Con-

In October of 1947, two months before his death, W. B. Riley watches the laying of the cornerstone of Memorial Hall

vention were unable or unwilling to grant the locals a share of denominational power and thus forced them out of the organization and, eventually, into the Conservative Baptist Association. The fundamentalist exodus was not limited to Minnesota. Throughout Riley's empire Northwesterners pulled their Baptist churches out of the Northern Baptist Convention and, in many cases, into the new denomination. One fundamentalist leader observed a few years after Riley's death that "the Conservative Baptist work in Wisconsin, Illinois, Iowa, and the Dakotas is often to be directly attributed to the influence of Dr. W. B. Riley."[64]

Not only is this, then, a story of grass-roots rebellion against an unresponsive national organization, but it is also a powerful example of the strength of W. B. Riley's personality within the empire he had created. The grand old man of midwestern fundamentalism, as we have seen, clearly orchestrated the Minnesota Baptist revolt. He organized the fundamentalist takeover of the state convention; he devised the alternative funding proposal, or Minnesota plan; he single-handedly conducted the negotiations with the denomination; and with his calls to action and letter of withdrawal from the denomination, he ensured that the state's Baptist churches would leave the NBC en masse.

In short, the Minnesota Baptist rebellion may justly be termed Riley's rebellion. But the mastermind behind the revolt died in 1947, before the final withdrawal from the denomination. Riley left behind a thriving fundamentalist network in the upper Midwest, including Northwestern Bible and Missionary Training School, Northwestern Evangelical Theological Seminary, and Northwestern College of Liberal Arts; a state convention controlled by Northwesterners; and numerous fundamentalist churches in the region dependent upon Northwestern. From all appearances this impressive enterprise rested on a sturdy foundation and would continue to function without the great man in command. But it was not to be. The Minnesota Baptist withdrawal from the national denomination would prove to be not a harbinger of future success but, instead, a last hurrah. Soon after the revolt the decline of the Riley empire began. It was a rapid descent.

Epilogue

W. B. Riley died in 1947. Within ten years of his death the fundamentalist empire he had painstakingly constructed in the upper Midwest had split into hostile fiefdoms. The division occurred along the lines of two divergent, almost contradictory, strands within his thought. Throughout the twentieth century Riley attacked Northern Baptist Convention leaders as modernists who were slowly but surely destroying the denomination. At times he hinted that he and the fundamentalists would depart; in 1923 he observed: "It begins to be increasingly evident that the Baptists of the North cannot abide together. We doubt if two more conventions can occur before the division in faith [will] find expression in fact."[1] Riley, however, did not join the fundamentalists who left the NBC in the early 1930s and formed the General Association of Regular Baptists. In the early 1940s he was still resisting separation, proclaiming that "while there are instances in which the cause is advanced by division, there are ten cases to the contrary, which have retarded the advancement of the cause of Christ."[2] It was only on his deathbed that Riley finally separated from the modernists by personally withdrawing from the Northern Baptist Convention.

For most of his life Riley maintained both separatist rhetoric and moderate actions. But after his death the fundamentalist empire that he had created in the upper Midwest could not contain this contradiction; eventually the empire split. This division was not peculiar to Riley's empire. In the immediate postwar period there were rumblings of conflict within fundamentalism; by the second half of the 1950s the fundamentalist movement had divided into evangelicals, or "new evangelicals," and separatist fundamentalists. The latter group militantly refused to cooperate with modernist apostates and made separatism a test of orthodoxy. While their evangelical counterparts also opposed modernism, they did not insist on complete separation; while these new evangelicals also emphasized the importance of correct belief, they tolerated certain doctrinal differences, such as Pentecostalism. To the separatists, these positions were unacceptable com-

151

promises.[3] When the dispute exploded into open conflict in the mid-1950s, the focal point of the fighting was Billy Graham, whose willingness to cooperate with modernists in organizing evangelistic crusades, among other failings, represented to the separatists everything that was wrong with their more moderate opponents.[4]

The fate of Riley's empire followed closely the national pattern — growing contentiousness in the late 1940s and early 1950s, and then open division between the separatists and the nonseparatists, or evangelicals, in the latter half of the 1950s. The early rumblings from the upper Midwest were particularly loud, providing clear hints (as we now can see) of the coming split in the fundamentalist movement. In this regard, what makes the demise of Riley's empire particularly interesting is that it was Billy Graham who succeeded W. B. Riley as president of the Northwestern schools.

In February 1945 Billy Graham spoke at a Youth for Christ rally in the Minneapolis Auditorium. W. B. Riley was seated on the dais, and the aging fundamentalist warrior was terribly impressed with the youthful evangelist. The next morning Riley called George Wilson, Northwestern's business manager and Youth for Christ director, and said, "Where did you get that young man? He's a comer!" It was not long before Riley began to pursue this rising star for the presidency of Northwestern.[5] But Graham was reluctant to accept the post. He was only in his twenties, and his evangelistic career was just taking off; he had serious doubts about his own administrative abilities; and according to his official biographer, he had some concerns about being identified with Northwestern. Graham's primary goal was "to bring men everywhere to Christ," and apparently he was hesitant about being associated with a school which at times seemed more concerned with mounting militant attacks on modernism than with spreading the gospel.[6]

But the stubborn old crusader was used to getting his own way. In August 1947 Graham paid a visit to Riley's bedside. Riley pointed an emaciated finger at the young evangelist and pronounced, "Billy, you are the man to succeed me. I've known it for a long time. You will be disobeying God if you don't!"[7] Graham was not able to resist this prophetic commission from the patriarch of fundamentalism. He reluctantly accepted the post of vice-president, agreeing to fill the post of president if Riley died during the next few months. That December Riley was dead, and Graham took leadership of the Northwestern empire.[8]

Graham's doubts about the wisdom of accepting Riley's call were well founded. In the beginning it appeared that the new president was a smashing success. By 1950 enrollment at the schools had jumped to 1169, up

442 from the last year of Riley's presidency.[9] This early jump in student population was a testament to Graham's personal magnetism, but it masked major problems with the Graham presidency. Graham did not have the administrative acumen of a Riley to accompany his evangelistic skills.[10] Even if he had matched Riley as an organizer, the fact was that while he wanted to be a successful college president, he was much more concerned with being a successful evangelist. As a result, he spent little time at his administrative duties, delegating most of the work to aides. Graham and his family continued to live in North Carolina; he would stop in at Northwestern for a few days or perhaps weeks and then return to the revival road. Even in February 1948, at the inception of his presidency, Graham spent two weeks at the schools and then left for a two-month evangelistic tour of Europe.[11] After his hugely successful revival campaign in Los Angeles in 1949, Graham spent even more time on the road and away from the educational institution over which he was presiding.

Graham's frequent absences from Northwestern limited his ability to cope with major problems besetting the school. Although Graham had not known it at the time, he had assumed the presidency of an institution rife with controversy. The central issue was the liberal arts college. When Riley founded the college in 1944 some administrators, alumni, and faculty believed that the new school marked a betrayal of Riley's original goal of educating individuals in the Bible and training them to serve in religious vocations. Others viewed the liberal arts college as a great opportunity for Northwestern to broaden and upgrade its educational offerings. This split roughly followed the lines of the coming separatist-evangelical split in the fundamentalist movement, with the opponents of the liberal arts college the separatists-to-be. While it appears that Riley wanted a balanced educational program, he could not quell the infighting over this issue.[12]

Billy Graham inherited this bitter infighting. His presidency only heightened the raging controversy, and not only because he was president in absentia. Graham clearly sided with the liberal arts crowd. As John Pollock observed, immediately after assuming the presidency Graham pushed to "reconstruct the program in order to create a second Wheaton, fully accredited, double-quick."[13] This was not a policy designed to placate the Bible school faction. To them, Graham's push for an accredited liberal arts college was simply a further abandonment of Northwestern's original emphasis on teaching the Bible. Believing that they were upholding the true standard of Riley's school, the attacks of these incipient separatists on the Graham administration became more insistent and vehement in the early 1950s. At the same time, enrollment began to drop, from the high of 1169 in 1950 to 838 in the spring of 1952.[14] According to a professor from those years, a primary reason for the drop was the "rampant infighting" between supporters and opponents of Graham's policies. Frustrated by the constant sniping of the Bible school faction and increasingly aware that he could not run Northwestern from afar, Billy Graham resigned his post in February 1952.[15]

But the disaffected contingent was no happier with subsequent administrations. Minneapolis minister, seminary dean, and board of directors member Richard V. Clearwaters led the militant minority. According to some observers, Clearwaters felt that he had "inherited the mantle" of leadership from Riley, and he was thus piqued that he was not chosen to serve as Northwestern's president.[16] Whatever Clearwaters' personal motives, as the 1950s advanced he and his colleagues became increasingly unhappy with what they saw as the administration's unwillingness to maintain a separation from apostasy. This failure was exemplified by the tendency to employ professors who were not sufficiently militant in their defense of the faith, and by the school's cooperation with modernist-infected denominations in evangelistic efforts, especially in the radio ministry. The separatists were also dismayed at the increasing emphasis on the liberal arts college to the exclusion of the other schools under the Northwestern umbrella.

The final break came in 1956. In that year the administration discontinued the seminary and, in effect, subordinated the Bible school to the liberal arts college. In response, separatist administrators and professors pulled out of Northwestern, actively supported in this move by many of the alumni. Clearwaters founded Central Baptist Seminary in his own Fourth Baptist Church in Minneapolis; one year later, in 1957, he and his separatist compatriots started Pillsbury Baptist Bible College in Owatonna. Both institutions continue to this day.[17]

With the separatists' withdrawal (or, depending on one's perspective, with the evangelicals' "departure from the original vision and purpose" of Northwestern),[18] Riley's empire was permanently rent. But in creating Pillsbury and Central the militants were not finished in their efforts to separate from apostasy. A few years later the Minnesota separatists also led a rebellion against the Conservative Baptist Association, the denomination created by the fundamentalist secession from the Northern Baptist Convention in the late 1940s. Most of the churches in the Minnesota Baptist Convention were affiliated with the CBA. In the early 1960s Clearwaters and other separatists became dismayed with what they saw as the compromising stance of the CBA. This was evidenced by the CBA's willingness to include within its organization churches that still affiliated with the American (formerly Northern) Baptist Convention, and the CBA's support of Billy Graham's crusades. In 1966 Clearwaters and the other extreme separatists left the CBA and created the New Testament Association of Independent Baptist Churches. Clearwaters' Central Baptist Seminary became the official seminary of the new organization. While the New Testament Association was a tiny organization on a national scale, in Minnesota it was in full control. In 1969 the Clearwaters group expelled from the Minnesota Baptist Convention all churches that did not join them in radical separation from apostasy, that is, those that did not leave the Conservative Baptist Association. The result of all this striving for purity was that by 1970 one could not distinguish Baptists in Minnesota without a scorecard, for they were fragmented into six groups — American Baptists, the Baptist General Conference (Swedish Baptists), the North American Conference (German Baptists), the General Association of Regular Baptists, the Fellowship of Minnesota Conservative Baptist Churches, and the New Testament Association of Independent Baptist Churches.[19]

This is the separatists' story. In the evangelical wing of what had been Riley's empire, the moderates in charge of the Northwestern schools decided in 1956 to make Northwestern essentially a liberal arts college. Twenty-two hours of Bible and missions courses were still required of all students, but these requirements were markedly reduced within a few years. This decision to de-emphasize Bible training alienated many of the alumni, who moved their support to Pillsbury and Central Seminary. The liberal arts college was left with a small constituency. By 1964 the once-proud Northwestern had only one hundred students and a lot of outstanding debts. The school shut its doors in 1966. Northwestern's radio station continued, however, and through its efforts the wife of a Minnesota pizza mogul was converted. Her donations to the moribund school allowed the purchase of a beautiful old Catholic property in a Twin Cities suburb, and Northwestern began again in 1972. The new Northwestern was also a liberal arts college; perhaps in response to the failure of the original college to make a go of it as a purely liberal arts school, all students now were required to have a second major in Bible. Ten years after being resurrected, Northwestern had 884 students in attendance, many of whom, as might be expected, were from evangelical (as opposed to separatist fundamentalist) backgrounds.[20]

No love is lost between the two wings of Riley's former empire. The evangelicals view the group that supports the New Testament Association, Pillsbury, and Central as hypercritical isolationists. The separatists view the supporters of the Conservative Baptist Association and the new Northwestern as co-opted compromisers. On each side of the divide there are those who claim that they and their compatriots are the true heirs of William Bell Riley. Given the divergent strains within Riley's thought, the two groups' arguments are equally strong. The legacy of William Bell Riley is carried on in both separatist and evangelical churches of the upper Midwest.

The division in Riley's empire is an important story, particularly because it provides a microcosmic look at the split that occurred within American fundamentalism in the 1950s. But to concentrate solely on the disputes among Riley's heirs is to miss the magnitude of his accomplishment in the upper Midwest, a remarkable success that was achieved in the face of great adversity. In spite of the fact that his national crusades against modernism, evolutionism, and the "Jewish conspiracy" were dismal failures and in the midst of a religious depression gripping mainstream Protestantism, W. B. Riley and his fundamentalist supporters created a formidable regional organization. Riley's Northwestern Bible and Missionary Training School was the hub of this enterprise. Northwestern staffed fundamentalist churches in the upper Midwest with ministers who had been indoctrinated in militant fundamentalism and inculcated with a passion to save souls. More than this, the Minneapolis Bible school also provided these churches with lay training, educational materials, traveling evangelists and student volunteers. In short, Northwestern served as a denominational surrogate for fundamentalist churches in the upper Midwest.

The role of Northwestern Bible and Missionary Training School in its region strongly supports the heretofore untested thesis that Bible institutes were crucial to the survival and growth of American fundamentalism after the devastating defeats of the 1920s. It is also important to note that Northwestern and the network of fundamentalist churches dependent upon it were dominated by one man—W. B. Riley. Baldly stated, W. B. Riley was the emperor of the fundamentalist empire he had created in the upper Midwest. His role in the Minnesota Baptist revolt and the demise of the Northwestern network after Riley's death underscored the fact that W. B. Riley had created a regional religious empire centered around himself.

He certainly was not alone in doing so. In the years since Riley numerous conservative Protestant leaders have constructed local or regional (or, on occasion, national) religious empires around themselves.[21] Because it is the prototypical fundamentalist fiefdom, Riley's empire provides valuable insights into this phenomenon. As his midwestern network makes clear, personality-based religious empires have certain organizational advantages. For instance, a charismatic leader is able to arouse intense loyalty in his or her followers. Riley inspired such devotion that decades after his death many Northwesterners still rhapsodized about his virtues and talked proudly about having followed him into battles against the modernist enemy.[22] Such loyalty is, generally speaking, mere fantasy in more formally-structured, bureaucratic religious organizations. Moreover, like all auto-cratic social structures, personality-based empires have the potential to be remarkably efficient. For example, when a fundamentalist church in the upper Midwest needed a minister or an evangelist or a Vacation Bible School worker, all it had to do was place a call or write a letter to Riley, and the need would be filled. The result was that Riley's organization maintained much more control over its churches than the denominational bureaucra-cies it replaced.

While fundamentalist empires do have some organizational advantages, there are also disadvantages. Most obvious is the simple truth that some-day the great leader will die. When that happens, the odds are that his or her great enterprise will not stay intact. The divisions in Riley's empire in the 1950s are prime evidence of the fragility of personality-based reli-gious organizations.

There are other problems. Given that a prime tenet of Reformation the-ology is that all human beings are sinners, it seems un-Protestant to invest so much religious authority in one person. Certainly it is dangerous to do so. When power is concentrated in one person, enormous temptations and enormous possibilities for corruption result. Religious leaders are not exempt from this general principle. There are numerous recent examples of the pitfalls of accumulated power among those at the top of religious empires, including the experiences of Jim and Tammy Bakker and the PTL Club and, more ominously, Jim Jones and the People's Temple.[23] Of course, regarding the case at hand, W. B. Riley did not bilk millions out of the faithful for his own personal use, nor did he induce mass suicide. On the other hand, he did engage in behind-the-scenes machinations within the Minnesota Baptist Convention that, at times, were more befitting a politi-cal boss than a man of God. More important, it is quite possible that Riley's position as czar of midwestern fundamentalism contributed to the vicious anti-Semitism of his later years. Alone at the top of his personal religious empire, the unquestioned hero for truth with an army of devoted follow-ers, Riley was without peer or restraint. Perhaps the decades of unchecked power and the unrestrained adulation of his followers corrupted his think-ing, thus contributing to the elderly Riley's tendency to view farfetched and horrible ideas as reasonable. But whether or not Riley's role as fun-damentalist autocrat contributed to the vicious anti-Semitism of his later years, the fact that he perpetrated and promoted such notions is prime evidence that Riley, like Jim Jones and the Bakkers, should not have been trusted with an inordinate amount of religious authority.

There is no question that, for good and for ill, Riley dominated the empire he created. This is not to say, however, that his fundamentalist fiefdom was strictly a top-down enterprise. Riley's empire had enormous grassroots support. Thousands and thousands of rural, town, and city people in the upper Midwest enthusiastically accepted the fundamentalist message preached by "Riley's boys" (and "Riley's girls") and joined and actively (often zealously) participated in churches pastored by Riley's religious progeny. In the process they blissfully ignored the numerous defeats endured by the national fundamentalist movement and the numerous expert pronouncements regarding the irrelevance or the imminent death of fundamentalism.

The simplest and most obvious explanation of this grass-roots support is that the inhabitants found life in Riley's empire to be satisfying. Certainly Riley and company gave midwesterners much that mainstream Protestantism did not (and probably could not) give. While the traditional denominations downplayed dogma, Northwestern-trained fundamentalists provided absolute and certain truth. While the mainstream denominations closed rural churches or combined them with churches from different traditions, Bible school graduates opened once-closed churches and gave them a clear and distinctive religious identity. And while the leadership of the mainstream denominations seemed but distant and gray bureaucracies, the fundamentalists were led by the eminently accessible and exceedingly magnetic hero of the faith, W. B. Riley.

Perhaps most important, Riley's fundamentalists gave their followers a sense of community. Northwestern-trained ministers created churches in which the communicants shared the same fundamentalist dogma and language and the same oft-stringent rules regarding appropriate behavior. More than this, these Bible school graduates implemented extensive schedules of activities; church members hence spent enormous amounts of time together, in worship services, Sunday School classes, revival meetings, missions meetings, prayer meetings, choir meetings, men's/women's/youth meetings, daily Vacation Bible School classes, and more. The results of these shared beliefs and shared experiences were churches that were, as one member said about the First Baptist Church of Granite Falls, "just like one big family."[24]

This sense of community extended beyond the walls of the individual churches. Fundamentalist congregations in the Northwestern network joined together to hold revival services, sponsor church camps, and engage in local missions activities. Moreover, inhabitants of Riley's empire came together to worship at the annual Northwestern Bible Conference and to attend Northwestern-sponsored Bible classes. And of course, many sent their children to Northwestern Bible School, where students formed their own bonds of fundamentalist community.

Fundamentalists in Riley's empire were united by more than common beliefs and activities and their devotion to Riley and active support of Northwestern. Perhaps as important as these positive factors in fostering a sense of community was the fact that midwestern fundamentalists also shared common enemies. Riley and his cadre of militant ministers repeatedly hammered home the notion that fundamentalists, in the upper Midwest and elsewhere, were united in holy and desperate combat against a host of dangerous and evil antagonists threatening the church and the nation. These enemies included modernists, evolutionists, and (at least according to Riley) Jewish Communists. In effect, midwestern fundamentalists were, their leaders articulated, a community of the saved besieged by and at war with the forces of the damned.[25]

Contemporary fundamentalist fiefdoms are similar to Riley's empire in their emphasis on dangerous enemies (secular humanists and others) and in their sense of tightly knit community (particularly at the congregational level). Moreover, while they are often personality-centered, these contemporary enterprises are also similar to Riley's empire in that they are not simply top-down affairs. The grass-roots support is very strong.[26] Thus, when local or regional or national fundamentalist chieftains are tarred by scandal, enmeshed in feuds, or taken away by death, their empires will be shaken and perhaps broken, but the fundamentalist movement will go on. Certainly this was the case with Riley's empire. After Riley died his followers fought and his empire split. But new institutions were formed, old institutions were reshaped, and the fundamentalist tradition continued (and continues) in the region.

In 1921 W. B. Riley informed liberal opponents that they should "cease from shoveling in dirt on living men," for the fundamentalists "refuse to be buried."[27] Seven decades later, the funeral for fundamentalism, in the upper Midwest and in America at large, seems a long, long way off.

Appendix

Notes

Bibliography

Index

Appendix

World's Christian Fundamentals Association Doctrinal Statement, 1919

I. We believe in the Scriptures of the Old and New Testaments as verbally inspired of God, and inerrant in the original writings, and that they are of supreme and final authority in faith and life.

II. We believe in one God, eternally existing in three persons, Father, Son and Holy Spirit.

III. We believe that Jesus Christ was begotten by the Holy Spirit, and born of the Virgin Mary, and is true God and true man.

IV. We believe that man was created in the image of God, that he sinned and thereby incurred not only physical death, but also that spiritual death which is separation from God; and that all human beings are born with a sinful nature, and, in the case of those who reach moral responsibility, become sinners in thought, word and deed.

V. We believe that the Lord Jesus Christ died for our sins according to the Scriptures as a representative and substitutionary sacrifice; and that all that believe in Him are justified on the ground of His shed blood.

VI. We believe in the resurrection of the crucified body of our Lord, in His ascension into heaven, and in His present life there for us, as High Priest and Advocate.

VII. We believe in "that blessed hope," the personal, premillennial and imminent return of our Lord and Saviour Jesus Christ.

VIII. We believe that all who receive by faith the Lord Jesus Christ are born again of the Holy Spirit and thereby become children of God.

IX. We believe in the bodily resurrection of the just and the unjust, the everlasting blessedness of the saved, and the everlasting, conscious punishment of the lost.

Notes

Introduction

1 Mark Schorer, *Sinclair Lewis: An American Life* (New York: McGraw-Hill Co., 1961), 440–42, 447–51, 455–63; James Benedict Moore, "The Sources of *Elmer Gantry*," *The New Republic*, August 8, 1960, p. 17; Charles Allyn Russell, *Voices of American Fundamentalism: Seven Biographical Studies* (Philadelphia: Westminster Press, 1976), 231n.

2 According to Lewis' biographer, Lewis and company were staying at a resort on Big Pelican Lake. Riley's mistake is understandable, however, considering that there is a Long Lake only a few miles to the south. Schorer, *Sinclair Lewis*, 458; William Bell Riley, "Blatant Birkhead," *The Northwestern Pilot* 25 (August 1945): 328–29.

3 "W. B. Riley" was how he often signed his articles and books, and he will usually be referred to thusly within the text of this work.

4 William R. Hutchison, *The Modernist Impulse in American Protestantism* (Cambridge: Harvard University Press, 1976), 2. Hutchison's *Modernist Impulse* is the most important work dealing with modernism/liberalism.

5 Ferenc Szasz has observed that "modernism" and "liberalism" were interchangeable terms. For the most part fundamentalists used the former, and hence so will I. Ferenc Morton Szasz, *The Divided Mind of Protestant America, 1880–1930* (University: University of Alabama Press, 1982), 99–100; Russell, *Voices*, 15–16; Hutchison, *Modernist Impulse*, 1–11; Kenneth Cauthen, *The Impact of American Religious Liberalism*, 2d ed. (Washington: University Press of America, 1983), 3–25; Martin E. Marty, *Modern American Religion*, vol. 1, *The Irony of It All, 1893–1919* (Chicago: University of Chicago Press, 1986), 25–43; Szasz, *Divided Mind*, 1–41. Particularly valuable is Szasz's discussion of the transmission of modernist ideas from scholars to the populace.

6 Fundamentalists were (and are) a subgroup within the large and extremely diverse world of evangelicalism. With their fellow evangelicals they emphasized, among other things, the Bible as the final authority, personal faith in Christ as the only route to eternal salvation, the great importance of a conversion experience and a transformed life, and the urgent need for evangelism and missions. What set fundamentalists apart from other evangelicals was, first and foremost, their aggressive antimodernism. As we will see in chapter 2, fundamentalists often delivered their most blistering attacks on those who agreed with them on doctrine but who failed to demonstrate the requisite militancy. For a superb discussion of evangelicalism and the place of fundamentalism within it, see George M. Marsden, "The Evangelical Denomination," in *Evangelicalism and Modern America*, ed. George M. Marsden (Grand Rapids, Mich.: Wm. B. Eerdmans Co., 1984), vii–xix.

165

7   H. Richard Niebuhr, "Fundamentalism," in *The Encyclopedia of the Social Sciences*, ed. Edwin R. A. Seligman (New York: Macmillan Co., 1931), 6:526–27; Frederick Lewis Allen, *Only Yesterday* (New York: Harper and Row, 1931), 199–206; Stewart Cole, *The History of Fundamentalism* (New York: Richard Smith, 1931), esp. 35–40, 336–37; Richard Hofstadter, *Anti-Intellectualism in American Life* (New York: Random House, 1962), 117–36; Richard Hofstadter, *The Paranoid Style in American Politics and Other Essays* (New York: Knopf, 1965), 77–82; Norman F. Furniss, *The Fundamentalist Controversy* (New Haven: Yale University Press, 1954), esp. vii, 177–79; William E. Leuchtenburg, *The Perils of Prosperity, 1914–1932* (Chicago: University of Chicago Press, 1958), 217–24; William McLoughlin, "Is There a Third Force in Christendom?" *Daedalus* 96 (Winter 1967): 45. For a much fuller discussion of this aspect of the historiography of fundamentalism, see William E. Ellis, "Evolution, Fundamentalism, and the Historians: An Historiographical Review," *The Historian* 44 (November 1981): 15–35; George M. Marsden, *Fundamentalism and American Culture: The Shaping of Twentieth-Century Evangelicalism, 1870–1925* (New York: Oxford University Press, 1980), 4, 199–200.

8   Paul A. Carter, "The Fundamentalist Defense of the Faith," in *Change and Continuity in Twentieth-Century America: The Twenties*, ed. John Braeman, Robert H. Bremner, and David Brody (Columbus: Ohio State University Press, 1968), 186–87.

9   The most influential works in this revisionist historiography are George Marsden's *Fundamentalism and American Culture* and Ernest Sandeen's *The Roots of Fundamentalism: British and American Millenarianism, 1800–1930* (Chicago: University of Chicago Press, 1970). Other important general studies include Russell, *Voices;* Szasz, *Divided Mind;* and Timothy P. Weber, *Living in the Shadow of the Second Coming: American Premillennialism, 1875–1982* (Grand Rapids, Mich.: Zondervan Co., 1983).
    This but scratches the surface of the burgeoning historiography of fundamentalism. For a good (although soon-to-be-dated) overview of scholarly writings on fundamentalism, see Joel A. Carpenter, "Understanding Fundamentalism," *Evangelical Studies Bulletin* 4 (March 1987): 6–9.

10 Donald Tinder, "Fundamentalist Baptists in the Northern and Western United States, 1920–1950" (Ph.D. diss., Yale University, 1969), 255. The only full-scale biography is an extremely flattering portrait by Riley's second wife: Marie Acomb Riley, *The Dynamic of a Dream: The Life Story of Dr. William B. Riley* (Grand Rapids, Mich.: Wm. B. Eerdmans Co., 1938). In many ways this is an autobiography. Riley wrote the preface and first chapter, and probably edited most of the remainder. Never a modest individual, in the preface Riley even defended his biographer's adulations: "For those extravagances born of affection, Mrs. Riley has deftly made her own defence."

11 The primary exception is Joel A. Carpenter's doctoral thesis: "The Renewal of American Fundamentalism, 1930–1945" (Ph.D. diss., Johns Hopkins University, 1984). Carpenter's focus is on leaders and institutions at the national level, whereas much of this study emphasizes local and regional fundamentalism.

12 Ellis, "Evolution, Fundamentalism," 32. This emphasis on elites is not universal. See Walter Edmund Warren Ellis, "Social and Religious Factors in the Fundamentalist-Modernist Schisms among Baptists in North America, 1895–1934" (Ph.D. diss., University of Pittsburgh, 1974); and Gregory H. Singleton, "Fundamentalism and Urbanization: A Quantitative Critique of Impressionistic Interpretations," in *The*

New Urban History, ed. Leo F. Schnore (Princeton, N.J.: Princeton University Press, 1975), 205–27.

13 Louis Gasper, *The Fundamentalist Movement* (The Hague: Mouton, 1963), 15–22; George W. Dollar, *A History of Fundamentalism* (Greenville, S.C.: Bob Jones University Press, 1973), 214–49; Marsden, *Fundamentalism and American Culture,* 192–94; Tinder, "Baptists," esp. 379–442; William A. BeVier, "A History of the Independent Fundamental Churches of America" (Th.D. diss., Dallas Theological Seminary, 1958); Joseph M. Stowell, *Background and History of the General Association of Regular Baptist Churches* (Hayward, Calif.: Gospel Tracts Unlimited, 1949); Robert T. Handy, "The American Religious Depression, 1925–1935," *Church History* 29 (March 1960): 3–16; Joel A. Carpenter, "Fundamentalist Institutions and the Rise of Evangelical Protestantism, 1929–1942," *Church History* 49 (March 1980): 64–65. It should be noted that very little work has been done regarding the demographics of the shift from the mainstream denominations to the fundamentalist churches. Observers such as Handy have pointed out that "many, probably a majority, of the supporters of sectarian movements were formerly adherents of the older and larger Protestant denominations," but it seems that little systematic analysis has been conducted to allow for more precise statements regarding this transition. Handy, "Religious Depression," 10.

14 Ernest Sandeen asserted that "no analysis of the structure of the Fundamentalist movement can proceed very far if the role of the Bible institute is ignored." He also spent one paragraph on Moody as a denominational surrogate. *Roots,* 241–43. See also Carpenter, "Fundamentalist Institutions," 66–68. Save for passing remarks, however, historians have all but ignored this institution. The standard work on the movement is a descriptive apologia by a former Bible school president: Safara Austin Witmer, *The Bible School College Story: Education with Dimension* (Manhasset, N.Y.: Channel Press, 1962). In the same vein, but quite useful, is Gene A. Getz, *MBI: The Story of Moody Bible Institute* (Chicago: Moody Press, 1969). Fortunately, Virginia Lieson Brereton has written an excellent study which should soon be published: "Protestant Fundamentalist Bible Schools, 1882–1940" (Ph.D. diss., Columbia University, 1981). In many ways the present study and Brereton's work are complementary. Brereton's emphasis is on Bible schools as educational institutions, whereas the present work deals with the role of a Bible school in the expansion of fundamentalism.

15 Samuel P. Hays, "The Structure of Environmental Politics since World War II," *Journal of Social History* 14 (Summer 1981): 719–21, 731; Samuel P. Hays, "The Social Analysis of American Political History, 1880–1920," *Political Science Quarterly* 80 (September 1965): 373–94. See also Samuel P. Hays, Preface to the Atheneum Edition of *Conservation and the Gospel of Efficiency: The Progressive Conservation Movement, 1890–1920,* 2d ed. (New York: Atheneum Books, 1969).

16 T. J. Jackson Lears, *No Place of Grace: Antimodernism and the Transformation of American Culture* (New York: Pantheon Books, 1981), 307.

Chapter 1: The Leader

1 William Bell Riley, quoted in Marie Acomb Riley, *The Dynamic of a Dream: The Life Story of Dr. William B. Riley* (Grand Rapids, Mich.: Wm. B. Eerdmans Co., 1938), 19–25.

2   M. A. Riley, *Dynamic*, 41–42.

3   Riley, quoted in M. A. Riley, *Dynamic*, 26–28. Experiences such as this one certainly played a role in the mature Riley's belief that through hard work anyone could escape poverty.

4   M. A. Riley, *Dynamic*, 31–33, 43–44.

5   Riley, quoted in M. A. Riley, *Dynamic*, 31–33.

6   M. A. Riley, *Dynamic*, 29–31, 39–40.

7   William Bell Riley, "My Alma Mater, A Fount of Modernism," *The Pilot* 23 (May 1943): 227; William Bell Riley, "Southern Seminary Lost to Southern Orthodoxy," *The Pilot* 22 (December 1941): 68.

8   Riley, "My Alma Mater," 227. Because of Riley's prominence, his charges that the Kentucky school had succumbed to "skepticism" and "Darwinism" caused a stir in the Southern Baptist Convention. See also William Bell Riley, "Das Barnett and the Southern Baptists," *The Pilot* 22 (October 1941): 9–10; William Bell Riley, "The Theology of Louisville Seminary," *The Pilot* 22 (March 1942): 174.

9   M. A. Riley, *Dynamic*, 171–72; Charles Allyn Russell has observed that it is ironic that "the broad and tolerant spirit of Moody did not appear to make a corresponding impact on Riley." Russell, *Voices of American Fundamentalism: Seven Biographical Studies* (Philadelphia: Westminster Press, 1976), 239n. This is true, but, to be fair, one must consider the changes that had occurred in American religion. It seems quite possible that Moody himself would have been much more rigid and intolerant if, like Riley, he had survived into the years of conservative-liberal warfare. In fact, by 1898, one year before the Chicago evangelist's death, Moody was calling on true Christians to separate themselves from modernists. Martin E. Marty, *Modern American Religion*, vol. 1, *The Irony of It All, 1893–1919* (Chicago: University of Chicago Press, 1986), 211–12.

10 This marked the end of W. B. Riley's formal education. A few years later Southwestern University, Jackson, Tennessee, awarded him an honorary doctorate of divinity. Henceforth Riley often signed his books and articles "Dr. Riley" or "W. B. Riley, D.D." M. A. Riley, *Dynamic*, 95.

11 M. A. Riley, *Dynamic*, 30–35, 48–49, 183–87. W. B. and Lillian Riley had six children: Arthur Howard (b. 1892), Mason Hewitt (b. 1894), Herbert Wilde (b. 1895), Eunice (b. 1901), William Bell, Jr. (b. 1904), and John Branson (b. 1906).

12 M. A. Riley, *Dynamic*, 50–51, 59–64.

13 William Bell Riley, quoted in "Four Anniversaries of a Great Christian Statesman," *The Northwestern Pilot* 27 (March 1947): 167.

14 Much of the following account of Riley at First Baptist comes from chapter 6, "The Dream Disturbed," of Marie Acomb Riley's *The Dynamic of a Dream*. As noted earlier, this book is essentially William Bell Riley's autobiography. This is particularly true of chapter 6, which, Marie Riley noted, was "carefully revised" by her husband, who assured her that he held "documentary evidence for every statement made which might require proof." M. A. Riley, *Dynamic*, 88.

15 Walter Edmund Warren Ellis, "Social and Religious Factors in the Fundamentalist-Modernist Schisms among Baptists in North America, 1895–1934" (Ph.D. diss., University of Pittsburgh, 1974), 103–4.

16 M. A. Riley, *Dynamic*, 64–65; Ellis, "Schisms," 104.

17 Riley, quoted in "Four Anniversaries," 167; M. A. Riley, *Dynamic*, 65, 73.

18 William Bell Riley, *The Crisis of the Church* (New York: Charles C. Cook, 1914), 178.

19 George Henry Ewing, "George Claude Lorimer," in *Dictionary of American Biography*, ed. Dumas Malone (New York: Charles Scribner's Sons, 1933), 11:412–13; Riley, quoted in "Four Anniversaries," 167. Interestingly, Lorimer preached the sermon at the June 1888 service in which Riley was installed as a minister of the First Baptist Church, Lafayette, Indiana. M. A. Riley, *Dynamic*, 35.

20 Virginia Lieson Brereton, "Fundamentalists as Popular Educators: The Bible Schools, 1880–Present" (Paper presented at meeting of the American Society of Church History, Holland, Mich., April 21, 1983), 3–4.

21 Ferenc Szasz has argued that Riley "was a social radical when he arrived in 1897, on the left, and a social radical when he died in 1947, but on the right." "Three Fundamentalist Leaders: The Roles of William Bell Riley, John Roach Straton, and William Jennings Bryan in the Fundamentalist-Modernist Controversy" (Ph.D. diss., University of Rochester, 1969), 92. The second half of Szasz's statement was correct: Riley did become increasingly reactionary through the years. In 1897, however, he was not a social radical on the left. See chapter 3 for further discussion of Riley's political views.

22 William Bell Riley, "Ananias — or the Dangers in Handling Wealth," quoted in Ellis, "Schisms," 107; Riley, quoted in "Four Anniversaries," 169. For another example of the First Baptist minister's belief that rich and poor should worship together, see Riley, *Crisis of the Church*, 180–85.

23 Ellis, "Schisms," 108.

24 M. A. Riley, *Dynamic*, 68–70. Mark Ketcham minimized the pew-rental issue because he could find no rental records in his examination of the church sources. Nevertheless, as Ellis clearly documented, Riley did make this resolution, certain wealthy members did oppose it, and the church did accept it. Perhaps it was primarily a symbolic gesture on Riley's part; if so, the opposition it engendered only demonstrates that symbolic gestures can be quite powerful. Mark S. Ketcham, "An Investigation of the Causes of the Separation of Trinity Baptist Church from First Baptist Church, Minneapolis, Minnesota," an unpublished paper discussed in Russell, *Voices*, 240n.

25 Riley, quoted in M. A. Riley, *Dynamic*, 69–71.

26 M. A. Riley, *Dynamic*, 71.

27 M. A. Riley, *Dynamic*, 71–72, 168; Russell, *Voices*, 87–88.

28 Evalyan Camp, interview with Ferenc Szasz, October 24, 1966, as reported in Szasz, "Leaders," 87.

29 M. A. Riley, *Dynamic*, 66, 87–88; Riley, quoted in "Four Anniversaries," 167.

30 Ellis, "Schisms," 110–19.

31 For instance, in his study of Los Angeles churches in the 1920s Gregory Singleton concluded that "'The Definitely Fundamentalist' and 'Sympathetic' [to fundamentalism] denominations were differentiated from the more established denominations and the total population by lack of power, lack of political participation, working-class roots, greater transiency, and higher arrest rates." Gregory H. Singleton, "Fundamentalism and Urbanization: A Quantitative Critique of Impressionistic Interpretations," in *The New Urban History*, ed. Leo P. Schnore (Princeton, N.J.: Princeton University Press, 1975), 224. See also Ellis, "Schisms," 284–88; and George M. Marsden, *Fundamentalism and American Culture: The Shaping of Twentieth-Century Evangelicalism, 1870–1925* (New York: Oxford University Press, 1980), 204–05.

32 M. A. Riley, *Dynamic*, 66–67.

33 M. A. Riley, *Dynamic*, 66–72; Ellis, "Schisms," 121.

34 Riley, quoted in M. A. Riley, *Dynamic*, 76–77.

35 M. A. Riley, *Dynamic*, 78.

36 M. A. Riley, *Dynamic*, 77–80; Ellis, "Schisms," 112–13.

37 Ellis, "Schisms," 114.

38 William Bell Riley, "Cohn vs. Riley," *The Pilot* 15 (May 1935): 218; M. A. Riley, *Dynamic*, 82–83.

39 M. A. Riley, *Dynamic*, 84–87; Ellis, "Schisms," 115–16, 119–22. Ellis also observed that "no significant [class] differentiation [ever] developed at Trinity Baptist Church."

40 M. A. Riley, *Dynamic*, 89.

41 "Forty Years of Service," *The Pilot* 17 (March 1937): 164; M. A. Riley, *Dynamic*, 181.

42 M. A. Riley, *Dynamic*, 172–82; Szasz, "Leaders," 87–89.

43 William Bell Riley, *Revival Sermons: Essentials in Effective Evangelism* (New York: Fleming H. Revell Co., 1939).

44 *Seattle Post-Intelligencer*, January 23, 1913, reported in Russell, *Voices*, 89.

45 *Waterloo Daily Courier*, as reported in M. A. Riley, *Dynamic*, 176.

46 In his book *Modern Revivalism, Charles Grandison Finney to Billy Graham* (New York: Ronald Press, 1959), William G. McLoughlin discusses six of these professional evangelists at length: William E. Biederwolf, J. Wilbur Chapman, Burke Culpepper, Rodney "Gypsy" Smith, Reuben A. Torrey, and Milan B. Williams (364–96). Of course, then came Billy Sunday.

47 M. A. Riley, *Dynamic*, 172–82; Szasz, "Leaders," 87–89.

48 William Bell Riley, *Ten Sermons on the Greater Doctrines of Scripture* (Bloomington, Ill.: Leader Publishing Co., 1891), 3–5.

49 Riley, *Ten Sermons*, 7–10.

50 Riley, *Ten Sermons*, 5–6; William Bell Riley, *The Finality of the Higher Criticism; or, The Theory of Evolution and False Theology* (N.p. 1909), 21.

51 Riley, *Ten Sermons*, 5–10.

52 Marty, *Modern American Religion*, 232–37. While he focused too much on the Princetonians as developers of the doctrine of inerrancy to the exclusion of other individuals and groups, Ernest Sandeen's general discussion of the ideas and development of the Princeton Theology is excellent: *The Roots of Fundamentalism: British and American Millenarianism, 1800–1930* (Chicago: University of Chicago Press, 1970), 103–31. For an insightful survey of evangelical biblical scholarship since 1880, see Mark A. Noll, *Between Faith and Criticism: Evangelicals, Scholarship, and the Bible* (San Francisco: Harper and Row, 1987).

53 Riley, *Ten Sermons*, 18–139.

54 William Bell Riley, "Facts for Fundamentalists," *The Pilot* 20 (June 1940): 267.

55 In 1896 Riley delivered a series of four sermons on Christ's Second Coming to his congregation at Calvary Baptist Church in Chicago. The next year at his new church in Minneapolis he presented a revised version of the four messages and also added another four sermons on this topic. Most of the subsequent discussion will be based on the eight sermons delivered in Minneapolis.

56 For excellent discussions of the history of dispensational premillennialism in the United States, see Marsden, *Fundamentalism and American Culture*, esp. 43–71; Marty, *Modern American Religion*, 218–32; Sandeen, *Roots*; and, particularly, Timothy P. Weber, *Living in the Shadow of the Second Coming: American Pre-*

millennialism, 1875–1982 (Grand Rapids, Mich.: Zondervan Co., 1983). For a provocative and persuasive critique of the widespread acceptance of dispensational premillennialism, see Douglas W. Frank, *Less than Conquerors: How Evangelicals Entered the Twentieth Century* (Grand Rapids, Mich.: Wm. B. Eerdmans Co., 1986), 60–102.

57 William Bell Riley, *The Promised Return* (Chicago: Star Printing Co., [1897?]), 5. Martin Marty has observed, quite rightly, that "no party had a heavier investment in inerrancy than the premillennialist. Only with an inerrant set of facts in the Bible could it hold together with absolute assurance." Marty, *Modern American Religion*, 236–37.

58 William Bell Riley, *The Evolution of the Kingdom* (New York: Charles C. Cook, 1913), 44. Riley was less direct about the apostasy within the institutional church in his sermons in the late 1890s, but the point is there. See William Bell Riley, *Present Signs of His Speedy Appearance* (Chicago: Star Printing Co., [1897?]), 5.

59 Riley, *Evolution of the Kingdom*, 71–98; Marsden, *Fundamentalism and American Culture*, 51–52.

60 Riley, *Promised Return*, 3.

61 Riley, *Present Signs*, 6–12; Riley, *Evolution of the Kingdom*, 120–30.

62 William Bell Riley, *The Hereafter; or, Heaven and Hell* (Chicago: Star Printing Co., [1897?]), 2–10.

63 Riley, *Present Signs*, 2–6. Forty-three years later Riley was still reading in current events indications that Christ's return was at hand: "Wars multiply, famines increase, false prophets flood the land with their philosophies, the darkness gathers; but Pre-millennialists know full well that all of this was taken into account of by the all-wise Christ who said, when we see *'these things beginning to come to pass . . . lift up your heads'*; and know that the day of your *'redemption draweth nigh.'"* William Bell Riley, "Facts for Fundamentalists," *The Pilot* 20 (June 1940): 267.

64 Marsden, *Fundamentalism and American Culture*, 70, 127–28; Sandeen, *Roots*, 225, 238.

65 George M. Marsden, "Defining Fundamentalism," *Christian Scholar's Review* 1 (Winter 1971): 141–51.

66 Marsden, *Fundamentalism and American Culture*, 224.

67 Winthrop Hudson, *Religion in America: An Historical Account of the Development of American Religious Life*, 4th ed. (New York: Charles Scribner's Sons, 1987), 258; Sydney E. Ahlstrom, *A Religious History of the American People* (New Haven: Yale University Press, 1972), 2:247.

68 M. A. Riley, *Dynamic*, 51–52.

69 Riley, *Finality of the Higher Criticism*, esp. 117–39. As the title makes clear, in his attack on modernism Riley focused not only on higher criticism but also on evolutionism. More on this in chapter 2.

70 Ferenc Morton Szasz, *The Divided Mind of Protestant America, 1880–1930* (University: University of Alabama Press, 1982), 81–83.

Chapter 2: The Crusade

1 Stewart Cole, *The History of Fundamentalism* (New York: Richard Smith, 1931), 325. Other accolades include: "the ablest leader of orthodox reaction during the early part of the twentieth century," Robert Sheldon McBirnie, "Basic Issues in

the Fundamentalism of William Bell Riley" (Ph.D. diss., State University of Iowa, 1952), 132; "the most important fundamentalist minister of his generation," Charles Allyn Russell, *Voices of American Fundamentalism: Seven Biographical Studies* (Philadelphia: Westminster Press, 1976), 105; "leading spokesman for the emerging movement," George M. Marsden, *Fundamentalism and American Culture: The Shaping of Twentieth-Century Evangelicalism, 1870–1925* (New York: Oxford University Press, 1980), 128; "organizing genius of American fundamentalism," Ferenc Morton Szasz, *The Divided Mind of Protestant America, 1880–1930* (University: University of Alabama Press, 1982), 89.

2   Marsden, *Fundamentalism and American Culture*, 141–64.

3   William Bell Riley, *The Menace of Modernism* (New York: Christian Alliance Co., 1917), esp. 32–75, 118, 76–104.

4   Ibid., esp. 43–68.

5   Ibid., 76–104.

6   The author is indebted to Joel A. Carpenter for providing an insightful reading of *The Menace of Modernism*. This paragraph borrows much from his observations. See also Carpenter's introduction to *Conservative Call to Arms*, vol. 21 of *Fundamentalism in American Religion, 1880–1950*, ed. Joel A. Carpenter (New York: Garland Publishing, 1988), xii–xv.

7   Burton J. Bledstein, *The Culture of Professionalism: The Middle Class and the Development of Higher Education in America* (New York: W. W. Burton, 1976); Alexandra Oleson and John Voss, eds., *The Organization of Knowledge in Modern America, 1860–1920* (Baltimore: Johns Hopkins University Press, 1979); Laurence R. Veysey, *The Emergence of the American University* (Chicago: University of Chicago Press, 1965); Robert Wiebe, *The Search for Order, 1877–1920* (New York: Hill and Wang, 1967). Regarding the impact of professionalization and secularization of knowledge on evangelicalism in America, see George M. Marsden, "The Collapse of American Evangelical Academia," in *Faith and Rationality: Reason and Belief in God*, ed. Alvin Plantinga and Nicholas Wolterstorff (Notre Dame, Ind.: University of Notre Dame Press, 1983), 219–64; Mark A. Noll, *Between Faith and Criticism: Evangelicals, Scholarship, and the Bible* (San Francisco: Harper and Row, 1987), esp. 32–36; and Darryl Hart, "'Doctor Fundamentalis': An Intellectual Biography of J. Gresham Machen, 1881–1937" (Ph.D. diss., Johns Hopkins University, 1988).

8   Riley, *Menace of Modernism*, 95.

9   R. Laurence Moore, *Religious Outsiders and the Making of Americans* (New York: Oxford University Press, 1986), 150–72.

10 Ernest Sandeen, *The Roots of Fundamentalism: British and American Millenarianism, 1800–1930* (Chicago: University of Chicago Press, 1970), esp. 132–61, 233–35; Reuben A. Torrey et al., "A Call for a Conference," *School and Church* 2 (May 1918): 85.

11 Riley, *Menace of Modernism*, 156; Marsden, *Fundamentalism and American Culture*, 157; Sandeen, *Roots*, 208–26; David A. Rausch, *Zionism within Early American Fundamentalism, 1878–1918: A Convergence of Two Traditions* (New York: Edwin Mellen Press, 1979), 106–8.

12 Some confusion exists over the precise year of this meeting. Cole, Sandeen, Russell, and Marsden claimed it was in 1918, while Szasz asserted it was in 1917. Neither side has provided definitive evidence. Marie Acomb Riley's biography contributed to the confusion: she specifically affirmed Cole's dating of the event, but then she

followed this with a claim that "the whole matter . . . drifted along for a year" until the 1918 premillennial conference in Philadelphia. Cole, *History of Fundamentalism*, 298–99; Sandeen, *Roots*, 243; Russell, *Voices*, 97; Marsden, *Fundamentalism and American Culture*, 158; Ferenc Morton Szasz, "Three Fundamentalist Leaders: The Roles of William Bell Riley, John Roach Straton, and William Jennings Bryan in the Fundamentalist-Modernist Controversy" (Ph.D. diss., University of Rochester, 1969), 129–30; Marie Acomb Riley, *The Dynamic of a Dream: The Life Story of Dr. William B. Riley* (Grand Rapids, Mich.: Wm. B. Eerdmans Co., 1938), 122–23.

13 Ernest Sandeen argued that while Riley's conference signaled that the "the millenarians had become Fundamentalists," all this really meant was that the group of millenarians had simply "dropped one badge and picked up another without altering its basic character or drive." Sandeen's thesis that premillennialism was the defining characteristic of this nascent fundamentalist movement is flawed in that it masks the antimodernism at the heart of Riley's efforts. Sandeen, *Roots*, 246–47.

14 William Bell Riley, "The World Premillennial Conference vs. The Coming Confederacy," *School and Church* 2 (January–March 1919): 92; Szasz, *Divided Mind*, 89–90. Curtis Lee Laws was the first to use the term "fundamentalist" as a group designation, in "Convention Side Lights," *The Watchman-Examiner* 8 (July 1, 1920): 834–35. In this article Laws called on "fundamentalists" to do "battle royal for the Fundamentals." Nevertheless, while the label had not yet been affixed, the fundamentalist movement in America actually began with the spring 1919 World Conference on the Fundamentals of the Faith.

15 William Bell Riley, *The Great Divide; or, Christ and the Present Crisis* (Philadelphia: Bible Conference Committee, 1919), 3; M. A. Riley, *Dynamic*, 123–25.

16 William Bell Riley, "The Christian Fundamentals Movement, Its Battles, Its Achievements, Its Certain Victory," *Christian Fundamentals in School and Church* 4 (October–December 1922): 5–6.

17 "Report of the World Conference on the Fundamentals of the Faith," *School and Church* 2 (July–September 1919): 172. For the full WCFA creed, see Appendix.

18 "Membership in the Christian Fundamentals Association," *Christian Fundamentals in School and Church* 4 (January–March 1922): 23; Riley, "Christian Fundamentals Movement," 6.

19 "Report of the World Conference," 169–80; Sandeen, *Roots*, 244–45.

20 "World Conference on the Fundamentals of the Faith," *School and Church* 2 (April–June 1919): 132; "Report of the World Conference," 180; "Minutes of the Meeting of the Executive Committee of Christian Fundamentals Association," *Christian Fundamentals in School and Church* 3 (July–September 1921): 15.

21 M. A. Riley, *Dynamic*, 129.

22 "Fourth Annual Convention: Christian Fundamentals Association," *Christian Fundamentals in School and Church* 4 (April–June 1922): 4; Szasz, *Divided Mind*, 93–94.

23 "Continent Wide Conferences," *School and Church* 2 (January–March 1920): 286.

24 "Minutes of the Meeting," 15; Riley, "Christian Fundamentals Movement," 4.

25 In 1947 the Accrediting Association of Bible Colleges was formed. An independent agency, the AABC had a membership of thirty-six Bible schools in 1960. Safara Austin Witmer, *The Bible College Story: Education with Dimension* (Manhasset, N.Y.: Channel Press, 1962), 45–46.

26 "Seventh Annual Convention of the World's Christian Fundamentals Association,"

Christian Fundamentals in School and Church 7 (January–March 1925): 4; M. A. Riley, *Dynamic,* 133; Russell, *Voices,* 99.

27 M. A. Riley, *Dynamic,* 128.

28 "Fourth Annual Convention," 4; William Bell Riley, "To My Brethren, Fundamentalist Editors," *Christian Fundamentals in School and Church,* 6 (April–June 1924): 11. It should be noted that Riley himself had little to do with J. Gresham Machen and John Roach Straton, and he had serious disagreements with T. T. Shields, J. C. Massee, and (as is discussed in the text) J. Frank Norris. For a general discussion of feuding within the fundamentalist movement, see Russell, *Voices,* 213–16.

29 "Dr. Riley's Illness," *Christian Fundamentals in School and Church* 7 (October–December 1924): 4–6; William Bell Riley, "An Open Letter from the Editor," *Christian Fundamentals in School and Church* 7 (January–March 1925): 5–6.

30 "Multiplying Fundamentalist Organizations," *Christian Fundamentals in School and Church* 8 (January–March 1926): 28.

31 Cole, *History of Fundamentalism,* 311–16.

32 William Bell Riley, "Frank Groner vs. Frank Norris, or Some Fundamental Facts," *Christian Fundamentals in School and Church* 5 (July–September 1923): 19–24; William Bell Riley, "Report of the Seventh Annual Convention, World's Christian Fundamentals Association," *Christian Fundamentals in School and Church* 7 (April–June 1925): 7–8.

33 William Bell Riley, "Fundamentalism and Religious Racketeering," *The Pilot* 19 (October 1938): 15–16; Russell, *Voices,* 230n, 243n. For a thinly veiled but nastier attack on Norris, see William Bell Riley, "The Ministry for My Day," *The Pilot* 22 (July 1942): 294.

34 Riley, "Christian Fundamentals Movement," 9–14; "The Coming Cleavage," *Christian Fundamentals in School and Church* 5 (July–September 1923): 31; [William Bell Riley], "The Ecclesiastical Black Hand," *Christian Fundamentals in School and Church* 5 (January–March 1923): 6.

35 Regarding the issue of separatism within the fundamentalist movement, see George M. Marsden, *Reforming Fundamentalism: Fuller Seminary and the New Evangelicalism* (Grand Rapids, Mich.: Wm. B. Eerdmans Co., 1987), esp. 6–7, 36–38; and Joel A. Carpenter, "The Renewal of American Fundamentalism, 1930–1945" (Ph.D. diss., Johns Hopkins University, 1984), 36–92. For early disavowals that Riley intended to lead a withdrawal from the Northern Baptist Convention, see William Bell Riley, "Is There to Be a Division in the Baptist Denomination?" *School and Church,* 2 (October–December 1919): 237–38; William Bell Riley, "Is There to Be a Division in the Baptist Denomination?" *School and Church* 2 (January–March 1920): 292–93. For further discussion of this issue, see the concluding section of chapter 2, and chapter 6.

36 Cole, *History of Fundamentalism,* 317.

37 For further discussion of this shift and its effect on the WCFA, see Szasz, *Divided Mind,* 107; and Russell, *Voices,* 100.

38 Marie Riley noted that her husband's first encounter with "an open champion of this philosophy" came at a Baptist ministers' meeting in Minneapolis, when a University of Minnesota professor delivered an address in support of evolutionism. In response, Riley gave a series of Sunday afternoon lectures against evolutionism. M. A. Riley, *Dynamic,* 101–2. His response eventually became part of his publication *The Finality of the Higher Criticism; or, The Theory of Evolution and False Theology* (N.p. 1909).

39 William Bell Riley, "The Theory of Evolution and False Theology," in Riley, *Finality of the Higher Criticism,* 71–92. See also Riley's sermon "Are the Sacred Scriptures Unscientific?" which is published in the same volume, 93–116.

40 Riley, *Finality of the Higher Criticism,* 88–91.

41 Ibid., 76.

42 Ibid., 81–82.

43 Marsden, *Fundamentalism and American Culture,* 19–20, 214–15. See also Ronald L. Numbers, "Creationism in 20th-Century America," *Science* 218 (November 5, 1982): 538–44. Numbers points out that in their opposition to evolutionism fundamentalists took a variety of positions. Riley accepted the least literal interpretation of Genesis available to fundamentalists, i.e., the so-called day-age interpretation, which held that, to quote Riley, "the days of Genesis are aeons, ages, geological days, days of God and not days of men." This interpretation allowed him to accept historical geology and much of evolutionary development. William Bell Riley and Harry Rimmer, *A Debate: Resolved, that the Creative Days in Genesis Were Aeons, Not Solar Days* (N.p. 1929), 5–17.

44 William Bell Riley, "The Evolution Controversy!" *Christian Fundamentals in School and Church* 4 (April–June 1922): 5–6.

45 Ibid.

46 William Bell Riley, "The Theory of Evolution: Does It Tend to Anarchy?" *Christian Fundamentals in School and Church* 4 (July–September 1922): 42.

47 William Bell Riley, "Debates on Evolution," *Christian Fundamentals in School and Church* 5 (January–March 1923): 20–21.

48 M. A. Riley, *Dynamic,* 113–15; Szasz, "Leaders," 209.

49 Reported in Szasz, "Leaders," 210. Parthenogenesis refers to reproduction by the development of a single sexual cell without fertilization by union of sexual elements.

50 "Dr. W. B. Riley of Minneapolis and Dr. Z. P. Metcalf of Raleigh State College in Debate," *Christian Fundamentals in School and Church* 4 (July–September 1922): 11–15; M. A. Riley, *Dynamic,* 115–16.

51 William Bell Riley, "Evolutionists Weary of Debate," *The Pilot* 21 (May 1941): 228; Szasz, "Leaders," 208.

52 William Bell Riley, "Debates on Evolution," *Christian Fundamentals in School and Church* 8 (January–March 1926): 54; letter from William Bell Riley to L. C. McAfee, June 5, 1925, Papers of William Bell Riley, Northwestern College Library, Roseville, Minn.

53 [William Bell Riley], "The Fourth Annual Convention of the Christian Fundamentalists," *Christian Fundamentals in School and Church* 4 (October–December 1922): 14–15.

54 William Bell Riley, "Shall We Tolerate Longer the Teaching of Evolution?" *Christian Fundamentals in School and Church* 5 (January–March 1923): 85–86. See also Riley, "Evolution Controversy!" 5.

55 "The Great Objectives of the Fort Worth Convention," *Christian Fundamentals in School and Church* 5 (April–June 1923): 25; M. A. Riley, *Dynamic,* 118; Szasz, *Divided Mind,* 111; Cole, *History of Fundamentalism,* 304–5; Edward J. Larson, *Trial and Error: The American Controversy over Creation and Evolution* (Oxford: Oxford University Press, 1985), 49–57. According to Larson, the first two anti-evolution laws were passed in Oklahoma and Florida, but it appears that the WCFA played little or no role in the passage of these laws.

56 William Bell Riley, "The World's Christian Fundamentals Association and the Scopes

Trial," *Christian Fundamentals in School and Church* 7 (October–December 1925): 37–38.

57   After Bryan's death Riley claimed that at Memphis Bryan had given a "partial pledge" to take over the WCFA presidency in 1926. William Bell Riley, "Bryan, the Great Commoner and Christian," *Christian Fundamentals in School and Church* 7 (October–December 1925): 5.

58   Ibid., 11.

59   C. Allyn Russell has observed that it was ironic that Bryan, "who had supported many a fundamentalist cause, and who had been used widely by the fundamentalists to champion their programs, was practically boycotted by the fundamentalist leaders at the Scopes trial." Other fundamentalists who did not attend included John Roach Straton, J. Gresham Machen, James M. Gray, and Billy Sunday. Russell, *Voices,* 184–85.

60   Riley, "World's Christian Fundamentals Association and the Scopes Trial," 39–40; Riley, "Bryan," 11.

61   "The Anti-Evolution League," *Christian Fundamentals in School and Church* 5 (January–March 1923): 16–17; "Minnesota Anti-Evolution League," *Christian Fundamentals in School and Church* 5 (April–June 1923): 31–32; "Riley Assails 'U' As Fostering State Atheism," *Minneapolis Tribune,* March 8, 1926.

62   M. A. Riley, *Dynamic,* 104–10; Ferenc Morton Szasz, "William B. Riley and the Fight Against Teaching of Evolution in Minnesota," *Minnesota History* 41 (Spring 1969): 201–16.

63   M. A. Riley, *Dynamic,* 118; Szasz, "Leaders," 266, 280; Larson, *Trial and Error,* 72–83.

64   Willard B. Gatewood, Jr., Introduction to *Controversy in the Twenties: Fundamentalism, Modernism, and Evolution,* ed. Willard B. Gatewood, Jr. (Nashville, Tenn.: Vanderbilt University Press, 1969), 40–41.

65   For descriptions of the fundamentalist-modernist battles in the various denominations, see Norman F. Furniss, *The Fundamentalist Controversy* (New Haven: Yale University Press, 1954), 103–76; Cole, *History of Fundamentalism,* 64–225; and Marsden, *Fundamentalism and American Culture,* 158–84.

66   Sydney E. Ahlstrom, *A Religious History of the American People* (New Haven: Yale University Press, 1972), 2:382–84. The best study of the Interchurch World Movement is Eldon G. Ernst, *Moment of Truth for Protestant America: Interchurch Campaigns Following World War One* (Missoula, Mont.: Scholar's Press, 1972).

67   William Bell Riley, "The Interchurch World Movement," *School and Church* 2 (April–June 1920): 320–25.

68   Laws, "Convention Side Lights," 834; Ernst, *Moment of Truth,* 160–65. The Northern Baptists and the Northern Presbyterians were not able to wash their hands entirely of the Interchurch in 1920. The denominations were left with the movement's enormous debts, and it took years to complete the payments. Ahlstrom, *A Religious History,* 2:384.

69   William Bell Riley, "The Conflict of Christianity with Its Counterfeit," *Christian Fundamentals in School and Church* 3 (July–September 1921): 10.

70   "Announcement for General Conference on Fundamentals," *The Watchman-Examiner* 8 (May 20, 1920): 652; Marsden, *Fundamentalism and American Culture,* 159, 166.

71   Homer DeWilton Brookins, "The Conference on Fundamentals," *The Watchman-Examiner* 8 (July 1, 1920): 838–40; William Bell Riley, "Modernism in Baptist

Schools," *School and Church* 3 (October–December 1920): 407–22. Note that Riley
toned down the title of his address for publication.

72 Brookins, "Fundamentals," 840; *Annual of the Northern Baptist Convention, 1920*
(Philadelphia: American Baptist Publication Society, 1920), 47–49, 60–61; Grant
Wacker, *Augustus H. Strong and the Dilemma of Historical Consciousness* (Atlanta: Mercer University Press, 1985), 115. As we will see, one of the statements
modifying the original proposal touched on an issue that proved to be crucial in
this matter of modernism in the schools: "Baptists have stedfastly [*sic*] . . . re-
fus[ed] to concur in the imposition of any doctrinal test by either political or ecclesiastical authority."

73 "Dr. Riley's Retirement from the School Committee," *School and Church* 2 (July–
September 1920): 399.

74 *Annual of the Northern Baptist Convention, 1921* (Philadelphia: American Baptist Publication Society, 1921), 92–93.

75 William Bell Riley, "Denominational Colleges and Destructive Criticism," *Christian Fundamentals in School and Church* 4 (October–December 1921): 3.

76 Ronald Nelson, "Fundamentalism and the Northern Baptist Convention" (Ph.D.
diss., University of Chicago, 1964), 74–75, 454. See also William Bell Riley,
"Seminaries and a Statement of Faith," *The Watchman-Examiner* 7 (January 2,
1919): 11; William Bell Riley, "The Question of Academic Freedom," *The Watchman-
Examiner* 11 (January 25, 1923): 116–17.

77 Riley, "Denominational Colleges," 3; "A Confession of Faith," *The Watchman-
Examiner* 9 (June 30, 1921): 805; Marsden, *Fundamentalism and American Culture*, 167, 171–72.

78 Homer DeWilton Brookins, "The Northern Baptist Convention," *The Watchman-
Examiner* 10 (June 29, 1922): pp. 814–16; *Annual of the Northern Baptist Convention, 1922* (Philadelphia: American Baptist Publication Society, 1922), 129–34.
The New Hampshire Confession was written in 1830 and consists of eighteen articles. Interestingly enough, Riley can not be accused here of attempting to force
his eschatological views on the NBC, for, in contrast with Riley's WCFA statement
of faith, this confession does not contain a statement of premillennialism.

79 Charles R. Brock, "Confessions of Faith at Indianapolis," *The Watchman-Examiner*
11 (July 6, 1922): 842; William Bell Riley, "Shall Northern Baptists Come to Peace
by Compromise?" *The Watchman-Examiner* 10 (May 18, 1922): 623; Riley, "Question of Academic Freedom," 116–17.

80 William Bell Riley, "Whipping Fundamentalist Leaders into Line, *Christian Fundamentals in School and Church* 5 (January–March 1923): 6–7.

81 Ibid.

82 Robert G. Delnay, "A History of the Baptist Bible Union" (Th.D. diss., Dallas Theological Seminary, 1963), 50–70. The absence of lay participation is also emphasized by Curtis Wayne Whiteman, "The General Association of Regular Baptist
Churches, 1932–1970" (Ph.D. diss., St. Louis University, 1982), 143.

83 "By-Laws and Resolutions of the Baptist Bible Union of America," *Christian Fundamentals in School and Church* 5 (July–September 1923): 43.

84 While the BBU might have been willing to begin new organizations, it did little
toward that end. The closest the Union came to starting a new agency was in 1925,
when Riley announced the formation of a BBU foreign mission society "which
will provide Baptists with an opportunity to invest their time, their prayers, and
their money, in a mission enterprise which shall be based upon the whole Bible."

Nothing came of this, since the BBU did little more than forward designated gifts to selected missionaries. William Bell Riley, "To All Baptists Who Believe the Bible to Be God's Word," *The Watchman-Examiner* 13 (November 19, 1925): 1497–98; Delnay, "Baptist Bible Union," 253.

85 Frank M. Goodchild, "The Fundamentalists and the Bible Union," *The Watchman-Examiner* 11 (April 19, 1923): 487–88; Frank M. Goodchild, "The Fundamentalists and the Bible Union," *The Watchman-Examiner* 13 (October 22, 1925): 1361–62.

86 "Disfranchising Our Paid Officials," *The Watchman-Examiner* 12 (May 15, 1924): 613–14; *Annual of the Northern Baptist Convention, 1924* (Philadelphia: American Baptist Publication Society, 1924), 51–52; "The Foreign Mission Situation," *The Watchman-Examiner* 12 (June 5, 1924): 709–10.

87 *Annual of the Northern Baptist Convention, 1925* (Philadelphia: American Baptist Publication Society, 1925), 79–94.

88 William Bell Riley, "The Baptist Foreign Missionary Society and Modernism," *Christian Fundamentals in School and Church* 6 (January–March 1924): 20–21; *Annual of the Northern Baptist Convention, 1925* (Philadelphia: American Baptist Publication Society, 1925): 94–96, 174–75.

89 William Bell Riley, "Baptist Foreign Mission Society or _____," *The Northwestern Pilot* 24 (January 1944): 126.

90 Homer DeWilton Brookins, "The Northern Baptist Convention, Washington, District of Columbia, May 25–30," *The Watchman-Examiner* 14 (June 3, 1926): 684–85. For evidence of FF-BBU conflict over this issue, see Frank M. Goodchild, "The Fundamentalist's Page," *The Watchman-Examiner* 14 (April 15, 1926): 467.

91 Marsden, *Fundamentalism and American Culture*, 182–83; J. C. Massee, "The Laodicean Lament," *The Watchman-Examiner* 14 (June 13, 1926): 693; Nelson, "Northern Baptist," 301–2.

92 As quoted in Cole, *History of Fundamentalism*, 80–81; Riley, "Fundamentalism and Religious Racketeering," 15. For a more vitriolic attack on "compromisers," see William Bell Riley, "Muste and the Committee of Nine," *The Pilot* 22 (May 1942): 228.

93 Joseph M. Stowell, *Background and History of the General Association of Regular Baptist Churches* (Hayward, Calif.: Gospel Tracts Unlimited, 1949), 28–29; Cole, *History of Fundamentalism*, 293–94.

94 William Bell Riley, "Facts for Fundamentalists," *The Pilot* 16 (January 1936): 110; Delnay, "Baptist Bible Union," 52–54; Nelson, "Northern Baptist," 416–17; Whiteman, "Regular Baptist Churches," 188–92.

95 In his thesis on Minnesota fundamentalism Dell Johnson asserted that "perhaps for personal reasons, Riley felt he could not have separated earlier [than 1947], for his ministry was often supported and aided in times of crisis by finances which came from the Mapes family (Cream of Wheat business). Pierce, a teacher and board member of Northwestern Schools since the 1920's, married into the Mapes family and frequently gave sums of money to . . . Northwestern Schools. Since Pierce was a convinced moderate and Riley was in need of school funds, Riley's actions were probably calculated." While it is certainly possible that money was an important motivator in the decision-making processes of William Bell Riley, Johnson failed to provide substantiating evidence. Dell G. Johnson, "Fundamentalist Responses in Minnesota to the Developing New Evangelicalism" (Th.D. diss., Central Baptist Seminary, 1982), 354–55.

96 William Bell Riley, "The Autonomy of a Baptist Church," *The Pilot* 19 (January 1939): 100; Delnay, "Baptist Bible Union," 61–62.

97 William Bell Riley, "Facts for Fundamentalists," *The Pilot* 16 (December 1935): 74; William Bell Riley, "Recovering Majority Baptist Rule," *The Pilot* 23 (August 1943): 313.

Chapter 3: The Conspiracy

1 Carey McWilliams, "Minneapolis: The Curious Twin," *Common Ground* 7 (Autumn 1946): 61–65. McWilliams was not the only observer of his time to comment on Minneapolis' extreme anti-Semitism. See also Charles I. Cooper, "The Jews of Minneapolis and Their Christian Neighbors," *Jewish Social Studies* 8 (1946): 31–38; and Selden C. Menefee, "What Americans Think," *The Nation* 156 (May 5, 1943): 764–68.

2 McWilliams, "Minneapolis," 61–65. According to McWilliams, the other "weird prophets" were Arthur Pachofsky, William D. Herrstrom, C. O. Stadsklev, and Luke Rader. For a summary of the views of the latter three, see Michael G. Rapp, "A Historical Overview of Anti-Semitism in Minnesota, 1920–1960" (Ph.D. diss., University of Minnesota, 1977), 120–67. Taking into account Riley's church, school, regional empire, and publications, none of the other anti-Semitic fundamentalists in Minneapolis had nearly the audience Riley did.

3 William Bell Riley, *Messages for the Metropolis* (Minneapolis: Winona Publishing Co., 1906), foreword.

4 Ferenc Morton Szasz, "The Progressive Clergy and the Kingdom of God," *Mid-America* 55 (January 1973): 3–20; William G. McLoughlin, *Modern Revivalism, Charles Grandison Finney to Billy Graham* (New York: Ronald Press, 1959), 364–99.

5 Riley, *Messages for the Metropolis*, foreword, 42–60.

6 Marie Acomb Riley, *The Dynamic of a Dream: The Life Story of Dr. William B. Riley* (Grand Rapids, Mich.: Wm. B. Eerdmans Co., 1938), 50, 61; "Four Anniversaries of a Great Christian Statesman," *The Northwestern Pilot* 27 (March 1947): 166–67.

7 This article was reprinted in Lincoln Steffens, *The Shame of the Cities* (New York: McClure, Phillips, and Co., 1904), 63–97. See also Carl H. Chrislock, *The Progressive Era in Minnesota, 1899–1918* (St. Paul: Minnesota Historical Society, 1971), 25–26.

8 William Bell Riley, *Riley versus Robinson: A Discussion of the Superintendency of Minneapolis Schools* (Minneapolis: W. B. Riley, [1944?]), 9–10; "Four Anniversaries," 167–68.

9 Riley, *Messages for the Metropolis*, 34. Riley certainly was not alone among conservative evangelicals in making such inflamed attacks on the saloon. For example, in a 1917 sermon Billy Sunday proclaimed: "The saloon is the sum of all villainies. It is worse than war or pestilence. It is the crime of crimes. It is the parent of crimes and the mother of sins. It is the appalling source of misery and crime in the land. And to license such an incarnate fiend of hell is the dirtiest, low-down, damnable business on top of this old earth." As quoted in Douglas W. Frank, *Less than Conquerors: How Evangelicals Entered the Twentieth Century* (Grand Rapids, Mich.: Wm. B. Eerdmans Co., 1986), 188.

10 Riley, as quoted in "Four Anniversaries," 168; M. A. Riley, *Dynamic*, 90–92. A

few years after this engagement, Riley and the federation fought a successful series
of battles to keep liquor sales limited to a certain section of the city.

11   Riley, *Messages for the Metropolis*, 129; M. A. Riley, *Dynamic*, 92.

12   Riley, *Messages for the Metropolis*, 165–83.

13   Ibid., 207–17.

14   Ibid., 222–29.

15   Most conservative evangelicals involved in "urban uplift" had a similarly limited
social vision. For a perceptive, albeit harsh, critique of dispensationalists as reformers, see Frank, *Less than Conquerors*, 96–102.

16   Otis L. Graham, Jr., *An Encore for Reform: The Old Progressives and the New
Deal* (London: Oxford University Press, 1967; reprint, 1968), 24–73, 166–81.

17   William Bell Riley, "The Great Divide; or, Christianity and the Present Crisis,"
The Watchman-Examiner 7 (June 26, 1919): 997.

18   George M. Marsden, *Fundamentalism and American Culture: The Shaping of
Twentieth-Century Evangelicalism, 1870–1925* (New York: Oxford University Press,
1980), esp. 85–93; David O. Moberg, *The Great Reversal: Evangelism versus Social Concern* (Philadelphia: J. B. Lippincott Co., 1972); Richard V. Pierard, *The
Unequal Yoke* (Philadelphia: J. B. Lippincott Co., 1970).

19   In a speech to civic leaders in 1947, Riley plaintively lamented that Minneapolis
scions still had not forgotten his early sermons: "Labor was poorly, I thought,
outrageously paid; therefore, I championed the cause of the poor. It estranged
the wealthy section of my church, and Minneapolis millionaires did not sympa-
thize with, and to this day, I guess, have not forgiven me. I have had Philadelphia
millionaires and California millionaires lend help to my school, but the Minneapolis millionaires, with one or two notable exceptions have passed me up cold (to
date), although for fifty years past I have been desperately fighting their cause,
in view of the encroachments of Communism, [which] all quite often takes the
form of Labor Unions." William Bell Riley, Speech given at a civic luncheon,
Radisson Hotel, Minneapolis, Minn., March 22, 1947.

20   William Bell Riley, *Ten Burning Questions* (New York: Revell and Co., 1932), 138;
M. A. Riley, *Dynamic*, 189.

21   William Bell Riley, "The Social Economy of Jesus Christ," *The Pilot* 18 (November
1937): 42–43.

22   William Bell Riley, "Facts for Fundamentalists," *The Pilot* 15 (March 1935): 160;
M. A. Riley, *Dynamic*, 189.

23   Riley, "Social Economy," 44; William Bell Riley, *The Four Horsemen; or, Prophecy
and the Approaching Slaughter* (Minneapolis, [1941?]), 10–11.

24   William Bell Riley, *The Philosophies of Father Coughlin* (Grand Rapids, Mich.:
Zondervan Publishing Co., 1935), 32–38.

25   William Bell Riley, "The Conflict of Christianity with Its Counterfeit," *Christian
Fundamentals in School and Church* 3 (July–September 1921): 6.

26   Leo P. Ribuffo, *The Old Christian Right: The Protestant Far Right from the Great
Depression to the Cold War* (Philadelphia: Temple University Press, 1983), 25–79,
110, 128–77.

27   William Bell Riley, "The Evolution Controversy!" *Christian Fundamentals in School
and Church* 4 (April–June 1922): 5–6; William Bell Riley, "The Theory of Evolution: Does It Tend to Anarchy?" *Christian Fundamentals in School and Church*
4 (July–September 1922): 36–42.

28   William Bell Riley, Sermon given at the First Baptist Church, Minneapolis, Minn.,

October 18, 1936. Reported by Charles I. Cooper and S.W., Box 54: "Subversive Activities: Minneapolis, 1936," Jewish Community Relations Council of Minnesota Papers, Minnesota State Historical Society, St. Paul, Minn. Much of the following discussion is based on these papers, hereafter cited as the JCRCM Papers. I am indebted to Michael G. Rapp, executive director of the Jewish Community Relations Council of Cincinnati, for pointing me to this source. In response to the prevalence of anti-Semitism in Minnesota, including the preaching and teaching of William Bell Riley, the Anti-Defamation Council of Minnesota was informally organized in 1936. In 1939 it was formally restructured as the Minnesota Jewish Council; in the 1950s the name was changed to the Jewish Community Relations Council of Minnesota. In the 1930s the primary purpose was to investigate and protest against anti-Semitic activities. In the 1940s the council turned its attention to discrimination in housing, hotels, etc.

29   McWilliams, "Minneapolis," 62-65. See also Cooper, "Jews of Minneapolis," 35-38.

30   That anti-Semitic themes had a certain resonance in the state as a whole was quite apparent in the 1938 gubernatorial election, in which Republican Harold Stassen benefited from nasty anti-Semitic attacks on the Farmer-Labor candidate Elmer Benson, who happened to have some Jewish advisers. While the level of Riley's involvement in the smear of Benson is not clear, there is no question that he was ecstatic with Stassen's victory: "For some years the triumph of *Communism in Minnesota*, under the name of *Farmer-Labor Party* . . . has attracted national attention. . . . [But] after six or eight years [Minnesota] found itself more than fed up on this impractical, graceless, godless, and expensive program! On the second Tuesday in November the State revolted to the extent of over 500,000 voters, reversing the majority given to its Governor two years ago, and turning a kindred majority over to young *Stassen* to make him Governor and reinstate the Republican Party." William Bell Riley, "Minnesota vs. California," *The Pilot* 19 (January 1939): 99. For a discussion of this election, see Hyman Berman, "Political Antisemitism in Minnesota during the Great Depression," *Jewish Social Studies* 38 (Summer-Fall 1976): 247-64.

31   Timothy P. Weber, *Living in the Shadow of the Second Coming: American Premillennialism, 1875-1982* (Grand Rapids, Mich.: Zondervan Co., 1983), esp. 154-57; Joel A. Carpenter, "The Renewal of American Fundamentalism, 1930-1945" (Ph.D. diss., Johns Hopkins University, 1984), 95-110.

32   Weber, *Second Coming*, 156-57, 185-203. In contrast with Weber, David A. Rausch does not see elements of anti-Semitism in dispensational premillennialism. In his book, *Zionism within Early American Fundamentalism, 1878-1918: A Convergence of Two Traditions* (New York: Edwin Mellen Press, 1979), Rausch argues that proto-fundamentalism was strongly philo-Semitic and pro-Zionist. Moreover, while the years after 1918 are not the emphasis in Rausch's book, in the final chapter he provides example after example of how the later fundamentalist movement was similarly supportive of the Jews. Interestingly enough, while he provides examples of Riley's Zionism in the 1910s, he completely ignores Riley when discussing the years after 1918. Any serious analysis of the relationship between fundamentalism and anti-Semitism in America will have to take into account the vicious views of the founder of the World's Christian Fundamentals Association.

33   Norman Cohn, *Warrant for Genocide: The Myth of the World-Conspiracy and the Protocols of the Elders of Zion* (New York: Harper Torchbooks, 1969), 61-65, 156-62; Ribuffo, *Old Christian Right*, 10-13.

34   William Bell Riley, *Wanted – A World Leader!* (Minneapolis, 1939), 42–43. Regarding problems with dating this book, see footnote 67. I am assuming the passage quoted here was written before 1939 because Lillian Riley died in 1931, and W. B. Riley's story involving her begins, "Less than eight years ago . . ."

35   See, for example William Bell Riley, "Christ Will Come Again! A Reply," *School and Church* 2 (April 1918): 69; and William Bell Riley, *Protocols and Communism* (Minneapolis: L. W. Camp, 1934), 4.

36   The exchangeability of these terms was even apparent in Marie Riley's biography of her husband. In a chapter entitled "The Conflict with Communism," she noted that "as a conservative in theology, Dr. Riley can do no other than oppose what he believes to be atheism in religion, modernism in theology and *Judaism in politics*" (emphasis mine). M. A. Riley, *Dynamic*, 189.

37   Riley, *World Leader*, 49; Riley, *Protocols and Communism*, 13–14.

38   William Bell Riley, "The Blood of the Jew vs. the Blood of Jesus," *The Pilot* 15 (November 1934): 25; Riley, *World Leader*, 71–81.

39   William Bell Riley, "Facts for Fundamentalists," *The Pilot* 15 (February 1935): 124. The section of this column in which the quote appears is entitled "The Jewish Web for the Gentile Fly."

40   William Bell Riley, *The Doom of World Governments* (Minneapolis, [1937?]), 5–10; Riley, *Protocols and Communism*, 5–6.

41   Riley, *Philosophies of Father Coughlin*, 57.

42   Riley, *Protocols and Communism*, 5–14.

43   William Bell Riley, "Facts for Fundamentalists," *The Pilot* 15 (September 1935): 311; William Bell Riley, "Facts for Fundamentalists," *The Pilot* 15 (February 1935): 126; William Bell Riley, "Christian Brethren Talk It Over," *The Pilot* 17 (October 1936): 3.

44   Riley, *Protocols and Communism*, 7–10.

45   Riley, *Philosophies of Father Coughlin*, 20.

46   William Bell Riley, "Why Recognize Russia and Rag Germany?" *The Pilot* 14 (January 1934): 109–10, 126.

47   William Bell Riley, "Facts for Fundamentalists," *The Pilot* 13 (July 1933): 298–99. The section of this column in which the quote appears is entitled "For Fear of the Jews."

48   "Germany," *The Pilot* 18 (November 1937): 46; Riley, *World Leader*, 45–46.

49   Riley, *Philosophies of Father Coughlin*, 18–24, 47–49; Alan Brinkley, *Voices of Protest: Huey Long, Father Coughlin, and the Great Depression* (1982; reprint, New York: Random House, 1983), 265–73.

50   William Bell Riley, "The Arrest of a Rifle Club," *The Pilot* 20 (March 1940): 171; William Bell Riley, "Blatant Birkhead," *The Northwestern Pilot* 25 (August 1945): 329.

51   Ribuffo, *Old Christian Right*, 87–118. For an example of Riley's *Defender* articles, see: William Bell Riley, "Is Anti-Communism Also Anti-Semitism?" *The Defender* 14 (November, 1939): 18.

52   Ralph Lord Roy, *Apostles of Discord: A Study of Organized Bigotry and Disruption on the Fringes of Protestantism* (Boston: The Beacon Press, 1953), pp. 40–41. For an example of a Dilling article in *The Pilot*, see Elizabeth Dilling, "What the Federal Council is Doing," *The Pilot*, 19 (December, 1938): p. 78. For an example of a Gilbert article in *The Pilot*, see Dan Gilbert, "The Anti-Christ Advance in the Colleges," *The Pilot*, 19 (November, 1938): 39–40.

53 Elizabeth Knauss, "Communism as Glimpsed Behind the Scenes in Sovietland," *The Pilot*, 13 (October, 1932): 20–22; Elizabeth Knauss, "Communism and the Protocols," *The Pilot*, 13 (November, 1932): 40–41; Elizabeth Knauss, "Communism and the Illuminati," *The Pilot*, 13 (December, 1932): 77–78; Elizabeth Knauss, "Communism and the Jewish Question," *The Pilot*, 13 (June, 1933): 271–272; William Bell Riley, "Facts for Fundamentalists," *The Pilot*, 14 (February, 1934): 143.

54 Ribuffo, *Old Christian Right*, 58–65.

55 Charles I. Cooper, "Summary [of S.W.'s investigation]," November 13, 1936; and S.W., "Report of October 20, 1936." Both in JCRCM Papers, Box 54: "Subversive Activities: Minneapolis, 1936."

56 William Bell Riley, Sermons given at the First Baptist Church, Minneapolis, Minn., October 11 and October 18, 1936, as reported by Charles I. Cooper and S.W., JCRCM Papers, Box 54: "Subversive Activities: Minneapolis, 1936."

57 William Bell Riley, *Shivering at the Sight of a Shirt* (Minneapolis, 1936).

58 Cooper, "Summary," JCRCM Papers; Cooper, "Jews of Minneapolis," 36.

59 One example: in 1943 Northwestern alumnus and South St. Paul Baptist minister Henry Van Kommer wrote two articles for the local newspaper decrying anti-Semitism. In the first one, "Jew Haters," Van Kommer directly contradicted his mentor: "Actually, Jews are no more likely to be involved in communism than are Gentiles. They do not have a larger percentage of criminals, nor of radicals. On the average, they are harder workers, they do not have so many people on relief, they give liberally to public causes, they are as patriotic and faithful citizens as are Gentiles. . . . The rousing of Christians against Jews, or of Gentiles against Jews is a wicked business that causes disunity, suspicion, and fear among the people and would bring about that state of mind which makes the public easier ruled by demagogues and Fascists or Nazis." JCRCM Papers, Box 17.

60 Weber, *Second Coming*, 184–203; David A. Rausch, "Our Hope: An American Fundamentalist Journal and the Holocaust, 1937–1945," *Fides et Historia* 12 (Spring 1980): 89–103; William R. Glass, "Fundamentalism's Prophetic Vision of the Jews: The 1930s," *Jewish Social Studies* 47 (Winter 1985): 63–76.

61 Quoted in Roy, *Apostles of Discord*, 45–47.

62 Carpenter, "Renewal of American Fundamentalism," 112–13; William Bell Riley, "Facts for Fundamentalists," *The Pilot* 15 (June 1935): 249–50.

63 [Keith L. Brooks?], "Let's Come Clean!," *American Prophetic League, Inc., Release No. 38* (January, 1942): 1.

64 "'The Protocols and Communism' No Longer on Sale," *The Pilot* 16 (July 1936): 302.

65 Riley, "Facts for Fundamentalists," *The Pilot* 15 (June 1935): 250; Riley, *World Leader*, 45–47.

66 William Bell Riley, "Cohn vs. Riley," *The Pilot* 15 (May 1935): 218; William Bell Riley, "Paul and Peter Voronaeff," *The Pilot* 19 (January 1939): 119; William Bell Riley, "Joseph Cohn's New Money-Getting Scheme," *The Northwestern Pilot* 26 (December 1945): 75. Keith Brooks wrote a spirited defense of Cohn and the American Board of Missions to the Jews, *Lies Have Wings: "Cohn Uncovered"—or Riley Unmasked—Which?*, a copy of which is in the JCRCM Papers, Box 61: "Rev. W. B. Riley, 1922–1942."

67 *World Leader* is undated. Some historians have placed the publishing date at 1936. While Riley may have written some or even most of the book in the mid-1930s, overwhelming internal evidence indicates that he published it in its final form in 1939. See Riley's *World Leader*, 16, 57–58, 62–63.

68 William Bell Riley, *Hitlerism; or, The Philosophy of Evolution in Action* (Minneapolis, [1941?]).

69 While I have not seen any evidence establishing that *Pilot* coeditor and WCFA associate Dan Gilbert shared Riley's blatant anti-Semitism, it certainly appears that he feared governmental prosecution. According to a May 4, 1942, letter from Keith Brooks, president of the American Prophetic League, to Samuel Scheiner, executive director of the Minnesota Jewish Council, early in 1942 Gilbert had become "deeply concerned about the turn of national affairs and probably a bit jittery about some things he had said publicly and written." In an effort to avoid being picked up by the government, he attempted to ally himself with the anti-Nazi American Prophetic League. As an indication of good faith, he gave Brooks a mailing list of three thousand individuals who needed to be "given right information on the Jewish question." Brooks sent the list to Scheiner, who promptly passed it on to the Anti-Defamation Council. Letter from Keith Brooks to Samuel Scheiner, May 4, 1942; letter from Samuel Scheiner to Keith Brooks, May 8, 1942; letter from Samuel Scheiner to Richard Gutstadt, May 8, 1942; letter from Richard Gutstadt to Samuel Scheiner, May 12, 1942. All in JCRCM Papers, Box 26: "Dan Gilbert."

70 [Brooks], "Let's Come Clean!" 1–2.

71 Ibid.

72 Letter from Samuel Scheiner to Keith Brooks, January 14, 1942; letter from Samuel Scheiner to Keith Brooks, January 20, 1942. Both in JCRCM Papers, Box 61: "Rev. W. B. Riley, 1922–1942." I do not know whether the Minnesota Jewish Council succeeded in having the article sent to all First Baptist members.

73 William Bell Riley, "Slogans to Silence Free Speech," *The Northwestern Pilot* 25 (March 1945): 163; William Bell Riley, "The Chucking of Upton Close," *The Northwestern Pilot,* 25 (September 1945): 335, 358.

74 William Bell Riley, "Persecution of Colonel Sanctuary and Others," *The Northwestern Pilot* 24 (August 1944): 366; [William Bell Riley?], "The End of the Famous Sedition Trial," *The Northwestern Pilot* 25 (March 1945): 163.

Chapter 4: The School

1 William Bell Riley, "The World Premillennial Conference vs. The Coming Confederacy," *School and Church* 2 (January–March 1919): 91–96.

2 "The Evolution of Northwestern," *The Pilot* 8 (November 1927): 4–5; Jessie Van Booskirk, "School Notes," *School and Church* 1 (February 1917): 25; "Praise God!" *The Pilot* 2 ([March?] 1922): 10; "The Northwestern Bible Training School," *Christian Fundamentals in School and Church* 5 (January–March 1923): 72.

3 "Opening Day," *The Pilot* 16 (October 1935): 3; "Northwestern's Forward Movement," *The Northwestern Pilot* 26 (January 1946): 107; "Northwestern Opening Reveals Largest Enrollment in History," *The Northwestern Pilot* 26 (September 1946): 334; "Northwestern Witnesses Ground Breaking," *The Northwestern Pilot* 26 (April 1946): 214.

4 Marie Acomb Riley, *The Dynamic of a Dream: The Life Story of Dr. William B. Riley* (Grand Rapids, Mich.: Wm. B. Eerdmans Co., 1938), 150–55. In the early years the school's board shared this function with the First Baptist board, because "the School was not able to buy [property] apart from the Church."

5 [William Bell Riley], *The City Temple* (Minneapolis, 1915), 4, a copy of which is in the Papers of William Bell Riley, Northwestern College Library, Roseville, Minn.; M. A. Riley, *Dynamic*, 148; Ernest Sandeen, *The Roots of Fundamentalism: British and American Millenarianism, 1800–1930* (Chicago: University of Chicago Press, 1970), 182, 209.

6 M. A. Riley, *Dynamic*, 152.

7 "Dr. Myron W. Haynes," *School and Church* 1 (January 1917): 5; "The School Building and the City Temple Block," *School and Church* 1 (May 1917): 82; M. A. Riley, *Dynamic*, 152. Marie Riley stated that with Haynes's resignation "Riley returned to the presidency." No substantive evidence exists, in her book or elsewhere, that Riley was president of the school before the Haynes episode. Moreover, all references to Riley before the early 1930s are to "superintendent Riley." See "Dr. Riley," *The Pilot* 1 (March 16, 1921): 47; "Our Faculty," *The Pilot* 8 (May 1928): 10; "In Memoriam," *The Pilot* 11 (September, 1931): 326.

8 "Dr. Riley," *The Pilot* 1 (March 16, 1921): 47.

9 M. A. Riley, *Dynamic*, 158; William Bell Riley, "The Northwestern Bible and Missionary Training School," *Christian Fundamentals in School and Church* 9 (January–March 1927): 63. Moyer succeeded Riley as pastor of First Baptist when the latter resigned that post in 1942. But Moyer died in 1944. "The Passing of Dean Robert L. Moyer," *The Northwestern Pilot* 25 (November 1944): 35.

10 "Friends and Funds," *School and Church* 1 (October 1917): 185–86; "The Northwestern Bible School Graduates," *School and Church* 2 (May 1918): 84; "The Northwestern Employment Department," *The Pilot* 20 (July 1940): 295.

11 "The Support of the Northwestern School," *The Pilot* 13 (December 1932): 103; "Giving," *The Pilot* 8 (November 1927): 10. In a 1926 article announcing the formation of a financial support group, the writer noted that the students paid only one-ninth of the expense of maintaining Northwestern. It should be noted, however, that this estimate took only tuition into account and not room and board charges. "Friendly Helpers' Association," *The Pilot* 7 (November 1926): 2.

12 Virginia Lieson Brereton, "Fundamentalists as Popular Educators: The Bible Schools, 1880–Present" (Paper presented at meeting of the American Society of Church History, Holland, Mich., April 21, 1983), 20.

13 "The Northwestern Bible School," *The Pilot* 15 (November 1934): 40; "To the Friends of Northwestern," *The Pilot* 18 (June 1938): 271.

14 Included in a January 1947 *Northwestern Pilot* article, "Facts in Great Figures," which celebrated Riley's fifty years in Minneapolis, was a record of financial contributions to the church and school. The following information from this article is relevant to our purposes:

Contributions

Years	Church	School	Total
1922–26	—	—	$955,534.89
1927–31	$495,830.29	$400,565.53	896,395.82
1932–36	280,011.91	263,753.87	543,765.78
1937–41	318,830.43	383,399.06	702,229.49

One major problem exists in comparing giving in the 1920s with giving in the 1930s. Price fluctuations, particularly the marked price deflation of the 1930s, do not allow for a simple dollar comparison between the decades. In an effort to deal with this problem, I used the wholesale price indexes as listed in the Census Bureau's *Historical Statistics of the United States: Colonial Times to 1970*, part 1 (Washington: Federal Bureau of the Census, 1975), 200. Conveniently enough, 1926 is the base year. I averaged the wholesale price index for each of the five-year periods listed above; using this average, I converted the contribution figures into 1926 dollars. The results are as follows:

Contributions in 1926 Dollars

Years	Church	School	Total
1922–26	–	–	$ 957,641.70
1927–31	$554,868.27	$448,260.44	1,003,128.70
1932–36	382,112.31	359,926.13	742,038.46
1937–41	390,819.35	469,966.98	860,786.33

15 "The President's Message," *The Pilot* 19 (May 1939): 278.

16 F. S. Groner, "An Appreciation of Our President," *The Pilot* 17 (May 1937): 253.

17 Charles Allyn Russell, *Voices of American Fundamentalism: Seven Biographical Studies* (Philadelphia: Westminster Press, 1976), 79; Brereton, "Popular Educators," 18–20.

18 Advertisement, *The Pilot* 10 (June 1930): 288; Advertisement, *The Pilot* 13 (April 1933): 224.

19 Ferenc Morton Szasz, "Three Fundamentalist Leaders: The Roles of William Bell Riley, John Roach Straton, and William Jennings Bryan in the Fundamentalist-Modernist Controversy" (Ph.D. diss., University of Rochester, 1969), 82.

20 "Financial Report," *Christian Fundamentals in School and Church* 3 (July–September 1921): 37–40; "The Bible School Finances," *School and Church* 2 (January–March 1920): 299–300; "Call unto Me —," *The Pilot* 7 (January 1927): 2; William Bell Riley, Speech given at a civic luncheon, Radisson Hotel, Minneapolis, Minn., March 22, 1947; M. A. Riley, *Dynamic,* 157–58.

21 "Fourth Annual Convention: Christian Fundamentals Association," *Christian Fundamentals in School and Church* 4 (April–June 1922): 4.

22 M. A. Riley, *Dynamic,* 193; Anna Rieger, completed questionnaire to author, August 29, 1986. Thanks to an Albert J. Beveridge Grant for Research in American History, awarded by the American Historical Association, and the cooperation of the Alumni Office of Northwestern College, I was able to obtain the addresses of alumni who attended Northwestern in the 1930s and 1940s. In the summer of 1986 I sent a questionnaire to 130 of these individuals. This questionnaire included questions about their experience at Northwestern, their relationship with Riley, and their ties with Riley and Northwestern after graduation. Much to my delight, seventy alumni responded. The information they provided helped me fill out this chapter and chapter 5.

23 Herbert Caneday, completed questionnaire to author, September 19, 1986; Linnea Hill, interview with author, Roseville, Minn., June 7, 1986.

24 Henry Van Kommer, completed questionnaire to author, September 23, 1986; George D. White, completed questionnaire to author, October 11, 1986; David Hammar, completed questionnaire to author, August 18, 1986.

25 Minnie Blixt Herrlinger, completed questionnaire to author, August 18, 1986; Anonymous correspondent, completed questionnaire to author, October 3, 1986.

26 Raymond Anderson, interview with author, Golden Valley, Minn., August 25, 1986; Fred Julius, interview with author, Shoreview, Minn., August 25, 1986.

27 M. A. Riley, *Dynamic*, 150.

28 [Riley], *City Temple*, 27; William Bell Riley, "The Bible School and That Blessed Hope," Sermon preached at the Founders' Week Conference, Moody Church, Chicago, February 5, 1936, reprinted in *The Pilot* 16 (March 1936): 164.

29 M. A. Riley, *Dynamic*, 146–47; William Bell Riley, *The Challenge of Minnesota Baptists* (N.p. [1944?]), 11.

30 William Bell Riley, "The Surplus of Preachers," *The Pilot* 14 (December 1933): 90.

31 This phenomenon is much noted but rarely discussed in depth, at least in the context of the fundamentalist-modernist conflict. See, for instance, Ferenc Morton Szasz's passing reference in *The Divided Mind of Protestant America, 1880–1930* (University: University of Alabama Press, 1982), 78. That the "crisis of the country church" did indeed exist is attested to by the numerous committee reports on the problem in the *Annuals* of the Northern Baptist Convention. More on this in chapter 5.

32 William Bell Riley, "We Met a Midwest Crisis," *The Northwestern Pilot* 28 (October 1947): 12.

33 Riley, "Surplus," 90; "The Northwestern Theological Seminary and the State Baptist Convention," *The Pilot* 23 (January 1943): 99.

34 Riley, "Surplus," 90.

35 William Bell Riley, *The Menace of Modernism* (New York: Christian Alliance Co., 1917), 151; William Bell Riley, "The Northwestern Schools," *The Pilot* 21 (November 1940): 48.

36 Riley, "Surplus," 90; Donald Tinder, "Fundamentalist Baptists in the Northern and Western United States, 1920–1950" (Ph.D. diss., Yale University, 1969), 256; Virginia Lieson Brereton, "Protestant Fundamentalist Bible Schools, 1882–1940" (Ph.D. diss., Columbia University, 1981), 261–62.

37 Riley, "Surplus," 90.

38 William Bell Riley, "The Ministry for My Day," *The Pilot* 22 (July 1942): 291; "Northwestern Bible and Missionary Training School Catalogue," *School and Church* 2 (July–September 1918): 13; Virginia Lieson Brereton, "Inside the Bible School: Classroom Teaching," chapter from revised dissertation, "Protestant Fundamentalist Bible Schools, 1882–1940," 4.

39 "Northwestern Bible School Notes," *Christian Fundamentals in School and Church* 6 (July–September 1924): 55; "What Northwestern Offers to Young People," *The Pilot* 10 (April 1930): 203; Advertisement, *The Pilot* 11 (January 1931): 98.

40 Anonymous correspondent, completed questionnaire to author, August 17, 1986; "Northwestern Bible School Notes," 55.

41 Fred Julius, interview with author, Shoreview, Minn., August 25, 1986; Kenneth E. Nelson, completed questionnaire to author, October 22, 1986.

42 William Bell Riley, "What Is Fundamentalism?" (Address delivered at the Ninth Annual Convention of the World's Christian Fundamentals Association, Atlanta, May 1, 1927), published pamphlet in Papers of William Bell Riley, Northwestern College Library, Roseville, Minn.

43 "Friends of Northwestern," *The Pilot* 10 (January 1930): 98; Axel Odegard, "Our Motto: II Timothy 2:15," *The Pilot* 1 (March 2, 1921): 38.

44 "The School," *The Pilot* 9 (April 1929): 2; "Our One-Year Course," *The Pilot* 8 (March 1928): 2.

45 "What Northwestern Offers," 203; "Missionary Training," *The Pilot* 6 (February 1926): 9.

46 "Let Us Help You?" *The Pilot* 11 (December 1930): 92; Arthur Karlstrom, "Northwestern Plans New Medical Missions Course," *The Pilot* 24 (May 1944): 250; "Northwestern to Excel in Music Field," *The Pilot* 26 (May 1946): 244.

47 One example is the series of articles by the virulent anti-Communist, Elizabeth Knauss: "Communism as Glimpsed behind the Scenes in Sovietland," *The Pilot* 13 (October 1932): 20–22; "Communism and the Illuminati," *The Pilot* 13 (December 1932): 77–78; "Communism and Youth," *The Pilot* 13 (January 1933): 105–6.

48 "Northwestern Plans a Russian Department," *The Pilot* 23 (December 1942): 68; "News from the Russian Department," *The Northwestern Pilot* 24 (March 1944): 179; [Vaclav Vojta], "We Are Ready . . . Send Us," *The Northwestern Pilot* 25 (March 1945): 170.

49 Vaclav Vojta, "Justifying My Opinion," *The Northwestern Pilot* 26 (December 1945): 74; "Northwestern Russian Department," *The Northwestern Pilot* 26 (August 1946): 293; "Looking upon the Fields," *The Northwestern Pilot* 27 (August 1947): 331. It should be noted that Northwestern's establishment of a Russian department in 1944 was just one example of the general increase in missions interest among fundamentalists during World War II. For more on this, see chapter 6, and Joel A. Carpenter, "The Renewal of American Fundamentalism, 1930–1945" (Ph.D. diss., Johns Hopkins University, 1984), 225–26.

50 "Further Development," *The Pilot* 15 (July 1935): 274; "God's Grace Manifested," *The Pilot* 16 (December 1935): 72–73; "Romance in Religion," *The Pilot* 17 (October 1937): 17.

51 William Bell Riley, "The Northwestern Evangelical Seminary," *The Pilot* 15 (May 1935): 220.

52 "Changing the Standard," *The Pilot* 2 (December 23, 1921): 82; Jessie Van Booskirk, "Last Year's Work," *School and Church* 1 (September 1916): 5.

53 "Changing the Standard," 82.

54 "Train for Service," *The Pilot* 9 (May 1929): 2; Mrs. E. P. Barrett, "Practical Outcome of Teacher Training," *The Pilot* 18 (June 1938): 270.

55 "Education for His Service," *The Pilot* 13 (December 1932): 67.

56 Jessie Van Booskirk, "School Notes," *School and Church* 1 (March 1917): 47; Leroy Gager, "Serving While Preparing," *The Northwestern Pilot* 25 (January 1945): 113; Virginia Lieson Brereton, "Inside the Bible School: Beyond the Classroom," chapter from revised dissertation, "Protestant Fundamentalist Bible Schools, 1882–1940," 1–3.

57 "Northwestern Practical Work at a Glance," *The Pilot* 22 (March 1942): 189; Henry Van Kommer, completed questionnaire to author, September 23, 1986.

58 "The Church in Thy House," *The Pilot* 13 (June 1933): 276.

59 "Northwestern Practical Work," 189; "A Practical Work Review," *The Pilot* 14 (May 1934): 250.

60 "Northwestern Practical Work," 189; Lawrence Ray Sanford, completed questionnaire to author, October 1, 1986; Anonymous correspondent, completed question-

naire to author, October 6, 1986; Elmer Dick, completed questionnaire to author, August 9, 1986.

61 Francis Tarrant, completed questionnaire to author, October 13, 1986.

62 Walter Bridge, "Northwestern – A Pioneer in Daily Vacation Bible Schools," *The Pilot* 19 (August 1939): 310.

63 Frank Bass, "Daily Vacation Bible Schools: Northwestern's Contribution to This Great Movement," *The Pilot* 22 (May 1942): 231–32, 254.

64 Brereton, "Popular Educators," 11.

65 "Statistics Show," *The Pilot* 15 (April 1935): 204.

66 "Catalogue Information Regarding the School," *School and Church* 2 (May 1917): 44–47; "Faculty and Courses," *The Pilot* 6 (October 1925): 4; Advertisement, *The Pilot* 11 (January 1931): 98.

67 "Northwestern Bible School Graduates," 83–84.

68 "A Survey of the Student Body," *The Pilot* 16 (March 1936): 183; "The Thrilling Story of Northwestern Schools," *The Pilot* 20 (December 1939): 67, 78; "Northwestern Employment Department," 295.

69 "Thrilling Story," 67; "Survey," 183.

70 "DOLLARS in your Pocket! Sell the New SCRAPE-EZ!," *The Pilot* 19 (February 1939): 160; "Northwestern Employment Department," 295.

71 "Northwestern Employment Department," 295.

72 Anonymous correspondent, completed questionnaire to author, August 1, 1986; Glenn Erickson, completed questionnaire to author, August 5, 1986.

73 Thirteen women graduates responded to my request for information regarding Northwestern, and they were uniformly and completely positive in their comments about Riley and his school. There were no complaints about sexist treatment at Northwestern, although one woman noted that after graduating "there was a decided difference in what I earned" as a missionary and pastor "in comparison with what a male was paid." Anonymous correspondent, completed questionnaire to author, August 6, 1986.

74 *The Pilot* 21 (November 1940): 60; E. Flora Roberts, "Frazee," *North Star Baptist* 12 (October 1927): 14–15; *The Pilot* 16 (August 1936): 333; *The Pilot* 13 (May 1933): 244; *The Pilot* 20 (May 1940): 244.

75 Minnie S. Nelson, "The Story of One of Our Women Preachers as She Herself Tells It," *The Standard* (September 1986): 8, as reprinted in Janette Hassey, *No Time for Silence: Evangelical Women in Public Ministry around the Turn of the Century* (Grand Rapids, Mich.: Zondervan Co., 1986), 60.

76 Reprinted in *The Pilot* 3 (February 8, 1923): 38. See also "Evangelism in Minnesota for the Season of 1916–17," *School and Church,* 1 (November 1916): 8; *The Pilot* 8 (April 1928): 13; *The Pilot* 8 (May 1936): 246; *The Pilot* 24 (January 1944): 117.

77 C. W. Foley, "Have You a Question?" *The Pilot* 12 (September 1931): 335.

78 [William Bell Riley?], "Further Development," *The Pilot* 15 (July 1935): 274. It should be noted that in this same article Riley expressly condoned the practice of women serving as missionaries. For a brief discussion of Riley's earlier views on woman's role, see Hassey, *No Time for Silence,* 23–24. Hassey notes that Riley supported female suffrage; however, sometime during the 1920s Riley changed his mind on this issue. For example, see William Bell Riley, "The Ideal Family," *The Pilot* 12 (September 1929): 10.

79   Hassey, *No Time for Silence*, 10, 137–43. It should be noted that because Hassey
     views fundamentalism as originating at the turn of the century, she sees the fun-
     damentalist movement as predating the narrowing of public ministry opportuni-
     ties for women, which occurred in the 1920s. I would argue that what she sees
     as fundamentalism is more accurately defined as proto-fundamentalism; hence,
     I see the restrictions on women as part and parcel of the emergent fundamentalist
     movement of the 1920s.

80   W. F. McMillan, "Have You A Question?" *The Pilot* 15 (February 1935): 143; Wil-
     liam Bell Riley, "Editorial Comment," *The Pilot* 17 (January 1937): 108.

Chapter 5: The Empire

1   Ernest Sandeen, *The Roots of Fundamentalism: British and American Millenarian-
    ism, 1800–1930* (Chicago: University of Chicago Press, 1970), 241–43.

2   While the college yearbook, *The Scroll*, occasionally included information about
    Northwestern alumni, most of the following statistical information about the spread
    of Northwestern-trained ministers, missionaries, and evangelists throughout North
    America comes from Northwestern's monthly magazine, *The Pilot*. I read every
    issue of *The Pilot*, from its first issue in 1920 through the issues published in 1948,
    one year after Riley's death. The magazine was a gold mine of information about
    the particulars of Riley's empire. Among other things, *The Pilot* kept remarkably
    close tabs on those alumni who were employed in church-related occupations. Con-
    versely, the magazine provided almost no information on graduates who were not
    in such jobs. This is no surprise, considering that Northwestern's raison d'être was
    the training of workers to serve in the advance of militant orthodoxy.

    From the information I gathered from *The Pilot*, I constructed a chart of Riley's
    empire: where evangelists, missionaries, and pastors were laboring; what missions
    agency they were working for or what church they were pastoring (and the de-
    nominational affiliation); and how long they stayed in one spot. I did not include
    all Northwesterners who were engaged in religious work; I did not keep track of
    the comings and goings of Northwestern alumni who served as youth workers,
    child evangelism directors, and the like. Nor did I include in my survey assistant
    pastors, primarily because I was not always certain that an individual so titled
    was more than just a part-time aide to the minister. My concern was with those
    alumni who were engaged in what is traditionally labeled "full-time Christian ser-
    vice" (although at times these alumni held other jobs) — pastors, evangelists, and
    missionaries.

    The result is a chart that approximates the spread of Northwestern influence
    in the United States. I say "approximates," because the chart is certainly flawed.
    For example, some individuals almost assuredly escaped the attention of *The Pilot*.
    (It does seem, however, that often these individuals were outside Northwestern's
    upper midwestern empire.) More often, gaps in personal histories occurred, and
    I was forced to devise methods to deal with the missing information. Sometimes
    an individual ceased to appear in the magazine altogether; when this happened
    I generally added three years to the final citation and then stopped, even though
    the individual may have still been working at the same church or for the same
    missions agency. Sometimes years passed without *The Pilot's* referring to an in-
    dividual, and then when he or she was finally mentioned, it was in reference to

work in a new location. If the text gave no clue about the date of the move, I assumed that most of the years in the gap period were spent at the last pastorate, for it seems that a graduate's move was often the occasion for a report in *The Pilot*.

If anything, the omissions in *The Pilot* lead me to underestimate the number of Northwestern alumni in religious work. (The chart is not reprinted due to the many omissions.) On the other hand, *The Pilot's* detailed information about alumni occupations enabled me to make some rough but helpful statistical observations about the locale, nature, and length of Christian service performed by Northwesterners, particularly Northwesterners serving in the upper Midwest.

3   "The Northwestern Theological Seminary and the State Baptist Convention," *The Pilot* 23 (January 1943): 109. It appears that the total given in this article did not include Northwestern missionaries in Canada, of whom there were at least eight in the mid-1940s.

4   William Bell Riley, "The Lighthouse of the Northwest," *The Pilot* 23 (March 1943): 163.

5   "Northern Minnesota—A True Mission Field," *The Pilot* 11 (December 1930): 86.

6   Hazel Gardner, "The Gospel in Northern Minnesota," *The Pilot* 16 (February 1936): 145; William Shillingsburg, quoted in "Northern Minnesota," 86.

7   Margaret Hendrickson, Letter to *The Pilot*, *The Pilot* [10 (March 1930)?]: 183; A. H. Norum, "Lo, the Poor Indian," *The Pilot*, 11 (May 1931): 249; *The Pilot* 13 (August 1933): 316.

8   I arrived at these totals by subtracting from the number of Northwestern pastors and missionaries serving in the upper Midwest (see table) those individuals who were working for a missions agency or teaching at a Bible school. I was not always able to ascertain denominational affiliations. Hence, it is possible that a few individuals I have included in this ministerial category were actually employed by missions agencies or were traveling evangelists. But the possibility that I overestimated the number of ministers is more than compensated for by the near-certainty that I completely missed some individuals in my count of Northwestern alumni serving in church-related occupations. The totals given here (and elsewhere in this chapter) regarding Northwestern-trained ministers in the upper Midwest differ slightly from the figures in my June 1988 *Church History* article. This is because in the interim I discovered further data on Northwestern alumni.

9   As noted above, I was not always able to find the denominational affiliation of a church at which a particular Northwesterner was serving as minister. These percentages thus refer to the proportion of Baptist churches among churches for which I was able to ascertain denominational affiliation. Nondenominational churches were included in this pool.

10   William Bell Riley, "We Met a Midwest Crisis," *The Northwestern Pilot* 28 (October 1947): 12; William Bell Riley, "Why Build Memorial Hall?" *The Pilot* 22 (May 1942): 235.

11   Hugh Hartshorne and Milton C. Froyd, *Theological Education in the Northern Baptist Convention: A Survey* (Philadelphia: Judson Press, 1945), 123. Donald Tinder has noted that Moody Bible Institute contributed to the total of Bible school graduates serving in pastorates in the upper Midwest, "but undoubtedly Northwestern was the biggest single contributor." Donald Tinder, "Fundamentalist Baptists in the Northern and Western United States, 1920–1950" (Ph.D. diss., Yale University, 1969), 259.

12   In computing this average, I excluded stints of working for a missions agency or Bible school, as well as pastoral stints for which I was forced to assign arbitrarily a termination date, those without a termination date (those that appeared to last past 1946), and those about which I lacked certain information regarding the church (location and/or denominational affiliation).

13   "Our Marching Clergymen," *The Pilot* 16 (August 1936): 307.

14   Fred Julius, interview with author, Shoreview, Minn., August 25, 1986. For an interesting discussion of the problems facing village and country churches, see Hartshorne and Froyd, *Theological Education,* 108–11, 117–20.

15   *The Pilot* 10 (January 1930): 132; *The Pilot* 11 (July 1931): 301; *The Pilot* 14 (January 1934): 114; *The Pilot* 16 (August 1936): 333; *The Pilot* 19 (January 1939): 118; *The Northwestern Pilot* 25 (April 1945): 214; *The Northwestern Pilot* 26 (November 1945): 44.

16   Granting the problems in using current data, I used Rand-McNally's 1980 list of metropolitan areas to indicate whether Riley's empire became more or less urban over time. I decided that to include Minnesota would skew the analysis, because some of the Minnesota ministers were current Northwestern students who were temporarily serving in Twin Cities pulpits as part of their "practical work experience"; upon graduation, many would become pastors of rural churches. Excluding Minnesota and excluding those ministers working for a missions agency, in the upper Midwest (Iowa, Nebraska, North Dakota, South Dakota, and Wisconsin) 6 percent of Northwestern ministers in Riley's empire were in metropolitan areas in 1925, while in 1945 the figure had jumped to 25 percent. *World Atlas: Census Edition* (New York, 1981), 123–46.

17   Sandeen, *Roots,* esp. xi–xii; and George M. Marsden, *Fundamentalism and American Culture: The Shaping of Twentieth-Century Evangelicalism, 1870–1925* (New York: Oxford University Press, 1980), 188, 201–2.

18   "Northwestern Theological Seminary and the State Baptist Convention," 99; Henry Van Kommer, "'Northwesterners' in Minnesota," *The Pilot* 18 (October 1937): 22.

19   Van Kommer, "Northwesterners," 22.

20   William Bell Riley, "Dr. Riley and His Boys: Allan Williams at Luverne," *The Pilot* 23 (November 1942): 56.

21   For extended discussions of this reform effort, see William L. Bowers, *The Country Life Movement in America, 1900–1920* (Port Washington, N.Y.: Kennikat Press, 1974); David Danbom, *The Resisted Revolution: Urban America and the Industrialization of Agriculture, 1900–1930* (Ames: University of Iowa Press, 1979); James H. Madison, "Reformers and the Rural Church," *Journal of American History* 73 (December 1986): 645–68; Mark Rich, *The Rural Church Movement* (Columbia, Mo.: Juniper Knoll Press, 1957); Merwin Swanson, "The 'Country Life Movement' and the American Churches," *Church History* 46 (1977): 358–73.

22   Madison, "Reformers," 665–68; Bowers, *Country Life,* 114. For two rather patronizing references to the resistance of rural people against the consolidation of their churches during the Great Depression, see the following volumes in the series *Studies on the Social Aspects of the Depression:* Samuel C. Kincheloe, *Research Memorandum on Religion in the Depression* (New York: Social Science Research Council, 1937), 134–35; and Dwight Sanderson, *Research Memorandum on Rural Life in the Depression* (New York: Social Science Research Council, 1937), 91–95.

23   Hartshorne and Froyd, *Theological Education,* 33–42; Tinder, "Baptists," 162–66.

24 Van Kommer, "Northwesterners," 22; *The Pilot* 20 (January 1940): 116–17; *The Pilot* 20 (June 1940): 277.

25 Harriet Gleason, "Pioneering in Central Wisconsin," *The Pilot* 17 (October 1936): 13; "Wisconsin Rural Mission," *The Pilot* 20 (May 1940): 227–28.

26 Gleason, "Pioneering," 14.

27 For examples, see "Pastors' Conferences," *The Pilot* 11 (May 1931): 248; "Iowa Fundamentalists," *The Pilot* 22 (May 1942): 251; "Business Meeting," *The Pilot* 8 (December 1927): 15; "Introducing Alumni Bible Conference," *The Pilot* 9 (February 1929): 5.

28 For examples, see "News Items," *The Pilot* 15 (August 1935): 295; "Chetek Baptist Assembly," *The Pilot* 23 (October 1942): 28; "East Iowa Bible Camp," *The Northwestern Pilot* 24 (September 1944): 388. For an interesting discussion of fundamentalist youth camps, see Tinder, "Baptists," 180–81.

29 "Northwesterners, We Are Proud of You," *The Northwestern Pilot* 25 (October 1944): 17.

30 Frank Bass, "Daily Vacation Bible Schools: Northwestern's Contribution to This Great Movement," *The Pilot* 22 (May 1942): 231.

31 "The Northwestern Bible Training School Bible Conferences," *School and Church,* 2 (July–September 1919): 192–93.

32 William Bell Riley, "Editorial Comment," *The Pilot* 17 (January 1937): 108; "Northwestern's Field Evangelist," *The Pilot* 17 (February 1937): 156.

33 "The Northwestern Bible Conference," *The Pilot* 19 (March 1939): 178; "Medicine Lake Bible Conference," *The Pilot* 14 (May 1934): 233.

34 "The Northwestern Bible Conference," *The Pilot* 13 (July 1933): 302.

35 "Summer School at Medicine Lake, August 14–28, 1939," *The Pilot* 19 (July 1939): 292; "Northwestern Bible Conference," *The Pilot* 13 (May 1933): 241; David Farrington, interview with Dell G. Johnson, as reported in letter from Johnson to author, July 3, 1984.

36 "Extension Classes in Teacher Training," *The Pilot* 18 (November 1937): 53; "Our Layman's Course," *The Pilot* 7 (May 1927): 4.

37 "Northwestern's Evening School," *The Pilot* 20 (November 1939): 53; "Modernism in the Minneapolis Church Federation," *The Pilot* 16 (October 1935): 3.

38 "Extension Classes," 53; Mrs. E. P. Barrett, "Pedagogy, Unit V of Teacher Training Course, Evening School," *The Pilot* 18 (January 1938): 109.

39 Marie Acomb Riley, "From the Editor's Desk," *The Pilot* 22 (October 1941): 3; "The President of Northwestern," *The Pilot* 13 (October 1932): 3; *The Pilot* 14 (July 1934): 290.

40 M. A. Riley, "Editor's Desk," 3; John Lundberg, "Do You Let Your People Know?" *The Pilot* 24 (December 1943): 69; L. C. Masted, "The Successful Church," *The Northwestern Pilot* 25 (June 1945): 265–66, 280.

41 "Don't Forget to Write," *The Pilot* 8 (January 1928): 15.

42 J. W. Welsh, "Northwestern's Extension Department," *The Pilot* 9 (April 1929): 6.

43 "Suggested Sources of Revenue," *The Pilot* 23 (December 1942): 76; "First Annual Northwestern Day," *The Pilot* 21 (September 1941): 351; "The Northwestern Bible and Missionary Training School," *School and Church* 1 (August 1917): 144.

44 "A Survey of the Student Body," *The Pilot* 16 (March 1936): 182.

45   William Bell Riley, "Good Prospects for Churches without Pastors," *The Pilot* 14
      (October 1933): 10; William Bell Riley, "The Demand for Ministers," *The Pilot*
      21 (June 1941): 259.

46   "Progress of Memorial Hall," *The Pilot* 23 (November 1942): 56; William Bell Riley,
      Looking for a Pastor? Perhaps We Can Help You (Minneapolis, [1942?]).

47   "Progress of Memorial Hall," *The Pilot* 23 (August 1943): 315; Riley, "Demand
      for Ministers," 259.

48   Stanley A. Anderson, completed questionnaire to author, July 26, 1986. Other
      alumni also mentioned pheasant hunting with Riley, including George Wilson,
      who was Riley's assistant in the 1940s. Wilson recalled: "Many times in the fall
      Dr. Riley would call me in the afternoon and say, 'George, let's go get 'em.' This
      meant hunting pheasants in Golden Valley near his home. In his 80's he could still
      shoot birds on the wing while I was just getting my gun up." George Wilson, com-
      pleted questionnaire to author, October 15, 1986.

49   Examples: William Bell Riley, "Twelve Days with Northwesterners," *The Pilot* 22
      (August 1942): 311; William Bell Riley, "Northwesterners Visited on Our Western
      Trip," *The Northwestern Pilot* 24 (April 1944): 227; Marie Acomb Riley, "My Day,"
      The Northwestern Pilot 25 (August 1945): 307, 319.

50   Richard V. Clearwaters, interview with Dell G. Johnson, as reported in letter from
      Johnson to author, July 3, 1984.

51   William Bell Riley, "Northwestern Boys as Church Builders," *The Pilot* 17 (August
      1937): 341–42.

52   The research in this section was made possible by an Albert J. Beveridge Grant
      for Research in American History, awarded by the American Historical Associa-
      tion. It was also made possible by the current pastor, Rev. Thorin Anderson, who
      graciously allowed me to examine all the extant records at the First Baptist Church
      of Granite Falls.

53   Carl and Amy Narvestad, *Granite Falls, 1879–1979: A Century's Search for Qual-
      ity of Life* (Granite Falls, Minn.: Granite Falls City Centennial Committee, 1979),
      1–20, 77–83.

54   *First Baptist Church of Granite Falls, Minnesota: Its 75th Anniversary* (Granite
      Falls, Minn.: Granite Falls Tribune, 1953), 4–7; Carl and Amy Narvestad, *A His-
      tory of Yellow Medicine County, 1872–1972* (Granite Falls, Minn.: Yellow Medi-
      cine County Historical Society, 1972), 174–75.

55   Minutes of Church Meetings of September 20, 1913, October 1, 1919, January 22,
      1920, and February 3, 1915; First Baptist Church of Granite Falls, Granite Falls,
      Minn.

56   Narvestad and Narvestad, *Yellow Medicine County*, 175; "Baptists Are Consider-
      ing Sale of Church Property," *Granite Falls Tribune*, March 2, 1927, p. 1; "Abstract
      of Baptist Church Property Dates Back to 1869," *Granite Falls Tribune*, March 23,
      1927, p. 1.

57   "Baptist Congregation Votes to Retain Church Property," *Granite Falls Tribune*,
      April 13, 1927, p. 1; Harvey Hill and Linnea Hill, interview with author, Roseville,
      Minn. June 7, 1986.

58   "Baptists Have Called Pastor," *Granite Falls Tribune*, September 7, 1927, p. 1; "Fed-
      erated Churches Hold the Last United Service," *Granite Falls Tribune*, Septem-
      ber 28, 1927, p. 1; *First Baptist Church*, 8.

59   "Church News," *Granite Falls Tribune*, May 23, 1929, p. 10; Minutes of Church

Meetings of June 29, 1930, and November 4, 1930, First Baptist Church of Granite Falls.

60 Until the early 1940s the Granite Falls pastor also pastored the Sparta church. The minister generally devoted most of his time to the Granite Falls work. For instance, according to the terms set forth when Nelson Crow was hired in 1939, "Sparta and Granite [Falls] would together call a pastor and that Sparta [would] have four services a month . . . [and] two days of visitation from the pastor." Crow's successor, Fred Julius, terminated the dual pastorate arrangement, resigning from the Sparta church in December 1942. Minutes of Church Meetings of June 29, 1939, July 2, 1939, July 6, 1939, December 30, 1942, January 17, 1943, First Baptist Church of Granite Falls.

61 Joe Pates, interview with author, Granite Falls, Minn., August 26, 1986; *First Baptist Church*, 8–11; George M. Wilson, letter to author, January 12, 1988.

62 This is not to say that there were not complaints about the brevity of pastors' stays. In his 1947–1948 "Report of the Board of Deacons" chair Elsworth Sandberg observed that "in the past there has been a shifting of pastors, each one staying two years or less. I do not believe short pastorates build churches. . . . We hope Rev. and Mrs. Alf Skognes will stay at least five years with us on this field." When Sandberg made this observation, Skognes had been in Granite Falls two years; in less than a year the Northwestern-trained minister was gone.

63 Joe Pates interview; George Knutson, interview with author, Maynard, Minn. August 26, 1986; "Annual Letter of the First Baptist Church of Granite Falls to the Southwestern Baptist Association, 1937"; "Annual Letter of the First Baptist Church of Granite Falls to the Southwestern Baptist Association, 1947."

64 A perusal of *Granite Falls Tribunes* in the late 1920s, 1930s, and 1940s reveals that the First Baptist Church was usually the only church conducting midweek services and sometimes the only church holding a Sunday evening service. The other churches included a Catholic church, three Lutheran churches, and the Congregational church.

65 "Church," *Granite Falls Tribune*, August 31, 1932, p. 7.

66 Raymond Anderson, interview with author, Golden Valley, Minn., August 25, 1986; "Church News," *Granite Falls Tribune*, June 20, 1928, p. 8; Minutes of Church Meeting of May 3, 1945, First Baptist Church of Granite Falls.

67 "Church News," *Granite Falls Tribune*, June 12, 1929, p. 3; Minutes of Church Meeting of March 6, 1944, First Baptist Church of Granite Falls; "Missionary from India Will Speak," *Granite Falls Tribune*, February 7, 1933, p. 7.

68 Minutes of Church Meeting of June 6, 1944, May 14, 1947, May 12, 1948, First Baptist Church of Granite Falls; "Church News," *Granite Falls Tribune*, March 28, 1928; Fred Julius interview; Raymond Anderson interview.

69 Advertisement, *Granite Falls Tribune*, March 16, 1933, p. 4; "Meetings at First Baptist Church," *Granite Falls Tribune*, March 23, 1933, p. 6; "Soldier Evangelist to End Series of Meetings Sunday," *Granite Falls Tribune*, March 30, 1933, p. 4; *Granite Falls Tribune*, April 10, 1933, p. 2. Much to the chagrin of the Granite Falls church members, eight months after these revival services Stauffer was arrested for the robbery of a Rochester, Minn., drugstore. In the trial it came out that Stauffer had become distraught over the fact that his son had contracted polio. Stauffer began to drink very heavily, and according to his testimony at the trial, it was in a drunken haze that he robbed the drugstore. Stauffer resigned his Blooming

Prairie, Minn., pastorate; heeding the advice of Northwestern alumni John Sie-
mens and Dudley Thimsen, among others, the church magnanimously voted to
refuse Stauffer's resignation. Joe Pates interview; "Pastor Is Given Suspended Jail
Term on Charge," *Austin Herald,* December 13, 1933, pp. 1, 7; "Column Left . . . ,"
Blooming Prairie Times, December 14, 1933; "Baptists Support Pastor; Reject His
Resignation," *Blooming Prairie Times,* December 21, 1933, p. 1.

70   Minutes of Church Meetings of October 25, 1934, July 17, 1934, January 23, 1944,
and December 26, 1943, First Baptist Church of Granite Falls.

71   This information comes from a review of church minutes and the annual financial
reports from the 1930s and 1940s. Because the financial records are not complete,
it is possible (but doubtful) that there was a year in which First Baptist did not
send money to Northwestern.

72   "Annual Letter of the First Baptist Church of Granite Falls to the Southwestern
Baptist Association, 1930"; "Annual Letter of the First Baptist Church of Granite
Falls to the Southwestern Baptist Association, 1932"; Minutes of Church Meeting
of November 25, 1938, First Baptist Church of Granite Falls.

73   Raymond Anderson interview.

74   Riley presented the ordination sermons for Arthur LeMaster and Raymond Anderson. Robert Moyer, dean of the Bible School, preached the ordination sermon for
Harvey Hill. *First Baptist Church,* 8–10; Minutes of Church Meeting of October 19,
1945, First Baptist Church of Granite Falls.

75   "Granite People Throng Church to Hear Dr. Riley," *Granite Falls Tribune,* August 7, 1929, p. 1.

76   Harvey Hill and Linnea Hill interview.

77   Ibid.

78   *First Baptist Church,* 10; Joe Pates interview; Minutes of Church Meetings of
May 4, 1944, October 25, 1945, October 30, 1947, and April 29, 1948, First Baptist
Church of Granite Falls. In an August 17, 1987, note to the author, Alf Skognes,
who pastored the Granite Falls church from 1946 to 1949, asserted that he had
opposed the church's separation from the Northern Baptist Convention. In this
instance, thanks to two decades of close affiliation with Northwestern, the congregation was more in keeping with Riley and his cadre than the Bible school alumnus in its pulpit.

79   "Minutes of Recognition Council Held at Granite Falls," March 15, 1966.

80   Thorin Anderson, interview with author, Granite Falls, Minn., August 26, 1986;
Thorin Anderson, letter to author, August 12, 1987.

Chapter 6: The Revolt

1   Henry Van Kommer, "'Northwesterners' in Minnesota," *The Pilot* 18 (October 1937):
15, 22.

2   Samuel P. Hays, "The Structure of Environmental Politics since World War II,"
Journal of Social History 14 (Summer 1981): 719–21, 731; Samuel P. Hays, "The
Social Analysis of American Political History, 1880–1920," *Political Science Quar-
terly* 80 (September 1965): 373–94.

3   Hugh Hartshorne and Milton C. Froyd, *Theological Education in the Northern
Baptist Convention: A Survey* (Philadelphia: Judson Press, 1945), 103–4. This figure underestimates the number of Bible institute graduates holding Northern Bap-

tist Convention pastorates, because it only refers to individuals whose education ended at a Bible institute. But as the authors of the study noted, in the 1930s and 1940s Bible institute graduates increasingly went "on after graduation to receive a theological degree." These individuals were not included in the 21.6 percent designated as Bible institute graduates. As noted in the text, Northwestern Evangelical Theological Seminary was one of the seminaries that Bible school graduates attended, since it was founded in 1935.

4   Hartshorne and Froyd, *Theological Education*, 103–4.

5   *Annual of the Northern Baptist Convention, 1916* (Philadelphia: American Baptist Publication Society, 1916), 214.

6   *Annual of the Northern Baptist Convention, 1935* (Philadelphia: American Baptist Publication Society, 1935), 151.

7   William Bell Riley, "Favor for the Forum," *The Pilot* 17 (May 1937): 253; William Bell Riley, "A Standardized Ministry," *The Pilot* 21 (July 1941): 290–92. In response to this familiar argument regarding the apostles, proponents of standardization quipped that "if for three years they could have sat under Christ's personal instruction, they would have been most happy to forego their collegiate and theological studies." *Annual of the Northern Baptist Convention, 1917* (Philadelphia: American Baptist Publication Society, 1917), 35.

8   William Bell Riley, "Bible Schools and the Standardization of the Ministry," *School and Church* 2 (July–September 1918): 23–26.

9   William Bell Riley, "The Baptist Ministers' Council," *The Pilot* 15 (April 1935): 183–84. See also Riley, "Favor for the Forum," 253; Riley, "Standardized Ministry," 290–92.

10 *Annual of the Northern Baptist Convention, 1916*, 214, 217; *Annual of the Northern Baptist Convention, 1917*, 34–36.

11 *Annual of the Northern Baptist Convention, 1918* (Philadelphia: American Baptist Publication Society, 1918), 87–90, 94; Robert Sheldon McBirnie, "Basic Issues in the Fundamentalism of William Bell Riley" (Ph.D. diss., State University of Iowa, 1952), 118–19.

12 *Annual of the Northern Baptist Convention, 1924* (Philadelphia: American Baptist Publication Society, 1924), 267–72.

13 For examples, see *Annual of the Northern Baptist Convention, 1928* (Philadelphia: American Baptist Publication Society, 1928), 187–93; *Annual of the Northern Baptist Convention, 1929* (Philadelphia: American Baptist Publication Society, 1929), 70–72; *Annual of the Northern Baptist Convention, 1931* (Philadelphia: American Baptist Publication Society, 1931), 88–89; *Annual of the Northern Baptist Convention, 1933* (Philadelphia: American Baptist Publication Society, 1933), 163–64; *Annual of the Northern Baptist Convention, 1935*, 151.

14 *Annual of the Northern Baptist Convention, 1938* (Philadelphia: American Baptist Publication Society, 1938), 133–34.

15 *Minnesota Baptist Annual, 1930*, 101–06 (mimeographed); "Friends of Northwestern," *The Pilot* 10 (January 1930): 98.

16 Richard V. Clearwaters, interview with Dell G. Johnson, reported in letter from Johnson to author, July 3, 1984.

17 "The Sixty-sixth Annual Convention," *North Star Baptist* 11 (November 1926): 3; unnamed Minnesota Baptist activist, Report on W. B. Riley, [1945?], Box 6:

"Letters from Leaders," Anna Canada Swain Papers, American Baptist Historical Society, Rochester, N.Y.

18 "Carleton College," *North Star Baptist* 11 (December 1926): 10–11; "Alumni Attend Baptist Convention," *The Pilot* 9 (November 1928): 17.

19 *Minnesota Baptist Annual, 1930,* 17; Dell G. Johnson, "Fundamentalist Responses in Minnesota to the Developing New Evangelicalism" (Th.D. diss., Central Baptist Seminary, 1982), 53–54.

20 Paul M. Harrison, *Authority and Power in the Free Church Tradition: A Social Case Study of the American Baptist Convention* (Princeton, N.J.: Princeton University Press, 1959), 195–97; *Minnesota Baptist Annual, 1935,* 17–25 (mimeographed). The Dane-Norwegian Conference, the Swedish Baptist Conference, and German Baptist Conference were not included in this examination of Minnesota associations.

21 Harvey Hill and Linnea Hill, interview with author, Roseville, Minn., June 7, 1986.

22 *Minnesota Baptist Annual, 1936,* 12–13 (mimeographed); William Bell Riley, "Wherein Fundamentalists Have Failed," *The Pilot* 23 (July 1943): 296; William Bell Riley, "Minnesota State Secretary," *The Northwestern Pilot* 26 (August 1946): 296.

23 Riley, "Minnesota State Secretary," 296.

24 George Knutson, interview with author, Maynard, Minn., August 26, 1986. Northwestern alumnus Raymond Anderson, who pastored Minnesota Baptist Convention churches in these years, recalled that "while he operated behind the scenes, there was no question that Dr. Riley was the leader of the state convention." Raymond Anderson, interview with author, Golden Valley, Minn., August 25, 1986.

25 As mentioned in a previous note, this [1945?] report can be found in the folder, "Letters from Leaders," in Box 6 of the Anna Canada Swain Papers at the American Baptist Historical Society in Rochester, N.Y. Ms. Swain was president of the Northern Baptist Convention in the mid-1940s.

26 Herbert Caneday, completed questionnaire to author, September 19, 1986. Also Stanley A. Anderson, completed questionnaire to author, July 26, 1986.

27 George Knutson interview; William Bell Riley, "The Denominational Division (Among Baptists)," *The Pilot* 20 (January 1940): 105. Riley does not specifically mention the Canby church in this article. The author is indebted to Rev. George Knutson for filling in the details.

28 In a letter appended to the questionnaire that he sent to the author on September 19, 1986, alumnus Herbert Caneday, who pastored three different churches in the MBC in the 1940s, made this interesting observation: "Dr. Riley's influence in Minnesota tended to strengthen and encourage, from early on — Fundamentalism . . . *within* the framework of the established denominations. The net result of that was a large proportion of theologically sound Baptist Churches within the MBC. . . . By comparison, the influence of the GARB [General Association of Regular Baptists, a fundamentalist denomination that originated in a separation from the NBC in the 1930s] remained very weak numerically in this state. The geographical areas that are farther removed from Minnesota were less influenced by his stay-in-and-clean-it-up stance. Both Iowa and Wisconsin have more GARB churches, while Illinois and Michigan have still greater numbers."

29 William Bell Riley, "The Minnesota Baptist Convention," *The Pilot* 23 (November

1942): 35; William Bell Riley, "Fundamentalism vs. Federal Church," *The Pilot* 23 (November 1942): 35–36.

30 William Bell Riley, "Fixed Points in Baptist Polity," *The Pilot* 23 (April 1943): 198.

31 Harrison, *Authority and Power,* 150–56.

32 Joel A. Carpenter, "From Fundamentalism to the New Evangelical Coalition," in *Evangelicalism and Modern America,* ed. George M. Marsden (Grand Rapids, Mich.: Wm. B. Eerdmans Co., 1984), 11; George M. Marsden, *Reforming Fundamentalism: Fuller Seminary and the New Evangelicalism* (Grand Rapids, Mich.: Wm. B. Eerdmans, 1987), 47.

33 Marsden, *Reforming Fundamentalism,* 48–50; Joel A. Carpenter, "The Fundamentalist Leaven and the Rise of an Evangelical United Front," in *The Evangelical Tradition in America,* ed. Leonard I. Sweet (Macon, Ga.: Mercer University Press, 1984), 257–88. It should be noted that one year before the establishment of the NAE, separatist fundamentalists led by Carl McIntire had founded their own organization, the American Council of Christian Churches. As George Marsden has pointed out, at the time "no one seems to have regarded the formation of the NAE [in 1942] as a sign that 'evangelicals' were now breaking from 'fundamentalists' over the principle of separatism." Marsden, *Reforming Fundamentalism,* 48. But while it was not seen as such at the time, the creation of two separate fundamentalist organizations portended the division to come. For more on this rift, see the epilogue.

34 Bruce Shelley, "The Rise of Evangelical Youth Movements," *Fides et Historia* 18 (January 1986): 47–63.

35 Joel A. Carpenter, "The Renewal of American Fundamentalism, 1930–1945" (Ph.D. diss., Johns Hopkins University, 1984), 225–26. See also Ralph D. Winter, *The Twenty-five Unbelievable Years, 1945–1969* (South Pasadena, Calif.: William Carey Library, 1970), esp. 47–73.

36 Frederick Anderson, chair, "A Statement by the Foreign Mission Society," *The Watchman-Examiner* 11 (November 15, 1923): 1468; Frederick Anderson, chair, "A Statement by the Board of Managers of the American Baptist Foreign Mission Society," *The Watchman-Examiner* 12 (January 17, 1924): 82–85; Homer DeWilton Brookins, "The Northern Baptist Convention: Milwaukee, May 26–June 3," *The Watchman-Examiner* 12 (June 12, 1924): 749; Donald Tinder, "Fundamentalist Baptists in the Northern and Western United States" (Ph.D. diss., Yale University, 1969), 333–34.

37 William Bell Riley, "The 'Inclusive Policy' Illustrated, and Disowned," *The Northwestern Pilot* 24 (August 1944): 367.

38 William Bell Riley, "Rule and Ruin: Dr. Fridell Chosen Baptist Foreign Secretary," *The Pilot* 23 (April 1943): 203; Bruce Shelley, *A History of Conservative Baptists* (Wheaton, Ill.: Wheaton Press, 1971), 30.

39 It should be noted that on Riley's home turf a group existed that followed a path similar to that of the Conservative Baptists — the Swedish Baptists. Organized in 1856 and strongest (as might be expected) in Minnesota, the small Swedish Baptist General Conference was a "participating organization" within the Northern Baptist Convention. As such, Swedish missionaries were under the supervision of the convention's Foreign Mission Society. But in 1944 General Conference Baptists, unhappy with the denomination's "inclusive policy" regarding missionaries, separated from the Northern Baptist Convention and established their own indepen-

dent organization. When in 1947 the Conservative Baptists were preparing to expand their mission society into a full-scale separate organization, there was talk
about affiliating with the Swedish Baptists. But according to the historian of the
Conservative Baptists, "the fact that the Conservatives already had their own missions society, and the fact of the Swedish linguistic background, kept the two groups
from organized unity." Shelley, *Conservative Baptists,* 52–54.

40   William Bell Riley, "The Conservative Baptist Foreign Board," *The Pilot* 23 (August 1943): 307; Shelley, *Conservative Baptists,* 30–34.

41   Richard V. Clearwaters, "Are We Unfair to Dr. E. A. Fridell?" *The Pilot* 23 (May
1943): 227; "Resolution Passed by the Minnesota Baptist Convention Executive
Committee," *The Northwestern Pilot* 24 (March 1944): 191.

42   Shelley, *Conservative Baptists,* 38–44.

43   William Bell Riley, "The Conservative Baptist Foreign Board," *The Pilot* 23 (August 1943): 307; Tinder, "Baptists," 351–53.

44   *Year Book of the Northern Baptist Convention, 1945* (Philadelphia: American Baptist Publication Society, 1945), 49–51.

45   *Year Book of the Northern Baptist Convention, 1944* (Philadelphia: American Baptist Publication Society, 1944), 45–46. Riley apparently understood the potential
import of this resolution. See William Bell Riley, "Voting in the Northern Baptist
Convention," *The Northwestern Pilot* 26 (May 1946): 246.

46   William Bell Riley, "Minnesota Plan neither Iconoclastic nor Revolutionary," *The
Northwestern Pilot* 26 (February 1946): 146–47; *Minnesota Baptist Annual, 1945,*
5–6 (mimeographed); McBirnie, "Riley," 123.

47   Riley, "Minnesota State Secretary," 296; *Minnesota Baptist Annual, 1945,* 5 (mimeographed).

48   Riley, "Minnesota State Secretary," 296.

49   Letter from E. H. Rhoades, Jr., to W. B. Riley, February 16, 1946. In the same vein:
letter from E. H. Rhoades, Jr., to W. B. Riley, July 24, 1945; letter from Reuben
Nelson to W. B. Riley, August 10, 1945; letter from E. H. Rhoades, Jr., to W. B.
Riley, August 29, 1945; letter from Reuben Nelson to W. B. Riley, April 15, 1946.
Box 6: "Minnesota," Reuben E. Nelson Papers, American Baptist Historical So-
ciety, Rochester, N.Y.

50   Letter from Reuben E. Nelson to E. H. Rhoades, Jr., May 7, 1946, Nelson Papers,
Box 6: "Minnesota."

51   Letter from E. H. Rhoades, Jr., to W. B. Riley, February 16, 1946, Nelson Papers,
Box 6: "Minnesota."

52   This is documented in Box 6 of the Nelson Papers.

53   Letter from W. B. Riley to Reuben E. Nelson, May 1, 1946, Nelson Papers, Box
6: "Minnesota."

54   Letter from E. H. Rhoades, Jr., to Reuben E. Nelson, May 7, 1946, Nelson Papers.

55   Harold E. Fey, "Fundamentalists Lose Grip on Northern Baptist Convention," *The
Christian Century* 63 (June 5, 1946): 725. This is an insightful piece, but the title
indicates that Fey or a *Christian Century* editor believed that before the Grand
Rapids convention the fundamentalists had controlled the NBC, which is a pa-
tently false proposition.

56   *Year Book of the Northern Baptist Convention, 1946* (Philadelphia: American Baptist Foreign Mission Society, 1946), 48, 96–97, 148–66; John W. Bradbury, "Report
of the Northern Baptist Convention," *The Watchman-Examiner* 34 (June 13, 1946):
605–16.

57 *Year Book of the Northern Baptist Convention, 1946* 96–97, 145–47; Fey, "Fundamentalists Lose Grip," 733.

58 *Year Book of the Northern Baptist Convention, 1946* 146–47; Harrison, *Authority and Power,* 154–55.

59 William Bell Riley, "A Document of Decision," *The Northwestern Pilot* 27 (April 1947): 218. Some fundamentalists within the Northern Baptist Convention, including Carl Henry and Harold Lindsell, felt that separating from the denomination was premature at this point. Marsden, *Reforming Fundamentalism,* 46.

60 *Minnesota Baptist Annual, 1946,* 9 (mimeographed).

61 In gratitude for his active support, in May 1947 the Conservative Baptist Association granted Riley an honorary seat on its executive committee, for life. Of course, Riley died that December. "Conservatives Make Dr. Riley Executive for Life," *The Northwestern Pilot* 27 (June 1947): 274.

62 Riley, "Document of Decision," 199, 218, 222; William Bell Riley, "Editor-in-Chief Resigns Life Membership in N.B.C.," *The Northwestern Pilot* 27 (June 1947): 275.

63 *Minnesota Baptist Annual, 1948,* 15 (mimeographed).

64 Warren Vanhetloo, "Your Editor's Viewpoint," *North Star Baptist* 32 (March 1958): 9.

Epilogue

1 William Bell Riley, "Darwinism—The Devil's Wedge," *Christian Fundamentals in School and Church* 5 (January–March 1923), 8. In the same vein: "The Coming Cleavage," *Christian Fundamentals in School and Church* 5 (July–September 1923): 29–31.

2 William Bell Riley, "The Problem of Denominational Loyalty," *The Pilot* 22 (October 1941): 19.

3 George M. Marsden, *Reforming Fundamentalism: Fuller Seminary and the New Evangelicalism* (Grand Rapids, Mich.: Wm. B. Eerdmans Co., 1987), esp. 3–11, 153–71. Although this earlier work places the evangelical-separatist split in the 1940s, also quite helpful is George M. Marsden, "From Fundamentalism to Evangelicalism: A Historical Analysis," in *The Evangelicals: What They Believe, Who They Are, Where They Are Changing,* ed. David F. Wells and John D. Woodbridge, 2d ed. (Grand Rapids, Mich.: Baker Book House, 1977), 147–49.

4 For a detailed discussion of Billy Graham's role as the focus of controversy in conservative Protestantism, see Farley Porter Butler, Jr., "Billy Graham and the End of Evangelical Unity" (Ph.D. diss., University of Florida, 1976).

5 John Pollock, *Billy Graham: The Authorized Biography* (New York: McGraw-Hill Co., 1966), 42–43. For an extended discussion of Riley's pursuit of Graham for the Northwestern presidency, see Dell G. Johnson, "Fundamentalist Responses in Minnesota to the Developing New Evangelicalism" (Th.D. diss., Central Baptist Seminary, 1982), 140–47.

6 Pollock, *Billy Graham,* 43–44. Actually, Pollock puts Graham's reluctance at being associated with Northwestern more strongly: Graham "was not sure he wished to be so closely identified with Midwest 'Fundamentalism,' because of the unfortunate connotation of the word." But as noted earlier, in the 1940s fundamentalism and evangelicalism were essentially synonyms, with the split between separatist fundamentalists and evangelicals not coming until the mid-1950s. It is thus quite possible that Pollock's (and Graham's?) account of Graham's reluctance to

go to Northwestern was colored by the fact that, while president of the school, Graham endured four years of sniping from those who would be on the separatist side when division came.

7   As reported by Pollock, *Billy Graham*, 42–43. For a slightly different version of this event, see Stanley High, *Billy Graham: The Personal Story of the Man, His Message, and His Mission* (New York: McGraw-Hill Co., 1956), 144–45.

8   "N.W. Names Billy Graham Vice-President-At-Large," *The Northwestern Pilot* 28 (October 1947): 20; Marie Acomb Riley, "Words of Appreciation and Tribute," *The Northwestern Pilot* 28 (March 1948): 189; Johnson, "Minnesota," 146–47.

9   "News from Northwestern," *North Star Baptist* 23 (December 1950): 22.

10 In Marshall Frady's *Billy Graham: A Parable of American Righteousness* Graham volunteers one humorous example of how he lacked the proper administrative mindset: as "an administrator, there were just a lot of things I didn't understand. For instance, the librarian came to me once and told me what she was making and said she had to have a raise, and I immediately told her, 'Why, you certainly do, you can certainly have it.' Just like that. The finance board went into a state of shock when they heard what I'd done." Frady, *Billy Graham: A Parable of American Righteousness* (Boston: Little, Brown and Co., 1979), 176.

11 High, *Billy Graham*, 145; "Graham Leaves for Two-Month Tour of Europe," *The Northwestern Pilot* 28 (March 1948): 200; Johnson, "Minnesota," 161–72.

12 The author is indebted to William Berntsen, who served as president of the new Northwestern from 1972 to 1985, for his insights into this controversy. Berntsen said in an interview in Roseville, Minn., on February 25, 1983: "I came to Northwestern in January 1946. Interested as I was in accreditation and in the degree-granting side of Northwestern, and being a 'liberal arts devotee,' I got myself into a hotbed of controversy and problems."

13 Pollock, *Billy Graham*, 45.

14 Johnson, "Minnesota," 179–214; "Dr. Graham Resigns School Post," *The Northwestern Pilot* 32 (March 1952): 187.

15 "Dr. Graham Resigns," 187; William Berntsen interview.

16 This point was made in a number of interviews and questionnaires. Interestingly, at Riley's death Clearwaters wrote an article entitled "The Passing of W. B. Riley," which was published in the January 1, 1948, issue of *The Watchman-Examiner*. At the end of the article Clearwaters recounts the last conversation he had with the dying Riley. According to Clearwaters, Riley's final words to him bespoke the dying man's trust: "Then, still holding my hand in his long, trembling, bony fingers that were now so cold, he looked up at me and said, 'Beloved, your ministry will suffer more severe tests than mine has ever known. I know that you will be found faithful. I have never seen you waver!'" Later in January 1948 this article was reprinted in *The Northwestern Pilot* but with the final passage excised. The excision may have been the doing of Riley's wife, who helped edit *The Pilot* and who opposed the notion of Clearwaters as her husband's natural successor.

17 Richard Elvee, "A Miracle Happens in Minneapolis," *The Northwestern Pilot* 36 (February 1956): 4; "News from Northwestern," *North Star Baptist* 30 (July 1956): 9; *North Star Baptist* 31 (October 1957): 24. For the separatist side in the Northwestern controversy see a former Pillsbury professor's thesis: Johnson, "Minnesota," 215–99.

18 Maynard Rogers, completed questionnaire to author, October 7, 1986.

19 Johnson, "Minnesota," 371–86, 421, 429–30; Bruce Shelley, *A History of Conser-*

vative Baptists (Wheaton, Ill.: Wheaton Press, 1971), 86–101; David O. Beale, *In Pursuit of Purity: American Fundamentalism since 1850* (Greenville, S.C.: Unusual Books, 1986), 284–85; Charles Allyn Russell, *Voices of American Fundamentalism: Seven Biographical Studies* (Philadelphia: Westminster Press, 1976), 103. In this complicated story of division after division, it is hard to understand why Clearwaters' group did not simply join with the General Association of Regular Baptists, the denomination which had formed in the early 1930s in the first major withdrawal from the Northern Baptist Convention. Both groups were equally militant in their demand for separation from apostasy. The only difference between the two groups seemed to be that the New Testament Association included in its doctrinal statement that the "days" mentioned in the Genesis account were twenty-four-hour days. According to Shelley, in "the minds of the leaders of the New Testament Association this appeared to be reason enough for the 'unique' place the NTAIBC [New Testament Association of Independent Baptist Churches] was called to fill on the religious scene." Shelley, *Conservative Baptists*, 102–3.

20   "News from Northwestern," *North Star Baptist* 30 (July 1956): 9; "Bible in College?: Why and How," *Northwestern College Bulletin* 14 (May 1966): 1; William Berntsen interview.

21   Russell, *Voices*, 213; George M. Marsden, *Fundamentalism and American Culture: The Shaping of Twentieth-Century Evangelicalism, 1870–1925* (New York: Oxford University Press, 1980), 61–62; Gabriel Fackre, *The Religious Right and Christian Faith* (Grand Rapids, Mich.: Wm. B. Eerdmans Co., 1982), 74–80.

22   Perhaps the most enraptured comments in the alumni questionnaires were written by Maynard Rogers (class of 1935): "SWEET MEMORIES OF Dr. Wm. Bell Riley: With joy, as flowers welcome the sun, will many remember him. With pleasure, as ears are pleased with music, will many recall him. With sweetness, as the taste of honey lingers in the mouth, will old hearts once young, remember him. With delight, as eyes gaze upon lovely landscapes, will many hold him in memory. With gratitude, as the rescued are grateful to the rescuers of modern days, will many hold him in memory." October 7, 1986.

23   Gabriel Fackre provides an incisive critique of personality-based religious empires in *The Religious Right and Christian Faith*, esp. 77–80. See also Richard Quebedeaux, *By What Authority: The Rise of Personality Cults in American Christianity* (San Francisco: Harper and Row, 1982).

24   Joe Pates, interview with author, Granite Falls, Minn., August 26, 1986.

25   For a superb and path-breaking discussion of religious groups that see themselves and are seen as being outside the main currents of American culture, see R. Laurence Moore's *Religious Outsiders and the Making of Americans* (New York: Oxford University Press, 1986), which includes a provocative chapter on fundamentalism.

26   For excellent discussions of contemporary fundamentalist communities see Nancy Tatom Ammerman, *Bible Believers: Fundamentalists in the Modern World* (New Brunswick, N.J.: Rutgers University Press, 1987); Frances Fitzgerald's chapter on Jerry Falwell in *Cities on a Hill: A Journey through Contemporary American Cultures* (London: Picador Press, 1986); and Alan Peshkin, *God's Choice: The Total World of a Fundamentalist Christian School* (Chicago: University of Chicago Press, 1986).

27   William Bell Riley, "Fundamentalism and the Faith of the Baptists," *The Watchman-Examiner* 9 (August 25, 1921): 1088.

Bibliography

Primary Sources

MANUSCRIPT COLLECTIONS

American Baptist Historical Society, Rochester, N.Y.
    Albert William Beaven Papers
    Reuben E. Nelson Papers
    Anna Canada Swain Papers
First Baptist Church of Granite Falls, Granite Falls, Minn.
    "Annual Letter of the First Baptist Church of Granite Falls to the Southwestern
        Baptist Association." 1930, 1932, 1937, 1947.
    Minutes of Church Meetings. 1913–1948.
    "Minutes of Recognition Council Held at Granite Falls," March 15, 1966.
    "Report of the Board of Deacons." 1947–1948.
Minnesota Historical Society, St. Paul, Minn.
    Jewish Community Relations Council of Minnesota Papers
Northwestern College Library, Roseville, Minn.
    Papers of William Bell Riley

WORKS OF WILLIAM BELL RILEY

Books and Pamphlets

The Challenge of Minnesota Baptists. n.p., [1944?].
Christianity vs. Socialism. n.p., n.d.
The City Temple. Minneapolis, 1915.
The Crisis of the Church. New York: Charles C. Cook, 1914.
A Debate: Resolved, that the Creative Days in Genesis Were Aeons, Not Solar Days.
    With Harry Rimmer. n.p., 1929.
The Doom of World Governments. Minneapolis, [1937?].
The Evolution of the Kingdom. New York: Charles C. Cook, 1913.
The Finality of the Higher Criticism; or, The Theory of Evolution and False Theology.
    n.p., 1909.
The Four Horsemen; or, Prophecy and the Approaching Slaughter. Minneapolis, [1941?].
The Gospel for War Times. Los Angeles: Bible Institute of Los Angeles, 1918.
The Great Divide; or, Christ and the Present Crisis. Philadelphia: Bible Conference
    Committee, 1919.
The Hereafter; or, Heaven and Hell. Chicago: Star Printing Co., [1897?].
Hitlerism; or, The Philosophy of Evolution in Action. Minneapolis, [1941?].
Looking for a Pastor? Perhaps We Can Help You. Minneapolis, [1942?].
The Menace of Modernism. New York: Christian Alliance Co., 1917.

Messages for the Metropolis. Minneapolis: Winona Publishing Co., 1906.

Painting America Red. Wichita: Defender Tract Club, [1940?].

The Philosophies of Father Coughlin. Grand Rapids, Mich.: Zondervan Publishing Co., 1935.

Playing the Fool, and Purposing Reform. Minneapolis, 1897.

Present Signs of His Speedy Appearance. Chicago: Star Printing Co., [1897?].

The Promised Return. Chicago: Star Printing Co., [1897?].

Prophecy and the Red Russian Menace. Minneapolis: L. W. Camp, [1932?].

Protocols and Communism. Minneapolis: L. W. Camp, 1934.

Revival Sermons: Essentials in Effective Evangelism. New York: Fleming H. Revell Co., 1939.

Riley versus Robinson: A Discussion of the Superintendency of Minneapolis Schools. Minneapolis: W. B. Riley, [1944?].

Shivering at the Sight of a Shirt. Minneapolis, 1936.

Socialism in Our Schools: Sovietizing the State through Schools. Minneapolis: [L. W. Camp?], [1923?].

Ten Burning Questions. New York: Revell and Co., 1932.

Ten Sermons on the Greater Doctrines of Scripture. Bloomington, Ill.: Leader Publishing Co., 1891.

Vagaries and Verities; or, Sunday Nights in Soul-Winning. Minneapolis: Hall, Black, and Co., 1903.

Wanted—A World Leader! Minneapolis, 1939.

What Is Fundamentalism? N.p. 1927.

   Articles

"The Adorable Lord." *The Pilot* 20 (February 1940): 141.

"All Non-New Dealers Endangered." *The Pilot* 23 (October 1942): 3, 21, 24.

"An Appraisal of the Layman's Commission." *The Pilot* 13 (January 1933): 122–24.

"Are the Scriptures Scientific?" *The Pilot* 17 (June 1937): 261–63; *The Pilot* 17 (July 1937): 297–98, 308.

"The Arrest of a Rifle Club." *The Pilot* 20 (March 1940): 171.

"Atheism, the Enemy of Civilization." *The Pilot* 13 (October 1932): 17–19.

"An Attack by the 'Christian Century.'" *Christian Fundamentals in School and Church* 4 (April–June 1922): 8–10.

"Attempted Debate with Dean Noe." *Christian Fundamentals in School and Church* 7 (July–September 1925): 11–19.

"The Autonomy of a Baptist Church." *The Pilot* 19 (January 1939): 100.

"The Baptist: A By-Partisan [*sic*] Denomination." *The Northwestern Pilot* 25 (February 1945): 143, 157–58.

"The Baptist Foreign Missionary Society and Modernism." *Christian Fundamentals in School and Church* 6 (January–March 1924): 20–21.

"BAPTIST FOREIGN SOCIETY or _____." *The Northwestern Pilot* 24 (January 1944): 126–27.

"The Baptist Ministers' Council." *The Pilot* 15 (April 1935): 183–84, 196.

"Baptist Ministers' Covenant and Northwestern Graduates." *The Northwestern Pilot* 25 (April 1945): 199.

"Baptist Modernists and Hitler Methods: The New Deal in Baptist Polity." *The Pilot* 23 (June 1943): 265, 286.

"Baptist Polity vs. Autocracy or Burocracy [*sic*]." *The Pilot* 23 (May 1943): 233, 239.

"Baptist State Convention." *The Pilot* 23 (October 1942): 3.

"Baptists [*sic*] Heterodoxy." *School and Church* 2 (April–June 1920): 334–35.

"Bartimaeus; or, The Conversion of a Blind Beggar." *The Pilot* 19 (September 1939): 338–40.

"The Bible Conference Trip." *The Pilot* 14 (June 1934): 268–69.

"The Bible School and That Blessed Hope." *The Pilot* 16 (March 1936): 164–66, 188–89.

"Bible Schools and the Standardization of the Ministry." *School and Church* 2 (July–September 1918): 23–26.

"The Big Baptist Opportunity." *The Pilot* 21 (February 1941): 139.

"Biola and the Bible; or, Dr. MacInnis Resigned." *The Christian Fundamentalist* 2 (January 1929): 9–10.

"Biola Boiling." *The Christian Fundamentalist* 1 (May 1928): 5–10.

"Blatant Birkhead." *The Northwestern Pilot* 25 (August 1945): 328–29.

"The Blood of the Jew vs. the Blood of Jesus." *The Pilot* 15 (November 1934): 24–26.

"Bob Jones College, Cleveland, Tennessee." *The Pilot* 21 (August 1941): 317, 334.

"The Book Makers." *The Pilot* 20 (August 1940): 308–10; *The Pilot* 20 (September 1940): 341, 349–50.

"The Book of the Prophets." *The Northwestern Pilot* 25 (August 1945): 298, 322, 328.

"Book Reviews." *The Pilot* 17 (August 1937): 342.

"Breaking the Bible School Defense Line." *The Christian Fundamentalist* 1 (April 1928): 5–9, 25.

"Brooks Threatens Critics of Biola." *The Christian Fundamentalist* 1 (June 1928): 13–14.

"Bryan, the Great Commoner and Christian." *Christian Fundamentals in School and Church* 7 (October–December 1925): 5–11, 37.

"Buchmanism; or, The Oxford Group Movement." *The Pilot* 13 (February 1933): 155.

"California Churches Visited." *The Pilot* 21 (February 1941): 131.

"Can the Compromiser Be a Reformer?" *The Northwestern Pilot* 24 (March 1944): 168.

"The Centralization of Power in the Baptist Denomination." *The Pilot* 23 (July 1942): 290.

"The Challenge of Orthodoxy." *School and Church* 2 (July–September 1920): 361–72.

"The Challenge of Youth." *The Pilot* 14 (April 1934): 203–5, 221.

"The Challenge to Carry On." *The Pilot* 21 (April 1941): 202–4, 221.

"Character Slanders by Pseudo-Communists." *The Pilot* 20 (September 1940): 340, 346.

"Charles Haddon Spurgeon." *The Northwestern Pilot* 26 (May 1946): 227.

"Christ, the Pre-eminent Authority." *The Pilot* 18 (August 1938): 308–10.

"Christ and the Changing Order." *Church and School* 1 (September 1916): 12–17.

"Christ the Child of Prophecy, Matthew 2." *The Pilot* 24 (December 1943): 70–72, 74–75.

"Christ versus San Francisco Conference." *The Northwestern Pilot* 26 (October 1945): 3.

"Christ Will Come Again! A Reply." *School and Church* 2 (April 1918): 63–71.

"Christian Action Crusade." *The Pilot* 22 (August 1942): 312.

"Christian Brethren Talk It Over." *The Pilot* 17 (October 1936): 3.

"The Christian Fundamentals Movement, Its Battles, Its Achievements, Its Certain Victory." *Christian Fundamentals in School and Church* 4 (October–December 1922): 4–14.

"Christmas Letter from Our President to the Alumni." *The Pilot* 21 (December 1940): 93.

"Christ's Estimate of Childhood." *The Pilot* 17 (December 1936): 69–71, 94.

"The Chucking of Upton Close." *The Northwestern Pilot* 25 (September 1945): 335, 358.

"The Church's Divorced Teammate." *The Pilot* 18 (February 1938): 142.

"Clear Creek in the Kentucky Mountains." *The Pilot* 23 (September 1943): 343.

"Cohn vs. Riley." *The Pilot* 15 (May 1935): 218, 220, 239.

"The Column on Columnists." *The Pilot* 22 (January 1942): 99.

"A Column on the Columnists." *The Northwestern Pilot* 24 (June 1944): 279.

"The Coming Cleavage." *Christian Fundamentals in School and Church* 5 (July–September 1923): 29–31.

"The Conference at Wallace Lodge." *The Watchman-Examiner* 14 (January 28, 1926): 117.

"The Conflict of Christianity with Its Counterfeit." *Christian Fundamentals in School and Church* 3 (July–September 1921): 3–12.

"The Conflict of Christianity with Its Counterfeits." *The Pilot* 22 (November 1941): 42–43.

"The Conservative Baptist Foreign Board." *The Pilot* 23 (August 1943): 307.

"A 'Conservative's' Introduction." *The Pilot* 23 (September 1943): 338.

"Consistency – A Jewel." *The Northwestern Pilot* 27 (September 1947): 381.

"Corporate Control: The Peril of American Education." *Christian Fundamentals in School and Church* 4 (October–December 1921): 21–29.

"The Cost of War." *The Pilot* 16 (February 1936): 140.

"The Court Case of the Princeton, Indiana, Church." *The Pilot* 20 (March 1940): 169–70, 174.

"A Critical Interpretation Corrected." *The Pilot* 21 (October 1940): 31.

"Critics Answered." *The Northwestern Pilot* 26 (November 1945): 35.

"Critics in the Fundamentalist Family." *The Northwestern Pilot* 27 (August 1947): 344, 348.

"Dallas Baptists." *The Pilot* 18 (April 1938): 214.

"Daniel and the Doom of World Governments." *The Pilot* 14 (October 1933): 17–19, 31; *The Pilot* 14 (November 1933): 49, 62.

"Darwinism – The Devil's Wedge." *Christian Fundamentals in School and Church* 5 (January–March 1923): 8–10.

"Das Barnett and the Southern Baptists." *The Pilot* 22 (October 1941): 9–10.

"Debates on Evolution." *Christian Fundamentals in School and Church* 5 (January–March 1923): 20–21.

"Debates on Evolution." *Christian Fundamentals in School and Church,* 8 (January–March 1926): 54–55.

"The Demand for Ministers." *The Pilot* 21 (June 1941): 259.

"Denominational Colleges and Destructive Criticism." *Christian Fundamentals in School and Church* 4 (October–December 1921): 3–4.

"Denominational Dictatorship." *The Pilot* 22 (March 1942): 170–71.

"Denominational Dictatorship." *The Pilot* 22 (April 1942): 197.

"The Denominational Division (Among Baptists)." *The Pilot* 20 (January 1940): 104–5.

"Distinctive Principles of Baptists." *The Pilot* 20 (April 1940): 206, 216.

"Divine Healing Discussion." *The Pilot* 16 (March 1936): 163.

"Divinely Ordered Divisions." *The Northwestern Pilot* 24 (May 1944): 260, 274.

"The Division among the Southern California Conservatives." *The Northwestern Pilot* 25 (April 1945): 198–99.

"Dr. George Vallentyne's [sic] Celebrate 50th Wedding Anniversary." *The Northwestern Pilot* 26 (April 1946): 198–99.

"Dr. Riley and His Boys: Allan Williams at Luverne." *The Pilot* 23 (November 1942): 56.

"Dr. Riley Replies to Dr. Campbell Morgan." *The Christian Fundamentalist* 2 (August 1928): 13–15.

"Dr. W. B. Riley Elected President, Minnesota Baptist Convention." *The Northwestern Pilot* 25 (November 1944): 57.

"Dr. W. B. Riley's 41st Anniversary Sermon." *The Pilot* 18 (April 1938): 204, 208.

"Dr. W. B. Riley's Resignation." *The Pilot* 21 (April 1941): 195.

"Dr. Walter Judd and the First Baptist Church." *The Pilot* 23 (January 1943): 110, 120.

"A Document of Decision." *The Northwestern Pilot* 27 (April 1947): 199, 218, 222.

"Eastern Baptist Theological Seminary." *The Pilot* 21 (June 1941): 267, 282.

"The Ecclesiastical Black Hand." *Christian Fundamentals in School and Church* 5 (January–March 1923): 4–6.

"An Echo from the Baptist Minister's Covenant." *The Northwestern Pilot* 25 (August 1945): 311.

"Editorial Comment." *The Pilot* 17 (January 1937): 108–10.

"Editor-in-Chief Resigns Life Membership in N.B.C." *The Northwestern Pilot* 27 (June 1947): 275.

"The Editor's Restoration and Return." *Christian Fundamentals in School and Church* 7 (April–June 1925): 6–8.

"The End of the Famous Sedition Trial." *The Northwestern Pilot* 25 (March 1945): 163.

"Epitomizing the Northern Baptist Convention Held in Los Angeles." *The Pilot* 19 (August 1939): 316–17.

"The Errors of E. Stanley Jones." *The Pilot* 17 (April 1937): 196–99, 222.

"Evolution — A False Philosophy." *The Pilot* 20 (November 1939): 40–42; *The Pilot* 20 (December 1939): 76–77.

"The Evolution Controversy!" *Christian Fundamentals in School and Church* 4 (April–June 1922): 5–6.

"Evolutionists Weary of Debate." *The Pilot* 21 (May 1941): 228.

"Exposure of Imposters." *The Northwestern Pilot* 25 (September 1945): 335.

"Exposure of Imposters." *The Northwestern Pilot* 26 (January 1946): 99.

"Facts for Fundamentalists." *The Pilot* 13 (December 1932): 92–93.

"Facts for Fundamentalists." *The Pilot* 13 (April 1933): 208–9.

"Facts for Fundamentalists." *The Pilot* 13 (May 1933): 241.

"Facts for Fundamentalists." *The Pilot* 13 (June 1933): 273–75.

"Facts for Fundamentalists." *The Pilot* 13 (July 1933): 297–99.

"Facts for Fundamentalists." *The Pilot* 13 (August 1933): 315.

"Facts for Fundamentalists." *The Pilot* 14 (October 1933): 10, 15.

"Facts for Fundamentalists." *The Pilot* 14 (November 1933): 57–58.

"Facts for Fundamentalists." *The Pilot* 14 (February 1934): 142–43.

"Facts for Fundamentalists." *The Pilot* 14 (March 1934): 171, 173, 177.

"Facts for Fundamentalists." *The Pilot* 14 (May 1934): 234–35, 237.

"Facts for Fundamentalists." *The Pilot* 14 (July 1934): 295–96.

"Facts for Fundamentalists." *The Pilot* 14 (September 1934): 327, 334.

"Facts for Fundamentalists." *The Pilot* 15 (October 1934): 7–8.

"Facts for Fundamentalists." *The Pilot* 15 (February 1935): 123–26, 141–42.

"Facts for Fundamentalists." *The Pilot* 15 (March 1935): 160–62.

"Facts for Fundamentalists." *The Pilot* 15 (May 1935): 217.

"Facts for Fundamentalists." *The Pilot* 15 (June 1935): 249–51.

"Facts for Fundamentalists." *The Pilot* 15 (September 1935): 311–12.

"Facts for Fundamentalists." *The Pilot* 16 (October 1935): 9–10.

"Facts for Fundamentalists." *The Pilot* 16 (November 1935): 45–46.

"Facts for Fundamentalists." *The Pilot* 16 (December 1935): 74–75, 84.

"Facts for Fundamentalists." *The Pilot* 16 (January 1936): 107–10.

"Facts for Fundamentalists." *The Pilot* 18 (November 1937): 78–80, 87.

"Facts for Fundamentalists." *The Pilot* 18 (November 1937): 110–11.

"Facts for Fundamentalists." *The Pilot* 19 (November 1938): 48–49.

"Facts for Fundamentalists." *The Pilot* 19 (April 1939): 210–11.

"Facts for Fundamentalists." *The Pilot* 20 (June 1940): 266–69.

"Faith Vindicated." *The Pilot* 22 (January 1942): 99, 120.

"Faithful Handling of Annuity Funds." *The Pilot* 22 (November 1941): 49.

"Fallen Heroes of Fundamentalism: William Gladstone." *The Northwestern Pilot* 26 (March 1946): 174.

"The False Front of the Federal Council." (with Dan Gilbert). *The Pilot* 19 (October 1938): 12–14.

"The False Front of the Federal Council." *The Pilot* 19 (December 1938): 68.

"The False Front of the Federal Council!" [with Dan Gilbert?] *The Pilot* 19 (March 1939): 163, 166.

"The Fatal Weakness of Fundamentalism." *The Pilot* 22 (May 1942): 227–28.

"Favor for the Forum." *The Pilot* 17 (May 1937): 228, 253.

"The Fight Is On: Modernism vs. Fundamentalism." *The Pilot* 16 (November 1935): 47–48.

"The Five Miracles of Jonah." *The Northwestern Pilot* 24 (September 1944): 4–5, 22–23.

"Fixed Points in Baptist Polity." *The Pilot* 23 (April 1943): 198.

"47th Annual Meeting of Northwestern Bible Conference." *The Pilot* 22 (August 1942): 319.

"The Fosdick and Faunce Furors." *Christian Fundamentals in School and Church* 5 (July–September 1923): 26–28.

"A Foul Philosophy." *The Northwestern Pilot* 26 (December 1945): 67.

"Foul Politics in Case of Dr. Husted." *The Northwestern Pilot* 27 (November 1946): 55.

"The Fourth Annual Convention of the Christian Fundamentalists." *Christian Fundamentals in School and Church* 4 (October–December 1922): 14–16.

"Frank Groner vs. Frank Norris, or Some Fundamental Facts." *Christian Fundamentals in School and Church* 5 (July–September 1923): 19–24.

"From Fundamentalism to Communism." *The Pilot* 20 (October 1939): 5–6.

"From Our Editor's Desk." *The Northwestern Pilot* 26 (September 1946): 323, 347.

"From Our Editor's Desk." *The Northwestern Pilot* 27 (December 1946): 67, 88.

"From Our Editor's Desk." *The Northwestern Pilot* 27 (January 1947): 99, 118.

"From Our Editor's Desk." *The Northwestern Pilot* 27 (February 1947): 131.

"From Our Editor's Desk." *The Northwestern Pilot* 27 (June 1947): 263, 279, 282.

"From Our Editor's Desk." *The Northwestern Pilot* 27 (July 1947): 295.

"From Our Editor's Desk." *The Northwestern Pilot* 27 (August 1947): 327, 343.

"From Our Editor's Desk." *The Northwestern Pilot* 27 (September 1947): 359, 380.

"From Our Editor's Desk." *The Northwestern Pilot* 28 (October 1947): 3, 24.

"From Our Editor's Desk." *The Northwestern Pilot* 28 (November 1947): 35.

"From Our Editor's Desk." *The Northwestern Pilot* 28 (December 1947): 77.

"Fundamentalism and Religious Racketeering." *The Pilot* 19 (October 1938): 15–16.

"Fundamentalism and the Faith of the Baptists." *The Watchman-Examiner* 9 (August 25, 1921): 1087–88.

"Fundamentalism vs. Federal Church." *The Pilot* 23 (November 1942): 35–36.

"Fundamentalists Misrepresented." *The Northwestern Pilot* 24 (August 1944): 347.

"The Fundamentals Series in Sunday School Work." *Christian Fundamentals in School and Church* 5 (April–June 1923): 8–10.

"Further Development." *The Pilot* 15 (July 1935): 274.

"The Future of Magazines." *The Pilot* 13 (November 1932): 35.

"The General Association of Regular Baptist Churches." *The Pilot* 17 (August 1937): 342.

"The Gipsy Smith Meetings in Minneapolis." *The Pilot* 22 (March 1942): 167.

"The Gospel in the Gloaming." *The Northwestern Pilot* 25 (April 1945): 210–11.

"The Gospel in the Gloaming." *The Northwestern Pilot* 26 (December 1945): 73.

"The Great Divide; or, Christianity and the Present Crisis." *The Watchman-Examiner* 7 (June 26, 1919): 997–99.

"The Great Green Lake, Wisconsin, Grounds." *The Northwestern Pilot* 24 (May 1944): 243, 274.

"Harry Emerson Fosdick's Church." *The Northwestern Pilot* 25 (January 1945): 106.

"Heaven's Peace Proclamation." *The Northwestern Pilot* 28 (December 1947): 78–80.

"Honesty Essential to Christian Fellowship." *The Pilot* 14 (February 1934): 140–41.

"How Andover Was Bootlegged and Hijacked." *The Pilot* 23 (September 1943): 342, 350.

"The Ideal Family." *The Pilot* 12 (September 1929): 10–12.

"Incidents of Our Mexico Trip." *The Pilot* 22 (February 1942): 138–39.

"The 'Inclusive Policy' Illustrated, and Disowned." *The Northwestern Pilot* 24 (August 1944): 367.

"The Inter-Church World Movement." *School and Church* 2 (January–March 1920): 288–90.

"The Interchurch World Movement." *School and Church* 2 (April–June 1920): 320–25.

"Internationalism and the Anti-Christ." *The Northwestern Pilot* 26 (August 1946): 294, 308.

"The Interpretation of a Dream." *The Northwestern Pilot* 26 (March 1946): 163, 187–89.

"Introducing Mr. George Wilson, Our New Publication Manager." *The Pilot* 24 (November 1943): 35.

"Is Anti-Communism Also Anti-Semitism?" *The Defender* 14 (November 1939): 18.

"Is There to Be a Division in the Baptist Denomination?" *School and Church* 2 (October–December 1919): 237–38.

"Is There to Be a Division in the Baptist Denomination?" *School and Church* 2 (January–March 1920): 292–93.

"Isaiah the Prophet." *The Northwestern Pilot* 25 (March 1945): 181–82; *The Northwestern Pilot* 25 (May 1945): 235–36, 252.

"Jerusalem and the Jew." *School and Church* 1 (January 1918): 12–16.

"Jerusalem and the Jew." *The Northwestern Pilot* 26 (September 1946): 328, 338–40.

"John the Baptist—Pioneer Soul Winner." *The Pilot* 18 (March 1938): 169–71.

"Jonah at Sea." *The Northwestern Pilot* 24 (April 1944): 210, 228.

"Jonah in the Storm." *The Northwestern Pilot* 24 (July 1944): 320–21, 332–33.

"Jonah Overboard." *The Northwestern Pilot* 24 (September 1944): 382–84, 394.

"Joseph Cohn's New Money-Getting Scheme." *The Northwestern Pilot* 26 (December 1945): 75.

"Kagawa—A Prophet of the Antichrist." *The Pilot* 16 (April 1936): 196–200.

"Kagawa's Visit to Minneapolis." *The Pilot* 16 (February 1936): 139–40.

"Keith Brooks in the Hebrew Christian Alliance Quarterly." *The Northwestern Pilot* 25 (April 1945): 195, 214, 216.

"Latest Dream Looking Up!" *The Pilot* 22 (August 1942): 323.

"The Lighthouse of the Northwest." *The Pilot* 23 (March 1943): 163.

"Looking for a Pastor? Perhaps We Can Help You." *The Pilot* 22 (April 1942): 200, 217.

"The Lord Jesus Christ." *The Pilot* 13 (December 1932): 70–71, 80.

"The Lordship of Christ." *The Northwestern Pilot* 28 (October 1947): 4–5.

"The MacInnis Controversy." *The Christian Fundamentalist* 1 (June 1928): 12–13.

"The Making of a Gospel Minister." *The Pilot* 23 (October 1942): 4–5, 13–14.

"The Making of Ministers." *The Pilot* 21 (October 1940): 7–8.

"The Meaning and Value of Worship." *The Pilot* 21 (March 1941): 170–72, 180.

"The Meditations of an Old Man." *The Northwestern Pilot* 28 (January 1948): 114–15.

"Memorial Hall Campaign." *The Pilot* 22 (June 1942): 261.

"The Ministry for My Day." *The Pilot* 22 (July 1942): 291, 294, 298–300.

"Minneapolis Murders." *The Northwestern Pilot* 26 (October 1945): 3.

"The Minnesota Baptist Convention." *The Pilot* 23 (November 1942): 35.

"Minnesota Plan neither Iconoclastic nor Revolutionary." *The Northwestern Pilot* 26 (February 1946): 146–47.

"Minnesota State Secretary." *The Northwestern Pilot* 26 (August 1946): 296–97.

"Minnesota State Sunday School Convention." *The Pilot* 19 (December 1938): 67.

"Minnesota vs. California." *The Pilot* 19 (January 1939): 99.

"The Missionary Appeal in Promoting College Endowments." *Christian Fundamentals in School and Church* 5 (April–June 1923): 11.

"Modernism – Intellectually Inferior." *The Northwestern Pilot* 25 (June 1945): 263.

"Modernism in Baptist Schools." *School and Church* 3 (October–December 1920): 407–22.

"Modernism in the Philippines." *The Pilot* 17 (July 1937): 299.

"The Most Essential Knowledge." *The Pilot* 18 (September 1938): 341, 349–50.

"Muste and the Committee of Nine." *The Pilot* 22 (May 1942): 228, 243.

"My Alma Mater, A Fount of Modernism." *The Pilot* 23 (May 1943): 227, 248.

"My Beloved People." *The Northwestern Pilot* 27 (April 1947): 214, 221.

"National Association of Evangelicals for United Action." *The Pilot* 23 (November 1942): 53–54.

"Newspaper Ability to Falsely Impress the Public." *The Pilot* 20 (May 1940): 228.

"The Northern Baptist Convention." *The Pilot* 20 (July 1940): 294–95.

"Northern Baptist Convention, Atlantic City." *The Northwestern Pilot* 24 (February 1944): 143.

"The Northern Baptist Convention, Atlantic City." *The Northwestern Pilot* 24 (July 1944): 315, 332.

"Northern Baptist Convention vs. Minnesota Baptist Convention." *The Northwestern Pilot* 27 (November 1946): 54.

"Northern Convention Unity." *The Northwestern Pilot* 27 (November 1946): 35, 50.

"The Northwestern Bible and Missionary Training School." *Christian Fundamentals in School and Church* 9 (January–March 1927): 63.

"Northwestern Boys as Church Builders." *The Pilot* 17 (August 1937): 341–42.

"The Northwestern Evangelical Seminary." *The Pilot* 15 (May 1935): 220.

"Northwestern in Review: Reasons for Rejoicing." *The Pilot* 22 (June 1942): 261, 277.

"The Northwestern Schools." *The Pilot* 21 (November 1940): 44–45, 48.

"Northwesterners Visited on Our Western Trip." *The Northwestern Pilot* 24 (April 1944): 227.

"Northwestern's Defense of the Faith." *The Northwestern Pilot* 26 (January 1946): 107.

"Objections to Our Editorial." *The Pilot* 23 (December 1942): 68, 76.

"The Old World Trip of Dr. and Mrs. W. B. Riley." *The Pilot* 16 (September 1936): 347–48.

"The Only Solution to the Sordid World Problems." *The Northwestern Pilot* 26 (October 1945): 7–8, 11, 14, 22.

"An Open Letter from Dr. W. B. Riley to Friends of Northwestern." *The Pilot* 19 (June 1939): 259.

"An Open Letter from the Editor." *Christian Fundamentals in School and Church* 7 (January–March 1925): 5–6.

"Organized Christianity." *The Northwestern Pilot* 24 (July 1944): 319.

"The Origin and Object of Christian Obligation." *The Pilot* 13 (November 1932): 50–52.

"Our New State Secretary, E. P. Fosmark." *The Northwestern Pilot* 25 (June 1945): 269.

"Our President and Mrs. Riley's Western Trip." *The Northwestern Pilot* 25 (February 1945): 148–49.

"Our Sunday School." *The Pilot* 18 (October 1937): 11–13.

"Paul and Peter Voronaeff." *The Pilot* 19 (January 1939): 119.

"A Paying Investment." *The Pilot* 20 (August 1940): 320.

"Pegler's Pen Point." *The Northwestern Pilot* 25 (January 1945): 99.

"The Perils and Potentialities of the Reconstruction Period." *The Pilot* 23 (March 1943): 168–69, 173, 180, 188–89.

"Persecution of Colonel Sanctuary and Others." *The Northwestern Pilot* 24 (August 1944): 366.

"Personals from the Editor-in-Chief." *The Northwestern Pilot* 24 (February 1944): 132.

"Philadelphia Laymen and Fundamentalism." *The Pilot* 22 (June 1942): 260, 277.

"Points of Parallelism between Baptists and Presbyterians." *The Pilot* 15 (August 1935): 297–98.

"The Preacher's Impotence." *The Pilot* 18 (January 1938): 111–12.

"A Preacher's Solution of the Unemployment Problem." *The Pilot* 17 (August 1937): 334–35, 337.

"President's Prognostications." *The Pilot* 24 (October 1943): 31.

"The Prevalence of False Prophets." *The Northwestern Pilot* 25 (September 1945): 336–37, 356–57.

"The Problem of Denominational Loyalty." *The Pilot* 22 (October 1941): 16–17, 19.

"Progress of Southern Baptists." *The Pilot* 19 (July 1939): 294.

"Prophecy and Past History." *The Northwestern Pilot* 26 (November 1945): 40, 57.

"Prophecy and Past History." *The Northwestern Pilot* 26 (August 1946): 302–5.

"Prophecy and Premillennialism." *The Northwestern Pilot* 26 (April 1946): 201–4.

"Prophecy and Present Problems." *The Northwestern Pilot* 26 (January 1946): 101–2, 125–26.

"Prophecy and the Approaching Slaughter." *The Pilot* 22 (January 1942): 104–5, 108–9, 113.

"Prophecy and the Coming Kingdom." *The Northwestern Pilot* 26 (February 1946): 135, 148–51.

"A Prophet's Humility." *The Pilot* 17 (January 1937): 116.

"The Prophet's Praise." *The Pilot* 18 (February 1938): 139–40.

"The Prophets Themselves." *The Northwestern Pilot* 25 (February 1945): 132–34.

"Proposed Theological Seminary Building." *The Pilot* 22 (April 1942): 195.

"The Question of Academic Freedom." *The Watchman-Examiner* 11 (January 25, 1923): 116–17.

"The Racial Composition of the United States." *The Northwestern Pilot* 24 (May 1944): 243.

"Rebuilding a Baptist Association." *The Pilot* 22 (August 1942): 311–12.

"Recovering Majority Baptist Rule." *The Pilot* 23 (August 1943): 312–13.

"The Regular Baptists." *The Pilot* 16 (May 1936): 252.

"Reply to President Mullins's Open Letter." *The Watchman-Examiner* 12 (June 26, 1924): 822.

"Report of the Seventh Annual Convention, World's Christian Fundamentals Association." *Christian Fundamentals in School and Church* 7 (July–September 1925): 7–11.

"The Return, the Resurrection, and the Rapture." *The Northwestern Pilot* 27 (September 1947): 363, 378; *The Northwestern Pilot* 28 (October 1947): 8–9; *The Northwestern Pilot* 28 (November 1947): 44, 65.

"The Revival with Youth." *The Northwestern Pilot* 26 (February 1946): 131.

"The Rochester, New York, Resolution on Communism." *The Pilot* 15 (April 1935): 196.

"The Roosevelt Report of Progress." *The Northwestern Pilot* 25 (February 1945): 131, 150.

"Rule and Ruin: Dr. Fridell Chosen Baptist Foreign Secretary." *The Pilot* 23 (April 1943): 203, 220.

"The Scriptures on Divine Healing." *The Pilot* 15 (May 1935): 219.

"Secret Sins." *The Pilot* 16 (August 1936): 322–23.

"Secrets of Success: Forty Years of Christian Education." *The Pilot* 22 (December 1941): 76.

"A Selection of Merit." *The Pilot* 17 (July 1937): 300.

"Seminaries and a Statement of Faith." *The Watchman-Examiner* 7 (January 2, 1919): 11–12.

"Sending Out the Seventy." *The Pilot* 19 (June 1939): 290–92.

"Shall Northern Baptists Automatically Exclude Ultra-Conservatives?" *The Watchman-Examiner* 10 (May 11, 1922): 589–90.

"Shall Northern Baptists Come to Peace by Compromise?" *The Watchman-Examiner* 10 (May 18, 1922): 623–24.

"Shall We Tolerate Longer the Teaching of Evolution?" *Christian Fundamentals in School and Church* 5 (January–March 1923): 81–86.

"The Shortage of Paper." *The Northwestern Pilot* 27 (November 1946): 54.

"The Sickly Birth of Evolution." *The Northwestern Pilot* 26 (October 1945): 3.

"The Signs of the Times in the Light of Sixty Years." *The Northwestern Pilot* 24 (February 1944): 149–50, 153–55.

"Sioux Falls College." *The Northwestern Pilot* 26 (January 1946): 106, 120.

"Sioux Falls College Controversy." *The Northwestern Pilot* 27 (October 1946): 22, 26, 28.

"Slinging Dirt in Iowa." *The Pilot* 16 (May 1936): 252.

"Slogans to Silence Free Speech." *The Northwestern Pilot* 25 (March 1945): 163.

"The Social Economy of Jesus Christ." *The Pilot* 18 (November 1937): 42–46.

"The Social Gospel in the Southern Baptist Convention." *The Pilot* 17 (June 1937): 279.

"Socialism in Northern and Southern Baptist Conventions." *The Pilot* 15 (August 1935): 291, 298.

"The Southern Baptist Seminary." *The Pilot* 23 (July 1943): 290.

"The Southern Convention." *The Pilot* 17 (June 1937): 279.

"Southern Points and People." *The Pilot* 23 (February 1943): 139, 143.

"Southern Seminary Lost to Southern Orthodoxy." *The Pilot* 22 (December 1941): 68, 89.

"A Standardized Ministry." *The Pilot* 21 (July 1941): 290-92.

"The State and the Ten Commandments." *The Northwestern Pilot* 24 (June 1944): 279.

"Studies in Prophecy." *The Northwestern Pilot* 25 (January 1945): 100-101.

"The Supreme Court and Our Constitution." *The Pilot* 17 (August 1937): 323.

"The Surplus of Preachers." *The Pilot* 14 (December 1933): 90-91.

"Swatting Fundamentalism While Professing Fundamentalism." *The Christian Fundamentalist* 1 (May 1928): 10-11.

"That Blessed Hope and the Resurrection Body." *The Pilot* 17 (March 1937): 173-76.

"The Theological War." *The Pilot* 16 (June 1936): 268-69.

"The Theology of Louisville Seminary." *The Pilot* 22 (March 1942): 164, 174.

"The Theory of Evolution: Does It Tend to Anarchy?" *Christian Fundamentals in School and Church* 4 (July-September 1922): 36-42.

"The Theory of Evolution: Does It Tend to Atheism?" *Christian Fundamentals in School and Church* 4 (April-June 1922): 14-21.

"Three Days in Cuba." *The Pilot* 19 (February 1939): 151.

"Three Steps Heavenward." *The Pilot* 13 (March 1933): 186-88.

"The Three Tenses of a Christian Experience." *The Pilot* 18 (May 1938): 234-37.

"To All Baptists Who Believe the Bible to Be God's Word." *The Watchman-Examiner* 13 (November 19, 1925): 1497-98.

"To My Brethren, Fundamentalist Editors." *Christian Fundamentals in School and Church* 6 (April-June 1924): 9-11.

"The Truth about Communism." *The Northwestern Pilot* 27 (August 1947): 349.

"Twelve Days with Northwesterners." *The Pilot* 22 (August 1942): 311.

"The Uncovering of Kagawa." *The Northwestern Pilot* 15 (August 1945): 295.

"The Undenominational Bible Training Schools." *Christian Fundamentals in School and Church* 5 (July-September 1923): 24-26.

"The Victims of Criticism." *The Northwestern Pilot* 24 (May 1944): 269.

"A Visit to Barron, Wisconsin." *The Northwestern Pilot* 25 (December 1944): 81.

"Voting in the Northern Baptist Convention." *The Northwestern Pilot* 26 (May 1946): 246, 249.

"W. B. Riley Quits Frank Norris." *The Pilot* 18 (April 1938): 205-6.

"W. B. Riley's Theological Position." *The Pilot* 18 (April 1938): 206.

"The War and Memorial Hall." *The Pilot* 23 (October 1942): 12.

"The Way to Win." *The Pilot* 15 (December 1934): 57, 72-73.

"We Met a Midwest Crisis." *The Northwestern Pilot* 28 (October 1947): 12.

"Welcoming Address at Banquet Hall in Honor of Rev. Walfred Danielson." *The Northwestern Pilot* 24 (May 1944): 270.

"What Is the Matter with the Oxford Movement?" *The Pilot* 15 (January 1935): 84-86, 109.

"What Will Conservatives Do?" *The Northwestern Pilot* 26 (July 1946): 261-62, 274.

"When Will Christ Come?" *School and Church* 2 (January-March 1919): 100-107.

"Wherein Fundamentalists Have Failed." *The Pilot* 23 (July 1943): 296, 302.

"Whipping Fundamentalist Leaders into Line." *Christian Fundamentals in School and Church* 5 (January–March 1923): 6–8.

"Who Are Fundamentalists?" *The Pilot* 16 (May 1936): 2.

"Why Baptists Do Not Give More to Their Own Denominational Schools." *The Northwestern Pilot* 24 (June 1944): 279.

"Why Build Memorial Hall?" *The Pilot* 22 (May 1942): 235, 253.

"Why Recognize Russia and Rag Germany?" *The Pilot* 14 (January 1934): 109–10, 126.

"Will the United States Be Propagandized into War?" *The Pilot* 19 (May 1939): 227.

"William Jennings Bryan University." *The Watchman-Examiner* 13 (September 3, 1925): 1150.

"The Work at Luverne, Minnesota, under Rev. Allan Williams." *The Northwestern Pilot* 25 (December 1944): 83.

"The World Conference on Fundamentals." *The Watchman-Examiner* 7 (May 1, 1919): 554.

"The World Premillennial Conference vs. The Coming Confederacy." *School and Church* 2 (January–March 1919): 91–96.

"The World's Christian Fundamentals Association and the Scopes Trial." *Christian Fundamentals in School and Church* 7 (October–December 1925): 37–48.

"World's Christian Fundamentals Association Convention." *The Pilot* 16 (June 1936): 267, 269.

"Youth and the Babel in Religion." *The Pilot* 17 (November 1936): 41–42.

"Youth for Christ." *The Northwestern Pilot* 25 (August 1945): 303.

"The Youth Movement Revival." *The Northwestern Pilot* 27 (September 1947): 369, 382.

CONTEMPORARY SOURCES

Annual of the Northern Baptist Convention, 1916, 1917, 1920, 1921, 1922, 1924, 1925, 1928, 1929, 1931, 1933, 1935, 1938. Philadelphia: American Baptist Publication Society, 1916, 1917, 1920, 1921, 1922, 1924, 1925, 1928, 1929, 1931, 1933, 1935, 1938.

[Brooks, Keith L.?] "Let's Come Clean!" *American Prophetic League, Inc., Release No. 38.* (January 1942): 1–2.

Minnesota Baptist Annual. 1930, 1935, 1945, 1946, 1948. (Mimeographed.)

Riley, Marie Acomb. *The Dynamic of a Dream: The Life Story of Dr. William B. Riley.* Grand Rapids, Mich.: Wm. B. Eerdmans Co., 1938.

Year Book of the Northern Baptist Convention, 1944, 1945, 1946. Philadelphia: American Baptist Publication Society, 1944, 1945, 1946.

NEWSPAPERS AND PERIODICALS

Austin Herald
Blooming Prairie Times
The Christian Century
Christian Fundamentals in School and Church
Granite Falls Tribune
Minneapolis Tribune
The Nation
North Star Baptist
Northwestern College Bulletin
The Northwestern Pilot
The Pilot

School and Church
The Watchman-Examiner

Secondary Sources

BOOKS, ARTICLES, AND DISSERTATIONS

Ahlstrom, Sydney E. *A Religious History of the American People.* 2 vols. New Haven: Yale University Press, 1972.

Allen, Frederick Lewis. *Only Yesterday.* New York: Harper and Row, 1931.

Ammerman, Nancy Tatom. *Bible Believers: Fundamentalists in the Modern World.* New Brunswick, N.J.: Rutgers University Press, 1987.

Beale, David O. *In Pursuit of Purity: American Fundamentalism since 1850.* Greenville, S.C.: Unusual Books, 1986.

Berman, Hyman. "Political Antisemitism in Minnesota during the Great Depression." *Jewish Social Studies* 38 (Summer–Fall 1976): 247–64.

BeVier, William A. "A History of the Independent Fundamental Churches of America." Ph.D. diss., Dallas Theological Seminary, 1958.

Bledstein, Burton J. *The Culture of Professionalism: The Middle Class and the Development of Higher Education in America.* New York: W. W. Burton, 1976.

Bowers, William L. *The Country Life Movement in America, 1900–1920.* Port Washington, N.Y.: Kennikat Press, 1974.

Brereton, Virginia Lieson. "Fundamentalists as Popular Educators: The Bible Schools, 1880–Present." Paper presented at meeting of the American Society of Church History, Holland, Mich., April 21, 1983.

Brereton, Virginia Lieson. "Protestant Fundamentalist Bible Schools, 1882–1940." Ph.D. diss., Columbia University, 1981.

Brinkley, Alan. *Voices of Protest: Huey Long, Father Coughlin, and the Great Depression.* 1982. Reprint. New York: Random House, 1983.

Butler, Farley Porter, Jr. "Billy Graham and the End of Evangelical Unity." Ph.D. diss., University of Florida, 1976.

Carpenter, Joel A. "From Fundamentalism to the New Evangelical Coalition." In *Evangelicalism and Modern America,* edited by George Marsden, 3–16. Grand Rapids, Mich.: Wm. B. Eerdmans Co., 1984.

Carpenter, Joel A. "Fundamentalist Institutions and the Rise of Evangelical Protestantism, 1929–1942." *Church History* 49 (March 1980): 62–75.

Carpenter, Joel A. "The Fundamentalist Leaven and the Rise of an Evangelical United Front." In *The Evangelical Tradition in America,* edited by Leonard I. Sweet, 257–88. Macon, Ga.: Mercer University Press, 1984.

Carpenter, Joel A. "The Renewal of American Fundamentalism, 1930–1945." Ph.D. diss., Johns Hopkins University, 1984.

Carpenter, Joel A. "Understanding Fundamentalism." *Evangelical Studies Bulletin* 4 (March 1987): 6–9.

Carter, Paul A. "The Fundamentalist Defense of the Faith." In *Change and Continuity in Twentieth-Century America: The Twenties,* edited by John Braeman, Robert H. Bremner, and David Brody, 179–214. Columbus: Ohio State University Press, 1968.

Cauthen, Kenneth. *The Impact of American Religious Liberalism.* 2d ed. Washington: University Press of America, 1983.

Chrislock, Carl H. *The Progressive Era in Minnesota, 1899–1918.* St. Paul: Minnesota Historical Society, 1971.

Cohn, Norman. *Warrant for Genocide: The Myth of the World-Conspiracy and the Protocols of the Elders of Zion.* New York: Harper Torchbooks, 1969.

Cole, Stewart. *The History of Fundamentalism.* New York: Richard Smith, 1931.

Cooper, Charles I. "The Jews of Minneapolis and Their Christian Neighbors." *Jewish Social Studies* 8 (1946): 31–38.

Danbom, David. *The Resisted Revolution: Urban America and the Industrialization of Agriculture, 1900–1930.* Ames: University of Iowa Press, 1979.

Delnay, Robert G. "A History of the Baptist Bible Union." Th.D. diss., Dallas Theological Seminary, 1963.

Dollar, George W. *A History of Fundamentalism.* Greenville, S.C.: Bob Jones University Press, 1973.

Ellis, Walter Edmund Warren. "Social and Religious Factors in the Fundamentalist-Modernist Schisms among Baptists in North America, 1895–1934." Ph.D. diss., University of Pittsburgh, 1974.

Ellis, William E. "Evolution, Fundamentalism, and the Historians: An Historiographical Review." *The Historian* 44 (November 1981): 15–35.

Ernst, Eldon G. *Moment of Truth for Protestant America: Interchurch Campaigns Following World War One.* Missoula, Mont.: Scholar's Press, 1972.

Ewing, George Henry. "George Claude Lorimer." In *Dictionary of American Biography,* edited by Dumas Malone, 11:412–13. New York: Charles Scribner's Sons, 1933.

Fackre, Gabriel. *The Religious Right and Christian Faith.* Grand Rapids, Mich.: Wm. B. Eerdmans Co., 1982.

First Baptist Church of Granite Falls, Minnesota: Its 75th Anniversary. Granite Falls, Minn.: Granite Falls Tribune, 1953.

Fitzgerald, Frances. *Cities on a Hill: A Journey through Contemporary American Cultures.* London: Picador Press, 1986.

Frady, Marshall. *Billy Graham: A Parable of American Righteousness.* Boston: Little, Brown and Co., 1979.

Frank, Douglas W. *Less than Conquerors: How Evangelicals Entered the Twentieth Century.* Grand Rapids, Mich.: Wm. B. Eerdmans Co., 1986.

Furniss, Norman F. *The Fundamentalist Controversy.* New Haven: Yale University Press, 1954.

Gasper, Louis. *The Fundamentalist Movement.* The Hague: Mouton, 1963.

Gatewood, Willard B., Jr., ed. *Controversy in the Twenties: Fundamentalism, Modernism, and Evolution.* Nashville, Tenn.: Vanderbilt University Press, 1969.

Getz, Gene A. *MBI: The Story of Moody Bible Institute.* Chicago: Moody Press, 1969.

Glass, William R. "Fundamentalism's Prophetic Vision of the Jews: The 1930s." *Jewish Social Studies* 47 (Winter 1985): 63–76.

Graham, Otis L., Jr. *An Encore for Reform: The Old Progressives and the New Deal.* London: Oxford University Press, 1967. Reprint. 1968.

Handy, Robert T. "The American Religious Depression, 1925–1935." *Church History* 29 (March 1960): 3–16.

Harrison, Paul M. *Authority and Power in the Free Church Tradition: A Social Case Study of the American Baptist Convention.* Princeton, N.J.: Princeton University Press, 1959.

Hart, Darryl. "'Doctor Fundamentalis': An Intellectual Biography of J. Gresham Machen, 1881–1937." Ph.D. diss., Johns Hopkins University, 1988.

Hartshorne, Hugh, and Milton C. Froyd. *Theological Education in the Northern Baptist Convention: A Survey.* Philadelphia: Judson Press, 1945.

Hassey, Janette. *No Time for Silence: Evangelical Women in Public Ministry around the Turn of the Century.* Grand Rapids, Mich.: Zondervan Co., 1986.

Hays, Samuel P. Preface to the Atheneum Edition of *Conservation and the Gospel of Efficiency: The Progressive Conservation Movement, 1890–1920.* 2d ed. New York: Atheneum Books, 1969.

Hays, Samuel P. "The Social Analysis of American Political History, 1880–1920." *Political Science Quarterly* 80 (September 1965): 373–94.

Hays, Samuel P. "The Structure of Environmental Politics since World War II." *Journal of Social History* 14 (Summer 1981): 719–31.

High, Stanley. *Billy Graham: The Personal Story of the Man, His Message, and His Mission.* New York: McGraw-Hill Co., 1956.

Hofstadter, Richard. *Anti-Intellectualism in American Life.* New York: Random House, 1962.

Hofstadter, Richard. *The Paranoid Style in American Politics and Other Essays.* New York: Knopf, 1965.

Hudson, Winthrop. *Religion in America: An Historical Account of the Development of American Religious Life.* 4th ed. New York: Charles Scribner's Sons, 1987.

Hull, Lloyd B. "A Rhetorical Study of the Preaching of William Bell Riley." Ph.D. diss., Wayne State University, 1960.

Hutchison, William R. *The Modernist Impulse in American Protestantism.* Cambridge: Harvard University Press, 1976.

Jeansonne, Glen. *Gerald L. K. Smith: Minister of Hate.* New Haven: Yale University Press, 1988.

Johnson, Dell G. "Fundamentalist Responses in Minnesota to the Developing New Evangelicalism." Th.D. diss., Central Baptist Seminary, 1982.

Kincheloe, Samuel C. *Research Memorandum on Religion in the Depression.* Studies on the Social Aspects of the Depression. New York: Social Science Research Council, 1937.

Larson, Edward J. *Trial and Error: The American Controversy over Creation and Evolution.* Oxford: Oxford University Press, 1985.

Lears, T. J. Jackson. *No Place of Grace: Antimodernism and the Transformation of American Culture.* New York: Pantheon Books, 1981.

Leuchtenburg, William E. *The Perils of Prosperity, 1914–1932.* Chicago: University of Chicago Press, 1958.

McBirnie, Robert Sheldon. "Basic Issues in the Fundamentalism of William Bell Riley." Ph.D. diss., State University of Iowa, 1952.

McLoughlin, William G. "Is There a Third Force in Christendom?" *Daedalus* 96 (Winter 1967): 43–68.

McLoughlin, William G. *Modern Revivalism, Charles Grandison Finney to Billy Graham.* New York: Ronald Press, 1959.

McWilliams, Carey. "Minneapolis: The Curious Twin." *Common Ground* 7 (Autumn 1946): 61–65.

Madison, James H. "Reformers and the Rural Church." *Journal of American History* 73 (December 1986): 645–68.

Marsden, George M. "The Collapse of American Evangelical Academia." In *Faith and Rationality: Reason and Belief in God*, edited by Alvin Plantinga and Nicholas Wolterstorff, 219–64. Notre Dame, Ind.: University of Notre Dame Press, 1983.

Marsden, George M. "Defining Fundamentalism." *Christian Scholar's Review* 1 (Winter 1971): 141–51.

Marsden, George M. "The Evangelical Denomination." In *Evangelicalism and Modern America*, edited by George Marsden, vii–xix. Grand Rapids, Mich.: Wm. B. Eerdmans Co., 1984.

Marsden, George M. "From Fundamentalism to Evangelicalism: A Historical Analysis." In *The Evangelicals: What They Believe, Who They Are, Where They Are Changing*, edited by David F. Wells and John D. Woodbridge, 142–62. 2d ed. Grand Rapids, Mich.: Baker Book House, 1977.

Marsden, George M. *Fundamentalism and American Culture: The Shaping of Twentieth-Century Evangelicalism, 1870–1925.* New York: Oxford University Press, 1980.

Marsden, George M. *Reforming Fundamentalism: Fuller Seminary and the New Evangelicalism.* Grand Rapids, Mich.: Wm. B. Eerdmans Co., 1987.

Marty, Martin E. "Fundamentalism as a Social Phenomenon." In *Evangelicalism and Modern America*, edited by George Marsden, 56–68. Grand Rapids, Mich.: Wm. B. Eerdmans Co., 1984.

Marty, Martin E. "Fundamentalists: What Do They Fear? Who's Afraid of Them?" Paper presented at Elizabethtown College, Elizabethtown, Pa., October 25, 1989.

Marty, Martin E. *Modern American Religion.* Vol. 1, *The Irony of It All, 1893–1919.* Chicago: University of Chicago Press, 1986.

Moberg, David O. *The Great Reversal: Evangelicalism versus Social Concern.* Philadelphia: J. B. Lippincott Co., 1972.

Moore, James Benedict. "The Sources of *Elmer Gantry.*" *The New Republic*, August 8, 1960, pp. 17–18.

Moore, R. Laurence. *Religious Outsiders and the Making of Americans.* New York: Oxford University Press, 1986.

Narvestad, Carl and Amy. *Granite Falls, 1879–1979: A Century's Search for Quality of Life.* Granite Falls, Minn.: Granite Falls City Centennial Committee, 1979.

Narvestad, Carl and Amy. *A History of Yellow Medicine County, 1872–1972.* Granite Falls, Minn.: Yellow Medicine County Historical Society, 1972.

Nelson, Ronald. "Fundamentalism and the Northern Baptist Convention." Ph.D. diss., University of Chicago, 1964.

Niebuhr, H. Richard. "Fundamentalism." In *The Encyclopedia of the Social Sciences*, edited by Edwin R. A. Seligman, 6:526–27. New York: Macmillan Co., 1931.

Noll, Mark A. *Between Faith and Criticism: Evangelicals, Scholarship, and the Bible.* San Francisco: Harper and Row, 1987.

Numbers, Ronald L. "Creationism in 20th-Century America." *Science* 218 (November 5, 1982): 538–44.

Oleson, Alexandra, and John Voss, eds. *The Organization of Knowledge in Modern America, 1860–1920.* Baltimore: Johns Hopkins University Press, 1979.

Peshkin, Alan. *God's Choice: The Total World of a Fundamentalist Christian School.* Chicago: University of Chicago Press, 1986.

Pierard, Richard V. *The Unequal Yoke.* Philadelphia: J. B. Lippincott Co., 1970.

Pollock, John. *Billy Graham: The Authorized Biography.* New York: McGraw-Hill Co., 1966.

Quebedeaux, Richard. *By What Authority: The Rise of Personality Cults in American Christianity.* San Francisco: Harper and Row, 1982.

Rapp, Michael G. "A Historical Overview of Anti-Semitism in Minnesota, 1920-1960." Ph.D. diss., University of Minnesota, 1977.

Rausch, David A. "Fundamentalism and the Jew: An Interpretive Essay." *Journal of the Evangelical Theological Society* 23 (June 1980): 105-12.

Rausch, David A. "Our Hope: An American Fundamentalist Journal and the Holocaust, 1937-1945." *Fides et Historia* 12 (Spring 1980): 89-103.

Rausch, David A. "A Rejoinder to Timothy Weber's Reply." *Journal of the Evangelical Theological Society* 24 (March 1981): 73-77.

Rausch, David A. *Zionism within Early American Fundamentalism, 1878-1918: A Convergence of Two Traditions.* New York: Edwin Mellen Press, 1979.

Ribuffo, Leo P. *The Old Christian Right: The Protestant Far Right from the Great Depression to the Cold War.* Philadelphia: Temple University Press, 1983.

Rich, Mark. *The Rural Church Movement.* Columbia: Mo.: Juniper Knoll Press, 1957.

Roy, Ralph Lord. *Apostles of Discord: A Study of Organized Bigotry and Disruption on the Fringes of Protestantism.* Boston: Beacon Press, 1953.

Russell, Charles Allyn. *Voices of American Fundamentalism: Seven Biographical Studies.* Philadelphia: Westminster Press, 1976.

Sandeen, Ernest. *The Roots of Fundamentalism: British and American Millenarianism, 1800-1930.* Chicago: University of Chicago Press, 1970.

Sanderson, Dwight. *Research Memorandum on Rural Life in the Depression.* Studies on the Social Aspects of the Depression. New York: Social Science Research Council, 1937.

Schorer, Mark. *Sinclair Lewis: An American Life.* New York: McGraw-Hill Co., 1961.

Shelley, Bruce. *A History of Conservative Baptists.* Wheaton, Ill.: Wheaton Press, 1971.

Shelley, Bruce. "The Rise of Evangelical Youth Movements." *Fides et Historia* 18 (January 1986): 47-63.

Singleton, Gregory H. "Fundamentalism and Urbanization: A Quantitative Critique of Impressionistic Interpretations." In *The New Urban History,* edited by Leo F. Schnore, 205-27. Princeton, N.J.: Princeton University Press, 1975.

Steffens, Lincoln. *The Shame of the Cities.* New York: McClure, Phillips, and Co., 1904.

Stowell, Joseph M. *Background and History of the General Association of Regular Baptist Churches.* Hayward, Calif.: Gospel Tracts Unlimited, 1949.

Swanson, Merwin. "The 'Country Life Movement' and the American Churches." *Church History* 46 (1977): 358-73.

Szasz, Ferenc Morton. *The Divided Mind of Protestant America, 1880-1930.* University: University of Alabama Press, 1982.

Szasz, Ferenc Morton. "The Progressive Clergy and the Kingdom of God." *Mid-America* 55 (January 1973): 3-20.

Szasz, Ferenc Morton. "Three Fundamentalist Leaders: The Roles of William Bell Riley, John Roach Straton, and William Jennings Bryan in the Fundamentalist-Modernist Controversy." Ph.D. diss., University of Rochester, 1969.

Szasz, Ferenc Morton. "William B. Riley and the Fight Against Teaching of Evolution in Minnesota." *Minnesota History* 41 (Spring 1969): 201-16.

Tinder, Donald. "Fundamentalist Baptists in the Northern and Western United States, 1920-1950." Ph.D. diss., Yale University, 1969.

Trollinger, William Vance, Jr. "One Response to Modernity: Northwestern Bible School and the Fundamentalist Empire of William Bell Riley." Ph.D. diss., University of Wisconsin–Madison, 1984.

Trollinger, William Vance, Jr. "Riley's Empire: Northwestern Bible School and Fundamentalism in the Upper Midwest." *Church History* 57 (June 1988): 197–212.

Veysey, Laurence R. *The Emergence of the American University.* Chicago: University of Chicago Press, 1965.

Wacker, Grant. *Augustus H. Strong and the Dilemma of Historical Consciousness.* Atlanta: Mercer University Press, 1985.

Wacker, Grant. "The Holy Spirit and the Spirit of the Age in American Protestantism, 1880–1910." *Journal of American History* 72 (June 1985): 45–62.

Weber, Timothy P. *Living in the Shadow of the Second Coming: American Premillennialism, 1875–1982.* Grand Rapids, Mich.: Zondervan Co., 1983.

Weber, Timothy P. "A Reply to David Rausch's 'Fundamentalism and the Jew.'" *Journal of the Evangelical Theological Society* 24 (March 1981): 67–71.

Weber, Timothy P. "A Surrejoinder to David Rausch's Rejoinder." *Journal of the Evangelical Theological Society* 24 (March 1981): 79–82.

Whiteman, Curtis Wayne. "The General Association of Regular Baptist Churches, 1932–1970." Ph.D. diss., St. Louis University, 1982.

Wiebe, Robert. *The Search for Order, 1877–1920.* New York: Hill and Wang, 1967.

Winter, Ralph D. *The Twenty-five Unbelievable Years, 1945–1969.* South Pasadena, Calif.: William Carey Library, 1970.

Witmer, Safara Austin. *The Bible College Story: Education with Dimension.* Manhasset, N.Y.: Channel Press, 1962.

QUESTIONNAIRES COMPLETED BY NORTHWESTERN ALUMNI

Stanley A. Anderson, July 26, 1986

Velma Coffey Anderson, August 12, 1986

Warren Anderson, July 29, 1986

Anonymous Correspondent, July 30, 1986

Anonymous Correspondent, July 31, 1986

Anonymous Correspondent, July 31, 1986

Anonymous Correspondent, August 1, 1986

Anonymous Correspondent, August 2, 1986

Anonymous Correspondent, August 6, 1986

Anonymous Correspondent, August 9, 1986

Anonymous Correspondent, August 17, 1986

Anonymous Correspondent, October 3, 1986

Anonymous Correspondent, October 6, 1986

Katherine R. Beard, August 11, 1986

Vernon R. Bliss, August 5, 1986

Mark G. Cambron, September 5, 1986

Ruth E. Campbell, July 30, 1986

Herbert Caneday, September 19, 1986

Chester J. Cording, August 29, 1986

Elmer Dick, August 9, 1986

Glenn Erickson, August 5, 1986

V. H. Ernest, October 18, 1986

Ella Patsch Ficke, September 22, 1986

Robert G. Gardner, July 30, 1986
Walter Gomez, August 7, 1986
Marion Haire, August 28, 1986
David Hammar, August 18, 1986
Ada Lou Hansen, August 4, 1986
Gordon Hansen, September 20, 1986
Margaret F. Hanson, August 12, 1986
Minnie Blixt Herrlinger, August 18, 1986
Gladys Eveland Johnson, August 11, 1986
Paul Lemke, October 6, 1986
Rex Lindquist, September 30, 1986
Frank McQuoid, September 22, 1986
B. J. Morford, September 22, 1986
Kenneth E. Nelson, October 22, 1986
Irwin L. Olson, October 9, 1986
Wallace A. Olson, September 23, 1986
Leonard H. Prentice, October 4, 1986
David L. Pritchard, October 4, 1986
Joy B. Quimby, September 26, 1986
Samuel H. Quiring, September 23, 1986
Tina Quiring, September 22, 1986
Anna Rieger, August 29, 1986
Maynard Rogers, October 7, 1986
Lawrence Ray Sanford, October 1, 1986
Frank Scorza, September 26, 1986
William Shillingsburg, October 10, 1986
Alf Skognes, September 22, 1986
Gordon C. V. Smith, September 21, 1986
Oswell L. Summers, November 17, 1986
Floyd Sutton, November 20, 1986
Andy A. Swanson, November 15, 1986
Francis Tarrant, October 13, 1986
Henry Van Kommer, September 23, 1986
Don M. Wagner, September 24, 1986
Lawrence Wagstrom, September 23, 1986
George D. White, October 11, 1986
George Wilson, October 15, 1986
Russell K. Wood, November 13, 1986

INTERVIEWS BY AUTHOR

Raymond Anderson, Golden Valley, Minn., August 25, 1986
Thorin Anderson, Granite Falls, Minn., August 26, 1986
William Berntsen, Roseville, Minn., February 25, 1983
Harvey Hill and Linnea Hill, Roseville, Minn., June 7, 1986
Fred Julius, Shoreview, Minn., August 25, 1986
George Knutson, Maynard, Minn., August 26, 1986
Joe Pates, Granite Falls, Minn., August 26, 1986

Index

Academic revolution (late nineteenth century), 36
Africa Inland Mission, 39
Ahlstrom, Sydney, 30
Allen, Frederick Lewis, 5
Allenby, General, 37
American Association for the Advancement of Atheism, 47
American Baptist Convention. *See* Northern Baptist Convention
American Baptist Foreign Mission Society: controversy over, 142–44. *See also* Northern Baptist Convention
American Bible League, 42
American Board of Missions to the Jews, 75, 79
American civilization: William Bell Riley's fears concerning, 34–35, 46, 49, chap. 3 *passim*
American Civil Liberties Union, 47, 49
American Jewish Committee, 75
American Prophetic League: organized, 78; attacks on fundamentalist anti-Semites, 80–81; Dan Gilbert's attempt to ingratiate himself with, 184*n69*
American Sunday School Union, 110
Ames, Amos Alonzo, 64
Anderson, Frederick, 142
Anderson, Raymond: Northwestern student, 90–91; Granite Falls (MN) minister, 127, 128, 130
Anderson, S. P., 138
Anderson, Stanley E., 124
Anderson, Thorin, 131
Anti-Defamation Council of Minnesota: investigation of William Bell Riley, 76, 77; history of, 76, 180*n28*; effort to enlighten members of First Baptist Church of Minneapolis, 81
Antievolutionism. *See* Riley, William Bell; World's Christian Fundamentals Association

Anti-Evolution League, 42
Antigo Journal, 105
Antimodernism. *See* Fundamentalism; Northern Baptist Convention; Northwestern Schools; Riley, William Bell; World's Christian Fundamentals Association
Anti-Semitism: of William Bell Riley, 6, 9, 61, 67–82 *passim*, 156, 157, 159; in Minneapolis, 62, 70, 179*n2*; in 1930s, 69; connections with dispensationalism, 70–71, 181*n32*; of certain fundamentalists, 71, 78; of Far Right spokespersons, 74–76; many fundamentalists opposed, 78, 80–81; in Minnesota, 181*n30*. *See also* American Prophetic League; Pelley, William Dudley; *Protocols of the Learned Elders of Zion*; Winrod, Gerald

Bakker, Jim and Tammy, 157
Baptist Beacon, 33, 57
Baptist Bible Union: organization of, 57; and Fundamentalist Fellowship, 57–58, 59–60, 177*n84*; campaign within Northern Baptist Convention, 58–59; demise of, 60
Baptist General Conference, 155, 199*n39*
Barber, Harold, 129
Bausman, A. L., 14
Beecher, Henry Ward, 4
Bible Institute of Los Angeles, 8, 37, 38, 88
Bible Institutes. *See* Bible Schools
Bible schools: origins of, 7–8; role in fundamentalist movement, 8, 38, 83–84, 108, 156; laity training, 8, 91, 93; in Great Depression, 88; ministerial training, 93; emphasis on Bible study, 94; emphasis on service, 99; graduates of, in Northern Baptist Convention, 112–13, 134, 135, 136, 197*n3*; mentioned, 35, 39, 41. *See also* Northwestern Schools

DATE DUE			